UNCIVILIZED

Learning to Trust My Untamed Nature
on the Appalachian Trail

A True Story
By Chris "Idaho Bones" Veasey

Arvada, CO 80003
www.readuncivilized.com

Printed and distributed in the United States of America

First Edition

10 9 8 7 6 5 4 3 2 1

Developmental Editor: Oksana Marafioti
Cover Design: Xavier Comas and his wonderful team

ISBN (paperback): 979-8-9886464-0-2
ISBN (hardcover): 979-8-9886464-2-6
ISBN (ebook - EPUB): 979-8-9886464-1-9

Author's Note: This work depicts actual events as best as memory can possibly offer. I recorded these experiences in real time. Some names and identifying details within have been changed to protect the privacy of individuals I have crossed paths with. Please respect that, as it was my tale to tell, not theirs.

To My Mom and Dad, Mike and Teri Veasey

Thank you for raising me right and for all your sacrifices. This book literally couldn't have happened without your love and support.

To My Amazing Wife, Annaleisa Veasey

You have been there every step of the way and I couldn't have made it to the finish line without your unwavering faith in me. You inspire me every day.

To All My Kickstarter Supporters

But especially:

Jack McMahon

Emily Atkin
Michael Bates
Bryan Benenati
Jason Bierig
Ian Brand
Mike Daggett
Jeung Hwa Danto
Matt Dondiego
Mark Erlenwein
Steven Foster
Ken Friednash
Marshall Ginn
Sam Hoffman

Alex Kagin
Michael King
Paige Martin
Adam Martin
Diane Meyers
Anthony Monaco
Dominic Morgan
Ashley Philips
Andrew Robertson
Jared Valentin
Jayson Valentin
Jay Vyas
Esme Yarnell

Contents

Prologue

Smoke combed my eyelashes in the humid fall air. I opened my eyes to take in the hazy trail ahead, the first of many switchbacks coming into focus before me. I blew out an enormous cloud and flicked the spent cannabis over the cliff to my left. My jangled nerves eased a little as I tightened the straps of my pack around my chapped waistline. I breathed deep, feeling the musty fog bristle against my nose hairs as my heaving load found rest in the small of my back. The formidable climb could be put off no longer.

The squeaks of my exhausted trekking poles were more pronounced in North Carolina's damp understory. Their fatigue mirrored my own as none of my steps had been easy since cleaning up breakfast that morning. I tried my best to ignore that every lunge felt like two as I rounded the second switchback. The scene of my smoke break seemed far too close and only about 60 feet lower than my current vantage point.

Each switchback tried in earnest to halt my march, getting weaker by the second, but I pressed on nonetheless. This climb was perplexingly harrowing, which made me want to put it in my wake all the more. Disobeying every cell in my body, I kept walking. I yearned for another break, to cast off my suffocating pack.

A gust engulfed me in dead leaves, each a crunchy little reminder of the rapidly changing season. Every day more leaves fell from the sky like sand in an hourglass, counting down the days I had to complete the Appalachian Trail. I'd fallen nearly a whole month behind schedule, which is why I'd grown so stubborn to tackle my daily climbs without taking any breaks.

Of those who attempt to hike the entire Appalachian Trail in one go, just 20% succeed. Only recently did it seem like I was at risk to leave it unfinished and fall into the vast majority.

"Not me," I panted through gritted teeth. "There's no way...in hell...I'm telling...everyone...I failed!"

I stabbed my trekking pole deep into the earth, staking a flag on my declaration, and only pausing for a breath. My knees seemed determined to force me to the ground for my own good. My feet questioned every stride.

Failure wasn't an option. I left for Appalachia deeply ashamed of my unfinished life pursuits, of the many projects I abandoned in my 20s. I feared judgment from my peers after making drastic career changes before quitting yet another unsatisfying desk job to test my wherewithal for 2,200 miles on the East Coast's famous footpath.

Completing the Appalachian Trail had become a denouement in my mind, a triumph of epic proportions that would redeem me and my forgotten pursuits. It wasn't meant to only salvage my reputation in the eyes of others: I needed to prove to myself that I was capable of finishing something grand. To endure when things got tough. To kiss the ground at the finish line.

As I climbed over a rock, my hand slipped down the trekking pole, leaving a streak of sweat behind. I went to grab the pole again only to realize I couldn't get a grip, nor feel any of my tingling fingers.

"No, please," I begged. "No, I need to finish."

My feet couldn't seem to agree on a proper stance as I stammered to catch sight of the summit. My mind was convinced that taking a small break to get my bearings equated to leaving the Appalachian Trail unfinished. My cardiovascular system waged war against my nervous system as I could hear the thuds of my pounding heart in my throbbing ears. Soon those thuds were all I could hear as my own words echoed feebly.

"I can't face everyone. I can't!"

I was thoroughly deaf once blackness crept in from the canopy and the ground below. The woods turned technicolor as the sky properly faded to black, my tunnel of sight growing smaller as gravity doubled. I unclipped my pack and braced for the dirt bound to take me in.

"I need to finish."

The silent words were whisked away in another gust as the last flamboyant colors of my distorted vision were engulfed by darkness.

I found the ground with grace as if the forest opened its arms to cradle me to the terrain below. Even so, nothing could keep me with the living.

My eyes closed as I left the world behind.

Chapter One

0 Miles Hiked, 2,189 Miles to Go
Days 1-5

4/14/17 – Ed Garvey Shelter, MD, 8 Miles Hiked – Day 1

The morning sun already brought the swelter of an afternoon blaze. Birds vanished around me, and the canal's shallow depths swallowed frightened turtles. I wanted to be a pillar of serenity, but the hum of engines in the balmy air forbade it. The first miles of my once-in-a-lifetime journey may as well have been along the New Jersey Turnpike.

"This was *not* in the brochure."

If there was a brochure, I hadn't seen it. If I had, it wouldn't have advised someone like me to do something like this.

A week prior, I'd never done a proper, overnight camping trip. I'd never even hiked more than ten miles in one click. After wrangling my gear from Craigslist, clearance outlets, and yard sales, I ventured into a suburban Virginia park to test out my kit for one night. The conclusion of my experiment brought a severe case of poison ivy developing while locked out of my car. The fiery rash stacked the chips against me for a trip where the odds of success were already slim. Less than 20% of those who attempt to hike the Appalachian Trail actually make it end to end.

Nevertheless, there I was, leaving a trail of sweat along West Virginia's C&O Canal, in a mad scramble to create distance between myself and the civilization I'd been rushing to leave behind.

My mind's eye parked me on a boulder in complete silence, gently kissed by the peeking sun. The yearning for that singular moment fueled the trail legs I hadn't yet developed to ignore the lactic acid as my lungs burned.

I was angry with those cars zooming by. Upset that a road dare encroach upon this sanctuary. Like a person resenting their roommate for being home when they have a date. Irrationality has no regard for proper causality.

Less than a mile in, an exhaustively familiar companion caught up.

A part of me hoped my anger would spare me its company on this trip. Another part knew all too well I would eventually be traveling with its many variants under the canopy, that 2,200 miles was far too long a distance to outrun them all.

Resentment haunted my past. Indignation fueled my future. Annoyance already slithered into my present.

Appalachia was supposed to mark the end of all that. I had no legitimate reason to be mad. Discontent molds reason as a sculptor smooths over clay, the grooves a distant memory, faded by the scrape of a trowel.

No villain eyes a scoundrel in the mirror, after all.

Once the road and cars were out of sight, I could hear the whines of my enormous pack pinballing along the trees of every switchback. At one turn, I spotted my flat rock 30 yards ahead.

Sun painted the gray stone and there wasn't a being to be found. A butt-sized patch of moss had my name on it.

Sedimentary chips glittered under the lush canopy. I couldn't hear any cars, planes, or voices. I couldn't hear anything at all.

I plopped down and gazed all around. Greens and yellows and browns. Eyes shut, I strained to push out every trace of air from my diaphragm. Musty oxygen rushed to meet my lungs.

Utter stillness soothed me and –

BUUUUUUUHHHHMMMM.

A semi truck's horn spoiled the moment and my feet were racing again.

Endless switchbacks cast doubt over my decision to make this my new daily activity. Drenched clothes and aching feet furthered those trepidations. I pondered the 80% of hikers whose walks end with a protruding thumb on the nearest road, well short of their grand finale.

Not me. Abandoning this trail was not an option. Haunted by abandoned business plans, forsaken cross-country relocations, and a hat trick of 9-5 catastrophes, the little pride I had left hinged on this journey's completion.

A rocky lookout beckoned me for a respite. Nestled between the colliding torrents of the Shenandoah and Potomac Rivers prominently stood St. Peter's bell tower in Harpers Ferry, WV. In its shadow two years prior, I had decided to hike the Appalachian Trail. We were standing in the AT Conservancy when my girlfriend Erica asked if she could join me. There were stars in her eyes as her soft hands squeezed mine.

The tower's chimes rang me back into the present, where I stood under the unforgiving sun with a one-person tent on my back.

Mercifully I found the ridgeline and my heart rate steadied. I took in views through spacious tree groves as my fears were washed away.

"I can do this," I muttered. "I'm going to finish."

A short eight miles in, I arrived at the shelter. I plopped down my pack, kicked off my shoes, and massaged my throbbing soles.

"Hi there!" A man who looked straight out of an L.L. Bean catalog was carrying firewood to the pit.

He was with a group of three boys engrossed in their respective chores. One was gathering kindling while the others prepared a bear line for the party's food.

"That yours?" he asked while nodding towards my overstuffed pack. When I nodded he continued, "How far ya going?"

"All the way," I said with shaky conviction.

"With that thing?" He let out a friendly guffaw. "I'd love to see what that pack looks like at the end. You'll get a shakedown soon enough, no doubt."

He had a right to laugh. I couldn't talk the talk. Carrying a platoon's worth of supplies on my back meant I was probably pretty far from walking the walk as well.

"Shakedown?"

"Well, you're gonna meet all sorts of people on this trail. Damn near all of 'em are gonna have opinions. Veteran thru-hikers, trail angels, hostel owners. Some of them want to help, a lot of them want to feel important. At any rate, a shakedown is when you take everything out of your pack with someone and debate what's essential and what's not."

I looked over at my *NO REFUNDS* 85-liter pack, stuffed to the gills.

"Won't my legs get used to the weight?"

"Sure will!" He smiled coyly. "But your feet won't. You wanna get that thing down as close to 40 as possible, and that's an absolute maximum! Including water and food. Y'gotta be a darn big fella to finish with anything heavier than that."

I hoped he wouldn't ask but knew I'd lie if he did. Weighing over 50 pounds, this thing was eligible for MMA in Thailand. And that's without water. I was already feeling its mass. Nothing tangible came to mind to dispense of, just sentiments and memories.

As the boy scouts prepared the fire I walked along the understory, still yearning for the solitude that eluded me all day.

My gait was slow and purposeful, and I reached out to touch natural features within my grasp (albeit with a lot more consideration following the ivy incident). I gazed at a particularly intricate tree for a while until the lighting suddenly changed.

Brilliant orange sunshine found its way through oak trees. The clouds once hiding the sun bled red and pink as they dispersed. The white daisies had all turned fuchsia, catching the dusky light. I leaned down to get a better look at the magic unfolding before me.

I breathed in fresh mountain air and faced the sun with eyes closed.

"Fuck!" I yelled, slapping my neck.

Several other mosquitoes came into orbit and I stomped through the bed of daisies back to the fire.

4/15/17 – Dahlgren's Campground, MD, 19 Miles Hiked – Day 2

The walk to Rocky Run was long and daunting. Feet throbbing, I leaned over to inspect the innocent looking dirt as I took a break. As my soles were suggesting, the path was much more nefarious than it appeared. The ground was so much harder than dirt, and between the cemented mud were pointy rocks blending in with the earth. I began to look forward to the many boulder fields that were shockingly easier on my feet.

I leapfrogged with a thru-hiker named Stamps who was covering 43 miles in one day.

"The Four State Challenge?" I asked him. "What's that?"

"On this section of the trail, Virginia, West Virginia, Maryland, and Pennsylvania are all relatively crammed together," Stamps explained. "If you hike 43 miles in 24 hours, you can set foot in all four states in a single day."

"How many people try that?" I asked, exasperated.

"Oh, I dunno. It's not terribly common, I know that much. And I'm sure most people don't make it."

Shame crept in as I realized this guy was literally hiking four times my distance. In 43 miles, he'd be passing nine shelters and three campsites. There are 260 shelters along the Appalachian Trails, ranging from the most rudimentary lean-to all the way up to a three story cabin with doors and plumbing. There are about half as many campsites without shelters, and 120 hostels that service thru-hikers. For every human hiking the trail, it's a *Choose Your Own Adventure* for where to lay your head. I myself planned to sleep mostly in my tent adjacent to shelters, with one hostel stay per week.

So are you gonna camp as soon as you get to the Pennsylvania border?" I asked.

"Pretty much! Hey," Stamps began. "Are you Shaman?"

Later that day, at the end of my meager 11-mile stroll, I struck up conversation with a thru-hiker named Grinder. She set up camp right near Dahlgren's entrance. Grinder started out of Georgia in late January and was averaging nearly 20 miles a day at the halfway point. After dinner, she came over with a friend she hadn't seen on the trail in over a month. Grinder spotted him on the nearby footpath thanks to a momentary upward glance.

"On the trail, timing is everything," explained her friend, Shaman.

He was putting the finishing touches on his meal: Gaffney hot dogs. "You eat this...every single day?" I asked.

"Every day," he replied, slicing away at the cheap protein. "The trail exhausts you. You're making choices constantly out here. Eating the same thing daily leaves energy for other dilemmas."

I remained silent, not wanting to seem disagreeable to the first thru-hikers I broke bread with. I knew that my morale would be drastically depleted if I were shoveling the same mush into my mouth for six months. Shaman's meal du jour was chicken flavored Rice A Roni with weiner bits, Adobo seasoning, and a package of Ramen.

Shaman earned his trail name before the trail at a Boy Scout camp. After a few campers spooked themselves out holding a seance, a frightened teenager turned to my Gaffney chomping friend to perform a cleansing ritual. Shaman lived up to the part fully, donning a bedsheet cloak, burning dried weeds, and chanting gibberish while walking the scene's perimeter.

After a few poltergeist-free days at the camp, the moniker Shaman stuck. It followed him to the trail like a ghost. S-H-A-M-A-N was etched into one of his two walking sticks.

Grinder, a graceful and smiley blonde, began the thru-hike with her father. When her mother needed her husband to come back after six weeks, Grinder ground on alone and had her boyfriend tag along for a week before he too broke for home.

This didn't go unnoticed by a fellow thru-hiker. "Two guys have left you out here? You just chew them up and spit them out! You're a real *grinder!*"

Whether that keen observer realized it or not, he had created a new identity.

I was delighted to meet Shaman after Stamps mistook me for him earlier. It made the whole experience feel more real. Like I was part of something bigger. The AT Class of '17.

Shaman and Grinder were NOBOs, northbound from Georgia to Maine. Most thru-hikers employ this method, though SOBOs do exist. Then people like me have to mess it all up with what's known as a "Flip-Flop." I planned to flip north to Maine from WV, then flop south to Georgia from where I began my flip in Harpers Ferry. No fancy acronym, just a flip-flopper.

When Erica and I were supposed to hike together, we had logistical reasons for flip-flopping. Plus this method is more environmentally friendly to the AT, and I'd seen Erica hug more than a few trees. Good thing I wasn't a jealous boyfriend. For some reason it never crossed my mind to simply go NOBO without her when we broke up. I wished I'd at least considered starting in Georgia. Now it seemed I'd bypassed a community of fellow thru-hikers with my unorthodox kickoff.

I tried to shrug off the need to fit in.

The old me wanted company, that was Chris's yearning. I was all too delighted to earn myself a brand new trail name and leave that man behind. A man accused of sex addiction by his ex-girlfriend. Chris had great ambition but little to no follow-through, with a string of unfinished projects in his wake. And what did Chris's friends think about the hike itself? This wasn't the first time he'd run away. He already used up his quarter life crisis in Honolulu and surely this new uprooting played like a rerun with outdated jokes.

I ached for a clean slate, but two days in, my overzealousness for a new identity was even turning *me* off. To earn a trail name, I'd have to put more trail behind me. Unless I wanted to end up with something like *Eager McBeaver.*

4/16/17 – Pine Knob Shelter, MD, 30 Miles Hiked – Day 3

The heat wave continued, but there was relief in other forms on my third day as a thru-hiker. Already less breaks were required for climbs, and I was able to stroll for six whole miles without stopping. With less pain in my feet and more oxygen in my blood, Appalachia presented more of that splendor I expected before my departure. I stopped for lunch on a rock overlooking a small town. A hawk ascended the thermals and as that same gust rustled the leaves around me, I found goosebumps along my arms.

The modest confidence I'd garnered that morning sparked pure ecstasy within. For the first time in as long as I could remember, I felt exactly where I belonged.

Finding an empty shelter several miles north, I made it my bed for the evening. Other hikers opted for tents instead. The adjacent fire pit primed me for social interaction, and a man dubbed Three Trees joined me by the flames for some time. I would have assumed such a title for someone of native descent. Instead, it belonged to a middle-aged, heavy set white man with an unwavering smile. A trio of teens found amusement in watching him set up his complicated tent, which requires tension among a triangle of load-bearing trees. Watching the fumbling inhabitant set it up, the girls deemed Three Trees an appropriate moniker.

His disposition was always cheerful, but his sentiments were less so, particularly after a climb. The only conversation topics Three Trees broached with me were his resentment of elevation gains and affinity for pizza. I never got a straight answer as to why he ventured out into the forest indefinitely, but it was hard to get him to shut up about toppings.

"What I wouldn't give for a slice of pepperoni in my jacuzzi," Three Trees bemoaned.

If I squinted, I could've seen the heavens reflecting off his dorky spectacles.

Three Trees was a bread delivery driver with a pension and a loving wife. He could look at the AT and say "I want" without taking his spouse, his Porsche, or his hot tub for granted. When he showed his enthusiasm, it was contagious. I observed Three Trees with utmost curiosity in my engagement of less enragement.

After witnessing the Dalai Lama speak eight years before, I became fascinated with the concept of true happiness.

An arena of one thousand attendees fell silent as his holiness took the stage. There was no introduction, no wave of his hand, only stillness. The Dalai Lama's smile was beaming yet soft, his magnified eyes curious yet knowing. I'd witnessed this kind of presence before, but not on this superhuman level.

I always thought of myself as a happy person, but the daily presence of anger cast serious doubt in my mind. The Dalai Lama didn't even feel anger as far as I was concerned. Like he'd been cured of the affliction entirely. When I heard him speak that early morning, that hypothesis dissolved with his holiness guiding thousands of uptight surburbanites through a breathing exercise. In his dreamy outbreath, I felt his anger. Many other emotions were there, but in his lulling sigh there it was.

Buddhism's leading mind wasn't immune to anger, I realized. These radiant souls more accurately cultivate a relationship of awareness with anger. They're practiced enough to refrain from letting it linger. To let it come and go makes for a more tranquil mind, but not a pristine one.

They also seem to sense it from farther away, seeing it coming like a train across a valley. They anticipate it chugging past but know well to stay off its tracks and help its safe passage on every trip.

The very same angry guests visit the Dalai Lama. He knows them just as well as I do, but wisely greets them with a smile.

The thought softened me. It renewed an infatuation with Buddhism that ultimately failed once more to stick. I'd regress for years to come but at least I had some affirmation that feeling so many negative emotions didn't seal my fate as a sad, fatalistic soul.

In keeping a closer eye on the jovial people coming and going from my life, I would reach the same conclusion that science has essentially proven: these folks are the real deal. Whether it's by virtue of genetic disposition, meditation, or favorable upbringing, these shiny happy people aren't full of it. Three Trees was as full of shit as he was of pizza, and there wasn't a Domino's for many, many miles.

He went to his tri-corner tent and a family joined me by the fire. The father, sporting a sharp tri-corner hat, worked as a ranger in Shenandoah National Park alongside his son.

"Saw 183 bears in the park last year," the father, Boomstick, said before taking a sip of whiskey. "Lots of mamas out there this spring, I expect you'll see some on your flop through Virginia. They're makin' a comeback, fer sure."

Boomstick got his trail name from his niece. Upon teaching her how to shoot a rifle, she proudly reported back to his brother:

"Daddy! I learned how to use the boomstick!"

Boomstick wasn't shy about his pride in having his son and wife on the trail.

"I'm a lucky man." Boomstick kissed his wife gently on the cheek. "Not everyday you find a woman willing to hike over mountains with ya."

On the Appalachian Trail, "hiker's midnight" is 9 pm. I felt the communal need to get horizontal by that time after another day of modest miles.

I let the fire die with grace and gazed beyond the embers at a sky evolving over magenta mountain ranges visible through still-bare trees.

I opened my eyes to complete blackness, in the dark as to how long my peepers were shut. Barely awake, a familiar rattle of pills filled my palm, which I slung towards my yawning mouth. I could tell that one was missing. Capsules for keeping my allergies and heartburn in check were accounted for, but the one for keeping my anxiety monster asleep was at large. My headlamp spotted the Lexapro on the floorboards like a vigilante after a prison break.

The pill was twice as big as a year prior when I started taking the SSRI.

"An antidepressant?" I repeated back to the first competent therapist I'd seen in eight years. "I'd rather not, I've been meditating every day and I'm going to quit my job."

"You should keep up the meditation, that's terrific. But I still

15

endorse you trying this for a while, so long as your primary care provider agrees. You scored a 19 on this assessment, which puts you well into the 'Severe Anxiety' category," he said.

"Out of what?"

"21. Chris, I understand your concern but it sounds like you've done what you can to adjust your lifestyle. Needing a little extra help is nothing to be ashamed of."

A few months later, after losing my girlfriend and apartment in one shot, the therapist recommended an even higher dosage. By then, I'd come to see the benefits of that little extra help I'd long been too proud to ask for.

I'd explained in my counseling sessions that I was perfectly willing to trade some of my dizzying emotional highs to encounter shallower rock bottoms. I felt deep down that there was a balance, and higher lows would require lower highs. I was bought in.

My wish largely came true at the cost of a few side effects. Sex was less interesting before the breakup, but I chalked that up to the expected half life of monogamy itself. I gained a few pounds and then welcomed some bonus mass with my prescription increase. I did seem to perspire a bit more. I deemed these consequences fair for my strengthened ability to face adversity. The trade-off went unconsidered until ringing in the New Year in 2017, three months before my hike.

It was at brunch during a visit back to Washington, DC where the conversation took on a strange dichotomy. It turned out that half a dozen of us were all taking Lexapro. Perhaps overhearing the initial rumblings of this commonality, one of the other six at the table confessed that he'd been taking Prozac for some time. He was in good company, because the remaining five attendees were in this latter camp as well.

All glasses were held high to toast the unilateral brokenness of our equilibriums.

One could almost hear the attempted drowning of inescapable stuckness beneath bottomless mimosas and SSRIs.

No one else appeared so alarmed by this unanimous suffering. I was alone in finding this shared trauma to be so problematic. Here were a dozen people on the youthful side of 30, all radiant in their own ways, each numbing themselves on a daily basis. We all had pills coursing through us like ranchers wrangling serotonin into our synaptic corrals, ensuring we could smile and dial our ways through every hungover minute of overtime.

This disturbed me. Not the drugs themselves, I'm a man of science after all. What disturbed me was the cavalier nature of young, relatively affluent first world adults taking antidepressants in droves.

I couldn't understand how it wasn't considered a crisis in this country. If *everyone* is serotonin deficient, isn't it high time we look at the bigger picture? Examine the cracks in our systems that keep us trapped in fight or flight hell every day?

Luckily I'd quit my 60+ hour a week job, but I was the lone escapee. Eleven of us were shoving down the Sunday Scaries into an abyss of champagne and pills.

I returned to New York wary of the pills prescribed to me. I wanted to improve my mental health on my own, without Big Pharma's aid. A detoxing was in order, but to put my body through such a change before leaving for Appalachia felt unwise. I resolved to wait until my environment was decidedly more chill on its famed footpath, and made it a goal to finish my thru-hike SSRI-free.

I tossed the Lexapro around in my palm, almost glistening under the cold stark light of my headlamp. I wasn't entirely sure why it was still in my hand.

A weaning off period was the blueprint, intended to take place a few months into my journey. I never intended to quit the pills cold turkey. Hearing the chalky pebble clamor around the floorboards stirred something in me that made me reconsider my perfectly responsible plan.

"Not yet," I said with a sigh. "It's far too soon."

In a half asleep daze on Day 3, I decided to stay on my prescribed course.

4/17/17 – Raven Rock Shelter, MD, 38 Miles Hiked – Day 4

Under the hot morning sun, an enjoyable stroll morphed into a searing minefield of boulders. After the jagged death slab portion of my day, I met an odd fellow by the name of Paul with Bunions. He used "cowboy" as a prelude for everything that might be deemed unorthodox.

"Looks like m'cowboy coffee's just as good as done."

He prepared his brew without a filter, pouring a little cold water over the ground beans to 'shock 'em on down.' Paul preferred to sleep on the bare ground, directly beneath the stars.

"Ain't nothin' like cowboy camping, I tell you hwat."

He had a specific THUMP for scaring off bears, with an exact force, at carefully timed intervals.

"Cowboy Kickin'. It's the oooh-nly way to scare off these furry daredevils. Ain't been shy o' cowboys in some time."

His outfit was Cowboy Chic, if I've ever seen such a thing. Denim on denim topping off some construction boots. No hat I reckon, but cowboy just the same. Though I couldn't picture him lassoing anything but a glassy-eyed hiker who's too polite to leave.

"How many miles ya got left?" Paul asked, spitting out the coffee grinds that refused to drown.

"Oh I dunno, around 2,100?"

"Ho-lee-cow! Ya just started then?" he said, shaking his head.

"Yeah..." I floundered, debating how much to open up to Mr. Bunions.

"Listen here, kid. Ya follow these little guides," he said while tapping a tree with a white blaze. "You'll be juuuust fine. Ya hear?"

My poles were the only sound as I trudged up the ridge, but Paul's words wouldn't stop echoing in my ears. *Follow these little guides.*

"Follow that and you'll end up in Georgia," my dad's childhood friend Jeff began. My whole life Jeff had yet to disappoint me on my requests for a hike, but this one was the best. "If you walk that way," he continued. "You'll end up in Maine."

My 8-year-old mind was blown. How could that be? We were in Pennsylvania!

"But what if you get lost?" I asked.

"It's impossible to get lost, these are called white blazes." He pointed above my head. "For over 2,000 miles, you just follow these little guides."

Thousands upon thousands of little white guides, like lanterns, reminding every one of us to walk. To keep walking.

It was the first time I'd set foot on the Appalachian Trail or even heard of it. I remember thinking I wanted to see every one of those guides. As girls and Pokemon came into my adolescence, the trail would come and go from my thoughts.

It was my now ex-girlfriend Erica, nearly 20 years later, who brought the footpath back into consciousness where it stayed. She spent weekends at the University of Virginia backpacking the Shenandoahs, following those little white guides, falling in love with the rolling blue ridges on both horizons.

She took me back soon after we met. Somewhere different from where Jeff took me but also the same. Erica saw the passion rise in me. She vowed to join me on that fading lifelong dream.

Hours after being reassured by Paul with Bunions, my confidence as a hiker was shattered once more.

Raven Rock was hardly a blip on my elevation map, but the final climb of my day thoroughly kicked my ass. I pulled out my phone and opened Guthook to check again.

Guthook was an app with a full interactive map of the Appalachian Trail. It had elevation profiles, checkpoints with comments from other thru-hikers including water sources, in depth information on trail towns and hostels, you name it. It was developed by a thru-hiker named Guthook, for thru-hikers, and has since been acquired and rebranded. Even on a second look in the app, Raven Rock Shelter didn't look to be at the end of a climb that killed me as much as it did. Yet there I was with jello for limbs.

I collapsed on a picnic table beside the shelter to catch my breath. Every bone, every muscle reminded me that I've never done anything like this before. My shoes were already wearing away at the front from my clunky hiking style. The skin on my arm, boiled from poison ivy, pulsated almost audibly.

Sure, it was hard to get *lost* with those little white guides, but following them wasn't exactly easy.

4/18/17 – Tumbling Run Shelter, PA, 51 Miles Hiked – Day 5

Several miles into the day, my cheeks hurt from smiling. All morning long, duets of little blue butterflies were dancing with each other in my orbit. Though my first few days burned like summer, the sights were distinctly out of a different season. Spring showers lurched over the ridge and luckily a shelter came into view shortly after.

Rain drops pummeled the roof as I wondered whether I could

strategically avoid precipitation for my entire hike with little breaks like this. Along with the unseasonable warmth I'd also been blessed with clear skies until that rainy afternoon.

Once the rain slowed down to a drizzle, I hiked through Pen-Mar Park and remembered I was strolling past the place where Stamps must have set up camp on my first day. It took me four days to log what he did in 24 hours. Would I ever get to that point as a long-distance hiker? Did I even want to?

The AT leads through historic Antietam, which was completely engulfed in green and silence. I stopped halfway over a bridge to bask in the stream below. The water's stillness reminded me of Monet's *Water Lilies*, casting the forest's greens into subtle technicolor haze over its calm surface. It was hard to believe that an oasis of Appalachian splendor could at any point be the scene of the bloodiest day in American military history. I looked at the nearby flowers and wondered how many of them had been crushed by corpses or sprayed in crimson.

The trail became more rock than dirt and my feet were throbbing something fierce when I finally reached Tumbling Run Shelter. I set up my tent adjacent to a bubbling stream and enjoyed dinner on a rock between the shores. After washing away dinner I cleaned what I dubbed the 5 P's: Pits, Package, Pooper, Peds, and Profile.

My campsite neighbor was covered in prison tattoos. Seeing him clumsily meander the campsite made me want to uproot my tent's stakes. Against my better judgment, I joined him by the fire which he built up hot enough to singe my leg hairs.

"Y'goin' the whole way?" he asked while never taking his eyes off the flames.

"That's the plan," I said, unwrapping the jolly rancher he offered to me. "I doubt I'll make it to New Jersey if Pennsylvania keeps it up with the jagged rocks."

"That's why they call it ROCKsylvania. No one makes it end to end with the same boots," he enlightened me.

"That right?" I sucked the jolly rancher for a few moments. "You pretty familiar with the trail?"

"I get out when I can, bought a house on the other side of the mountains years ago with Cocaine Money." He laughed and all I could hear besides the crackling fire was the rustling of his calloused hands against scruff. It was a sound I was familiar with. It was the sound of regret.

"Nice house, way nicer than I deserved. But my baby girl, she deserved it." He smiled and visibly loosened. "Baby Momma took the house and I said to her I said, 'I don't care, you can have the house, just don't take my daughter away.' She's 9. I love her, she knows I love her. When she's older, we'll spend more time together..."

I kept my skepticism to myself.

"She smart. Mom's evil and I can tell my daughter knows it. I can't blame her, though. For leavin'. I was in a bad way when she did me wrong. Haven't so much as seen blow since."

He clasped his hands tightly around his neck and rocked towards the fire. I felt a moment of panic and jumped slightly when he let out a tragic sigh.

"She gave me chances, she did. Said it was over when I finally went to prison. Third DUI, fuckin' idiot." He bit his lower lip and the roaring embers revealed scars under the face tattoos I hadn't noticed earlier. "Prison wasn't so bad, though. More like college, honestly. Lots of pot smokin'. The guards don't mind 'cause it keeps us calm. It's not like TV, there's hardly any fights in lockups for nonviolent crimes. Spent most of my time there playing guitar, guards called me Gibson."

Gibson didn't have a guitar on him but that wouldn't have surprised me. He had an old military pack, no less than seven pounds on its own. Inside were a Coleman tent and sleeping bag only suitable for car camping. His cookware was only suitable for kitchen cooking. Perhaps giving me S'mores *Pop-Tarts* was as kind as it was to shed weight. It made me feel better about my 49-pound behemoth.

"Had to keep it cheap for this trip. Been living off social security for 13 years since I suffered brain damage. Hit a poor 12-year-old girl with my truck when I was 18 while she was riding an ATV. Had bone stickin' right outta her thigh."

I managed to limit the evidence of my distress to slightly raised eyebrows.

"Threw my shirt over it to keep her from seein' it," he continued. "She was in shock but I figured it couldn't hurt... My brain ain't been the same since."

"I'm glad you're ok. At least you can get out here, right?" I was relieved my mouth was working because my brain was overloaded with fight or flight adrenaline.

"Fuck yeah, man!" He chippered up. "Gonna hike a couple more days til my girlfriend joins me. Hiking these mountains is bound to get that fat ass to lose some damn weight."

Chapter Two

65 Miles Hiked, 2,124 Miles to Go
Days 6-8

4/19/17 – Quarry Gap Shelter, PA, 65 Miles Hiked – Day 6

That's weird, I think I just saw a snake with legs.

I instinctively kept moving but then doubled back to discover what I thought I saw. An infantile snake had a fully grown toad by the head and arm. Battle was waging directly on the footpath.

Thinking that the struggle could last a while, I wanted to keep moving. Then I thought to myself: *If I don't watch this, then why the fuck am I even out here?*

Every time I thought the toad was dead, he'd furiously kick his legs, sending him and the snake airborne. I wondered why the snake didn't focus on suffocating the toad while its head remained in its mouth. Inexperience, perhaps.

I've always loved toads. So I was very tempted to intervene and set it free. I figured the AT's unofficial tagline *Leave No Trace*, probably also frowns upon playing god among the trail's reptiles and amphibians.

Upon clear victory, the snake fixed its gaze upon me. I could have sworn there was a slight nod of acknowledgment and respect there. That he knew I could have moved the needle any which way and appreciated my steadfast role as a curious spectator.

I reached out my thumb sideways over the snake's head. He coiled for a moment, watching my hand closely. My shoulders tensed, I narrowed my gaze and pointed my thumb towards the sky. A crowd noise escaped my mouth and I nodded in both directions to my imaginary coliseum.

Day 6: Gladiator impersonations for a snake. Hermitage was already taking hold.

Once the last frog leg was out of sight, I finally moved along, making great time to Rocky Run Shelter.

I plopped down on a rock and was overcome by complete silence. Following this was a sense of utter solitude. I'd begun to wonder whether I'd ever find such a state. It was beautiful.

I continued to Quarry Gap, every mile feeling like two. I trudged on through trees that looked increasingly like a rainforest. Even the bird calls started to match, and for a second, I wondered if I had fallen into a ditch and hit my head.

The added challenges didn't keep me from witnessing the beauty all around, but they didn't blind me to the ugliness, either. The trail passed some backyards rather closely, where there were two confederate flags for every rusty pickup. And I saw a whole lot of broken down Chevrolets.

"West Virginia and Pennsylvania..." I said, shaking my head. At least talking to myself was slightly less embarrassing than holding for applause from a snake. "Untamed natural beauty inherited by untamed natural assholes."

I spat on one truck in anger over how people don't appreciate what they've got. It would've been so pleasurable to get them to understand the irony in hanging these flags on the wrong side of the Mason Dixon. What a delight it would be to knock out some of their Mountain Dew rotted teeth.

A pit stop was essential. Anger turned to shame. I felt guilty for lumping all Mountaineers and Pennsylvanians in with these backward-thinking hillbillies. There were plenty of good people around. Sending them to the dentist wouldn't change any minds. That was Chris's anger. Whoever I was going to be out here, I didn't want it.

At 25 years old, my trips to the trailer in the Poconos were declining in frequency. I made the five hour drive from DC at least a couple times a year to keep the familiar Pennsylvania scene fresh in my mind.

I stood on the only sturdy plank left on our moss-ridden picnic table, surveying the nearby trailer lots. My cousin was wavering back and forth with squinted eyes, seeming to work out a long overdue puzzle beneath his Knicks cap while sipping Bud Heavy.

"Yo, Chris..." he began. "Are we white trash?"

I spotted the object of my elevated inspection and hopped into a stride towards an old cinder block about 40 yards away on a neighbor's abandoned property.

"Well, Matt. We can't play cornhole on this uneven ground. So I stood on that table that's older than you to find a bit of versatile concrete that I was sure I'd find *somewhere*."

I scooped up the large brick, feeling the aged stone bristle against my calloused hands. It hadn't held up a trailer in over a decade but it'd level out our lawn game just fine.

"The only thing standing between me and a cinder block...was a higher vantage point."

I swung it as I walked past our family's sun faded trailer, letting the reality of our situation sink in for Matt. I tucked it neatly under one of the board's legs and tested out its integrity by standing up on it.

"So to answer your question: Yes. We are certainly white trash."

I wasn't ashamed of that trailer. I must've brought 50 friends up to the Poconos to enjoy my family's idea of a cottage getaway. It was a serene spot beneath a lush oak canopy and a stone's throw away from a lovely stream. The firepit saw plenty of action beneath the rope Christmas lights that worked when they felt like it.

It wasn't trying to be more than it was.

No, that 25 year old trailer rarely incited any embarrassment from me.

The Poconos trailer always struck me as exactly what it was meant to be. It was a rustic escape from the bustling city and somewhere between camping and a hotel. It wouldn't have felt appropriate to dine on fancy plates with the good silverware.

It's impossible to fully explain the endemic rivalry of white trash on my native Staten Island, only 80 miles away: north shore vs. south shore. Their shared language is anger. And who wouldn't be in a perpetual foul mood when you have to pay $19 to cross the bridge back home every time you've mustered up the courage to leave the forgotten island borough? A big house or a boat doesn't exclude anyone from this unique ivory caste. And throwing Andrew Jackson at a toll attendant will piss off both camps just the same.

Aside from anger, ridicule of Jersey, and cuisine, the two shores have little in common.

If you were to walk anywhere from Richmond Terrace to Great Kills, you could take in the pleasantries of the north shore's brand. You might see offenses like Christmas decorations gathering mud in a March rain storm or a smattering of wind chimes that symphonize something awful above a sneering Marlboro smoker. He doesn't speak but you can still hear "Mind ya own fawkin' bizniss" as you pick up your pace. Once out of sight you have the ill tempered mutt to deal with in his backyard, snarling through the fence gaps made when he barged through a cheap aluminum slat for the last time. Once the dog finds another target of aggression you may eye a sea of blue tarps protecting everything from lawn mowers to a desk chair that would never find its way back into the house someday. A broken down '87 Chevy completes the menagerie, covering a patch of brown grass for no good reason. Maybe an all too common wood pile for the island with less than a dozen working fireplaces.

You might find yourself crossing the street after hearing a larger, madder dog next door, only to be nearly struck by a white certified pre-owned Infiniti. It's hard to hear the blaring gangster rap rattling the subwoofer compromised frame over the barking canines. As it speeds by with impressive volume, the proliferous repetition of the n-word shakes the bumper toting *TRUMP 2020: FUCK YOUR FEELINGS*. As if not ironic enough, the driver's dad assaulted another dad at his baseball game several years ago. Someone on the other team called him a fucking faggot after a strikeout. But surely his feelings weren't hurt.

In a rush, he streaks past Amboy road to the south shore. He's late for a meal that was never destined to start on time: a buffet of Italian deli features inching towards room temperature as his cousins argue over whose turn it is to unpack the feast. The mothers are dusting Pomeranian fur off their velour sweat suits while complaining that the deli hired another Mexican who doesn't have the decency to take food to your car. There's nowhere to park because one of his uncles upgraded to a Hummer with matching chrome grill and rims. The rest of his generation kicks tires, Bud Lights in hand, finding little jabs to incite cackling laughter but of course they could have bought the exact same vehicle had the lease on their Lexuses been up. The piece de resistance: at the press of a button, lights from under the car project spinning Yankees logos on both sides.

"I had to grease the greasy Puerto Rican under the table for it."

The strangest thing about growing up in this environment was that I knew I wanted no part of it, but I genuinely didn't know what else was out there. I assumed everyone was just about the same, maybe with a more traditional pronunciation of the letter "R." It never occurred to me that the rest of the country wasn't hoarding 30 years' worth of baby toys and flipping the bird every mile on their drive. Surely the rest of the country was just as angry about *something*. Hiding your anger was foreign to me. Not only did "Spit it out!" and "Youze got somethin' tuh say?" seem efficient, they felt natural. Why would anyone hang on to that kind of poison? It wasn't until I left for college that I realized all that venting of anger wasn't actually keeping the air clean. It was more so training embittered neurons to fire and wire together.

"Heyyy! I'm fuuuuzin heeeeuh!"

I opened my eyes in the Pennsylvania mountains and everything seemed brighter. Deep breaths preceded genuine appreciation.

"Thank you, universe," kept passing through my lips and felt more natural every time. Resentment gave way to adoration. One thought led to another, and I thought about god for the first time in a while.

Do I believe in god? What's god's verdict on me? Is god's verdict contingent on my faith in god's existence?

Catholicism raised me to believe god is pretty damn egotistical. Don't use his name in vain. Honor him while having blind faith and trusting Zombie Jesus will show us the way before answering the age-old question: *why does he lay eggs every Spring?*

In my teens, I transitioned from strong faith to agnosticism on my best day, and atheism on my worst. I stopped avoiding 'Goddamn' and 'Holy shit' and let the natural angst of young adulthood take hold. There was regular second guessing, and I wondered whether 'using his name in vain' would be the last pebble on the wrong side of the scale to leave me in eternal damnation.

Somewhere along this road of doubt I learned about Buddhism in history class. The ancient philosophy struck several chords with me but ultimately I deemed it to be "too emo." Life is suffering? Sure, but can't we call it something else? My diet was mostly taquitos and Slurpees for ~~Christ's sake~~ crying out loud.

What stuck with me for years was the Wheel of Karma. Long before reading about it in a textbook, I observed that *something* was keeping balance. Something was keeping score and righting wrongs whenever possible. I saw it in the miserable rich and the enthralled homeless. Among bullies and the meek. Bearing witness to this force propelled me to follow my conscience when it was daunting and no one was watching.

I had no hesitation in calling karma *karma*, but I didn't know what to call the greater being behind the curtain. One day, 'universe' seemed appropriate. I'd thank the universe, blame and question the universe, and manifest to it as best I could. Periodically, I'd wonder what god would think. Whether chalking up supreme power to 'the universe' would stroke their ego enough to let me through the pearly gates.

Repeatedly thanking the universe on trail brought this pondering back to my conscious surface. Beneath the gratitude was a bit of fear that I wasn't doing enough to secure a good afterlife.

At the top of a long climb, I was certainly feeling the *Life is Suffering* part of Buddhism. On the summit, far from the rusty pickups, I forced my poles into the hard ground.

"You know what?" I shouted to no one. "If god in all their infinite power can't press CTRL+F to 'find and replace' every mention of the U-word to get their ego fix...then fuck god and I don't want to be in heaven anyway."

I proceeded on with newfound resolve.

"I don't wish damnation upon every telemarketer who calls me 'Chris *Veezly.*'"

4/20/17–Pine Grove Furnace State Park, PA, 78 Miles Hiked – Day 7

I approached Pine Grove Furnace State Park bone tired. Another brutal day forced me to admit that my body was not yet prepared for a hike of this magnitude, particularly in Rocksylvania.

"Doesn't it feel like someone took out each rock on the path and deliberately angled them upwards?" I asked a fellow struggling hiker, who nodded in agreement.

I stopped at Tom's Run to prop my feet up and they screamed in agony when I started putting one foot in front of the other again.

Then a black hornet hit me square in the chest and I sprinted about 50 feet in the blink of an eye, pack and all. Fear: the great motivator.

At the edge of the state park stood a hostel known as The Mansion and its general store. Tourists with clean clothes passed in and out of their rooms as I stepped off the trail.

I pulled on the door of the Pine Grove Furnace General Store but it didn't budge. Five minutes past closing time. My heart was doubly shattered when I discovered the vending machine out front only accepted $1s.

I heard noises from inside the store and took a peek around the back to find an SUV with the trunk open.

"Excuse me," I said gently, trying my best not to startle the woman.

"Jesus CHRIST!" the store owner yelled with a palm on her chest.

"I'm so sorry!" I pleaded with hands up. "I was hoping to get a Coke and all I have is a five."

"What's your name?" she asked while opening the cashier drawer a few minutes later.

"Chris."

"Chris? What kinda trail name is that?" she asked.

"Don't have one yet," I replied while taking the singles. "Just started a week ago."

"Well I'm Michelle, I own the joint. You gonna do the half gallon challenge tomorrow or you hikin' through? I don't see many flip-floppers ready to eat that much ice cream in one sitting."

Before my hike, I'd read about the famed challenge, asking thru-hikers to eat 64 ounces of ice cream without yakking it back up. Nearly every hiker would arrive at the general store with 1,000 miles' worth of raging metabolism behind them. I had less than 80 in my wake.

The Half Gallon Challenge, taken on about halfway for NOBOs and southbound SOBOs alike, was the best known among a menagerie of unofficial challenges adopted by the AT community. It also struck me as an aptly gluttonous counterpoint to the taxing Four State Challenge that preceded it by mere miles.

I told Michelle that I'd love to partake in a hefty dairy breakfast but that all the campsites in the park seemed to come with a price tag. She told me where I could sneak my tent without any trouble, so I picked up my pack and stepped out onto her porch.

"Hey, look at that." Michelle picked up a cigarette from a table outside the entrance and held it out to me. "Your first bit of Trail Magic."

I've never been a smoker, but it felt like bad luck to pass up on the first gift left for me on the trail. I stuffed a couple frosty sodas in my bag and strolled beneath the darkening sky, taking in the minimum amount of puffs to keep the dart alive.

Trail Magic can be a variety of things, from a beer left in a stream to a timely ride into town. It's typically an item left by someone off trail for a thru-hiker, though there are no strict rules for what qualifies as such. People who regularly leave trail magic on the Appalachian Trail are called Trail Angels.

The cigarette's fumes made me sneeze, and the smell of nicotine already seeping into my shirt reminded me of my chain smoking uncle Mark. I pressed the cig into the dirt, desperate to prevent the stench from tainting my clothes any further.

Reluctant as I was, part of me was excited to leave Washington, DC for Staten Island in October 2016. I hadn't worked in four months and no longer had a lease keeping me tethered to the nation's capital. I had no obligations for the upcoming six months I would live with my parents before leaving for Appalachia in April 2017. The free time and some unique circumstances presented an opportunity: I could renovate and flip my grandmother's house before my hike.

I liked the thought of spending more time with my parents and helping them improve their quality of life. And the prospect of working with my hands to fix up my grandmother's house was invigorating.

My grandma had long been whiling away at her large and empty house in a codependent, alcohol fueled living arrangement with her middle son, Mark. After she experienced a number of falls and a stroke, I implored our entire family to get serious about selling the house and moving her somewhere viable for such a stage in life. Luckily none of the spills were down either of the treacherous sets of stairs in the three floor home, but, in my mind it was only a matter of time. If all of these reasons weren't good enough, she slyly procured a reverse mortgage years back. The house had become an equity toilet.

In my uncle Mark's mind, he was my grandmother's chef, her caretaker, her savior. Maybe sometimes he was one of those things, but mostly he was an enabler and a mooch with a lousy bedside manner. Though he enthusiastically agreed to my plan to renovate and sell the house when it was presented to him, he relentlessly pushed back his move out date every month thereafter. According to an agreement he signed the moment it was presented to him, he was supposed to be two months removed from the house in October. Yet there he was without a single box packed when I first brought my tools through the door. I knew he was going to continue squatting so in November I intended to show him that I meant business.

I intended to make living conditions as unpleasant as possible for him, to make him feel like he was living on a construction site. My power tools and saw horses remained in the common areas as I conducted walkthroughs with various contractors and real estate agents. The distress this was causing for the man who hadn't paid rent in over ten years was manifesting in increasingly problematic drinking episodes. I just kept plugging away at the projects that were within my control. It was grueling labor, but the end goal of providing for my aging grandmother (and then buying the finest hiking gear) kept me going.

One chilly December day, I spent the entire afternoon repairing drywall. One by one, I'd spackle over the voids of drunken Irish fists from room to room. Some required my jig saw, others required mesh. The slightest shake of my hand could undo an hour of work. My uncle seemed to know that as he cackled at the television, tossing each cigarette infused beer can into a growing pile of aluminum.

Later that evening I could hear Mark yelling inside his room. He eventually came out in a huff, reeking of cigarettes and weed, and I refused to engage. I cleaned up and headed home, hearing him scream more nonsense, not necessarily at my grandmother, but certainly within reach of her. My knuckles whitened over the steering wheel outside, waiting for the traffic light to change. I thought of the peace she'd find soon enough, away from the maniac she birthed 50 years ago.

The next morning I returned and couldn't believe my eyes. A fresh circle of black stared at me among a slew of whites. My heart raced but my breath was silent. I thought I heard a creak from Mark's doorway upstairs, and him waiting to hear a reaction from me wouldn't have shocked me in the slightest.

Creaky footsteps followed me to the hole as I was careful to make no sound; determined to rip from him the satisfaction of my rage. The slightest huff escaped my nostrils as I wondered how I could stay one step ahead of this white trash juggernaut to sell this house. Mark's squatting cost me three precious months and I had less than four to pull off a house-flipping miracle to take care of my grandmother.

I quietly pulled out my trowel.

The only sound to be heard was metal on plaster.

Not too far along in the Pennsylvania State Park, I found the spot Michelle described to me. I flicked the long abandoned cigarette into a firepit and looked for a stealthy spot to set up my tent.

It looked like someone had taken a plot of Earth straight out of the Pacific Northwest and plopped it down in the Keystone State. Enormous red pines stood at 100 feet tall, intertwining with their neighbors to leave me in the dark. I could see why the general store's jumpy owner sent me here.

Once camp was set up, I poured the bit of Hennessy I had left into my pot. When I set down the Cherry Coke mixer, I noticed a three-foot-tall stack of perfectly chopped wood to my right. I stood up and saw several more tinder towers as well as designating signs. I seemed to be right in the middle of some upcoming camping retreat.

I debated whether the wood could be considered more Trail Magic or stealing. I settled upon taking a few logs from each tower so as not to arouse suspicion the following day.

Loud cracks bounced among the trees as the flames consumed the perfectly chopped wood. A bittersweet feeling crept up within me. The solitude was beautiful, and exactly what came to desire, but it was inherently lonely. I thought of how special it would've been to have someone to share all the new experiences the Appalachian Trail had to offer, as I initially planned.

I stoked the modest flames and sipped my Hennessy cocktail.

"Why the fuck would anyone pay for this Cognac bullshit?" I muttered to no one as Tupac Shakur rolled in his grave.

At least being alone meant freedom and control. And the booze was all mine. I winced while taking the last gulp before rinsing my pot and holding it over the fire pit. By then only embers remained and silence fell over me. I ran my hand over the pot to rid the excess moisture. My callouses made the metal sing, the only sound to gently echo off the red trunks.

4/21/17 – James Fry Shelter, PA, 88 Miles Hiked – Day 8

Doing my best Winnie the Pooh impression, I hid behind a tree, wearing only a shirt. Pants dangling just out of reach, I tried to eye the Park Ranger's truck that was rolling by without exposing myself. I glimpsed enough to learn that he was turning into the cul de sac with a line of sight to my tent. If not that, at least my smelly garments hanging from paracord. Unable to decide whether it was better to eventually be caught pantless or to surrender myself fully clothed, I shimmied around the sticky bark, trying not to get my already irritated cheeks sappy.

A man walked to a shed, remained out of sight for thirty seconds, and returned to his pickup.

Did he spot me? Is he having a laugh at the paranoid naked guy behind a tree?

Finally he left the cul de sac and I returned to hiding my sack from the world. With renowned haste, I packed up and headed for my lactose packed breakfast.

I debated skipping the challenge, partially for feeling like an imposter and partially out of concern for my digestive system during the climb that followed. Ultimately I felt that my stomach could handle the load for the 13 miles after.

"Pick yer poison." Michelle nodded to the freezer full of ice cream.

I opted for Breyers Strawberry Cheesecake and got to work. There was a moment under the hot morning sun, about 35 ounces in, where I had the silliest thought that this could actually be a viable breakfast choice on more than one occasion. After carefully scraping enough out of the tub to avoid Michelle's dismissal, I proudly relinquished the empty vessel for inspection.

"I'M DONE!"

"Oh no you ain't," Michelle responded with a smile. "You've got another pint left!"

"...You're kidding..."

"Nope, read the sign!"

A simple math equation I hadn't noticed before.

1 tub ice cream + 4 scoops slow churn = HALF GALLON CHALLENGE

"This stuff's slow churned, more rich and creamy than that garbage. Full of real fat, too!"

When you've eaten 48 ounces of ice cream at 10 in the morning, 'creamy' and 'rich' are the last words you want to hear. 'Fat' was a word I couldn't argue with.

The final scoop plummeted down my esophagus like a stone and Michelle handed me my prize: a flat, wooden ice cream spoon that read *HALF GALLON CHALLENGE* in the same red ink you'd find telling a joke on a popsicle. She opened a musty looking book and handed me a pen. Atop the page was ~ *2017* ~ and I noticed that on the prior page was the last entry from Fall 2016.

"Wait...I'm the first one to complete it this year?"

"First attempt too," Michelle replied. "Today's our first day open of the season."

A mix of excitement and shame ran through me. It was thrilling to be a half gallon pioneer, but what about the folks who had hiked over a thousand miles for that right? It was a HALFway HALF gallon challenge, after all. What would they think of Chris, the newbie flip-flopping imposter out of Harpers Ferry? They'd probably consider him a joke worthy of a popsicle.

"Harpers Ferry, huh? Thought you at least started south of there," Michelle began. "What's that place like? Kind of a mecca for guys like you, isn't it?"

She had no idea.

I puttered about the weathered hardwood of the Appalachian Trail Conservancy and found a 3D model of the footpath. I plopped my finger on Harpers Ferry, imagining a giant fingernail crashing through the ceiling, squishing us all right there and then.

I traced it a few inches to the Delaware Water Gap, mere miles from where I grew up looking for bears and catching frogs. The tightness in my chest loosened as I recalled my dad's childhood friend Jeff pointing out those stark white blazes to me for the first time.

It was January 2015. Hearing enough of my resentments about my job and the mountain of debt I was climbing, my girlfriend Erica suggested we spend our two-year anniversary away from it all. Specifically in Harpers Ferry, WV. We hiked some of the Appalachian Trail, which led us right up to its Conservancy's headquarters in town. While Erica nerded out with one of the employees about civil engineering, something was shifting inside me.

Distant memory lingering, hand still resting on the model at the Conservancy, I looked up and saw a collage of photos. White blazes could be found in all of them, and I was once more filled with boyhood wonder. To think that there was one singular path from Georgia all the way up to Maine, and that a community of outdoor enthusiasts cared enough to maintain it...that notion gave me hope. I pondered all the different backgrounds and values of the people who had seen those blazes and how one trail could unite them all.

"Adventure."

"What's that, love?" Erica asked, placing her hand in mine.

"I'm gonna hike the Appalachian Trail," I said, patting the 3D model with enthusiasm.

"Oh yeah? Can I come with?" Erica asked with an infectious smile.

"Of course you can," I answered. "I can't think of a better adventure."

Had I accurately calculated the profound elevation changes of the day, I might've forgone the adventure known as the Half Gallon Challenge. A sharp cramping in my stomach suddenly eclipsed the pain in my feet and knees. Next thing I knew, I was redecorating some poor tree as far from the trail as I could go without shitting myself.

I did my best to abide by *Leave No Trace*, but this wasn't in the manual.

Several more unfortunate bouts awaited me ahead. On the last one, I pondered how much of the day I'd spent pantsless since being caught mid-laundry retrieval earlier in the day.

Mercifully, my digestive system found equilibrium right around the same time I reached the shelter. I struggled through the chore of retrieving and filtering water and chugged two liters of it. I passed out shortly after, hoping for a more comfortable morning.

Chapter Three

4/22/17 – Boiling Springs Campground, PA, 99 Miles Hiked – Day 9

The trail wore my feet down more by the day and the words of the Boy Scout Leader from day one rang in my ears. He warned me that my pack was too large to complete a thru-hike and his prophecy was unfolding before me. I needed to complete this hike and failure wasn't an option.

A Trail Angel left a scale at the State Gamelands trailhead, presumably for all the NOBOs and SOBOs eager to see how many pounds they left in their thousand mile wakes. I found more use in doing a bit of math to figure out how much my gargantuan pack actually weighed.

"55 pounds?" I exclaimed.

I decided a spring cleaning was in order. It was time to administer my own shakedown.

The first choices of what to eliminate from my pack were comically easy: a winter hat and gloves, a flashlight, and my kindle which rarely worked anyway.

Four pounds subtracted.

I tossed aside half my first aid kit. I squeezed out some ointments. I ditched my lacrosse ball. I duct-taped the selfie stick's clamp to my trekking pole, tossing the rest of the device. I discarded my French press kit and mug.

"48 pounds," I said with relief.

Without water and food, it was down to 36. So I decided to keep my hammock.

As luck would have it, I was due to pass by an outfitter in Boiling Springs the next morning. They'd have a hiker box, a container where thru-hikers could leave and take items as they please. I wrote the PIN for the temperamental Kindle on a piece of tape and stuck it to the screen. I threw all the other items I planned to leave behind into their own stuff sack and carried it by hand for a while to get a sense of my pack's new weight.

I descended the Appalachian Mountains into welcomed flatlands and found an empty campsite just shy of town, elated to have some time alone to recharge. As I set up my tent, fantasies filled my mind of a fire all to myself. The surrounding marshland almost discouraged me from making one, but I soon got to work on the damp tinder.

After over an hour, I finally gave up. For as long as I remember, I'd never capitulated in getting a blaze going. I've gotten fires roaring hours after a thunderstorm. I once set up a tarp canopy while it was actively pouring to appease a lady. I had a fire every single night of my hike thus far. I struck out when I needed one most.

The wood was damp to the core. The temperature was too low and the humidity too high. I collected some dead grass, knowing it wouldn't work. I wasted one of my firestarters.

With my feet soaked and the temperature flirting with 40, I still felt the heat on my cheeks from blowing into the heart of what seemed like a budding inferno. The aching in my lower back was hotter than the wood that briefly lit aflame.

Just another failure, I seem to thrive at those.

Between accepting that my pack was truly too full, and still not notching my daily miles into the teens, my monkey mind had me questioning my competence all day long. I was counting on a crackling fire to pull me back into the trail's wonder, away from the defeats looming over me.

I'd developed a new and annoying nightly ritual. Although I told myself I'd stay on Lexapro for at least a few more weeks, I began staring at the little pill in my hand every evening before bed. For minutes I would study it and contemplate tossing it far away, despite my attempt to eliminate a daily dilemma, as Shaman had advised me on Day 2.

My hand was shaking in that tent next to the Appalachian Trail, feet away from the scene of a fire that never was, the pill only hanging on by my wet palm. My hand wanted to move, but my heart disagreed.

"Why do I want this so badly? Why does the act of taking Lexapro feel like a failure?" I asked myself, wispy breath briefly taking the pill out of sight before me. "Why is it so important to find the peace that SSRIs grant me on my own? Within my own drug-free mind?"

I popped the happy pill into my sighing mouth. A day where I was haunted by self-doubt was not a time to see what my detoxed mind was capable of. I had 2,100 more miles to sort out my mental health, to figure out who the real Chris was.

Not that it mattered. I wouldn't be Chris for much longer.

4/23/17 – Darlington Shelter, PA, 116 Miles Hiked – Day 10

The outfitter in town, exactly one stream away from the AT, hosted a BBQ. I had the fortune of good timing. I stopped on the other side of a crystal clear stream to see dozens of trout fighting the current in foot deep water. Every feature of them was vibrant and it seemed utterly feasible to reach in and grab one.

"We're just..." began the lead singer of the classic rock cover band playing right up against the outfitter. After a well calculated pause he and his bandmates continued.

"--Two lost souls swimminginafishbowl..."

The trout, all seeming to sense a gap in the current, leapt with all their might in vain.

"Year after year."

I headed towards the outfitter to drop off my castaway belongings but the smell of barbecue immediately seduced me. After getting my order of mac and cheese bowl, topped with a mountain of brisket, I turned to head back to the stream.

"Hey, hold up. Are you a thru-hiker?" a sales woman asked from the food truck window.

"Sure am!" I replied.

"You weren't supposed to pay!"

"Wow," I began. "No worries, I appreciate it!"

"Would you eat another one?" she asked. "We have way too much food."

"Oh, absolutely."

I hadn't earned my stripes as a long-distance hiker, but my appetite was eons ahead of my legs on that matter. As the musicians riffed Pink Floyd for a perfectly acceptable eternity, I scraped the first BBQ bowl with gusto.

"So the legends are true," I muttered. "The trail provides."

As the guitarist stepped forward and wailed on his higher E string, my heart began to race and I wasn't sure why. Then the culprit came to mind. Pink Floyd had long been a classic rock favorite of mine, but it was my uncle Mark who introduced me to them. A tick in the GOOD column in a very complicated relationship.

My mind drifted to what he might be up to. I was nearly four months into my latest bout of cutting off all ties with the man.

"I'll do what I want!" my uncle Mark yelled from across the bar at an hour most people would consider too early for downing their first drink, let alone 10th. "It's my fawckin bruuuunch daaaaay!"

Raucous, troll-like laughs followed as he grabbed an uncomfortable server by the midriff. I sat in distressed silence among his fiancée's family who looked even less excited to be there than I was.

"Yo, Paul. How hot are my fiancée's daughtuhs?" His words were entirely too clear as I scrambled for a diversion. "Is there any law against my son hookin' up with his step sistuhs?"

I'd finally found the demographic for all those Porhhub ads.

Amazingly Mark surrounded himself with enough cronies, so the place didn't go silent for this legal inquiry. He was still harassing the server, who now took the long way around tables to avoid the birthday manchild. My cousin's horrified look beckoned me over.

"Grandma asked me to go to her house and get Uncle George to leave," Matt said, shaking his head.

My other favorite uncle and godfather was technically violating a restraining order by sleeping in his mother's house. It had been many months since my Uncle George legally slept under that roof. Being kicked out of his latest stint in rehab and blowing all his chances at a halfway house, he squatted to little protests; the rest of the family preferred this to homelessness. I had the dissenting opinion on that one.

Despite rarely knowing where he'd lay his head, George always found a way to pump iron. The man exhibited superhuman strength regularly. My dad stopped short with him in the passenger seat once, spider webbing the glass. George had a tiny little bump on his head.

That same head caused the trickiest and largest hole in the drywall that I'd repaired. He fell down the entirety of treacherous stairs that made me regularly fear for my grandmother's safety. The fall sent his head through both sets of plaster, fracturing two vertebrae. He walked out of the hospital three days later, and 10 more miles to my aunt's house.

One crisp fall evening George fought off five NYPD officers and got away. George landed haymakers on two of them, right in the face. Despite that affront, they abandoned their manhunt.

Now his mother was asking my 150-pound cousin to kindly squire him from the residence so Mark could "enjoy the rest of his birthday George-free."

I assured Matt that he wouldn't have to go alone. My dad came over to find out what was going on and we briefed him on the situation.

"You've gotta be kidding me," were the tired words that came before a gargantuan sigh from my dad. "All right, let's get this over with."

Rage swelled for the entire drive to the house. Twenty-four hours before, I was sipping mimosas with friends on a rooftop with the

Washington Monument in view. Now I feared for my life in the name of preserving Mark's precious brunch day. I had come home early for the event as a sign of good faith, hoping it would give me leverage in finally getting him out of the house for good.

My dad led us through the front door, and the smell of cheap vodka filled the air. George rushed to clear away the evidence, sending several empty beer cans onto the floor.

"George, let's go," my dad said calmly. "Gather your things, I'll drive you wherever you need to go. But you can't stay."

"What do you mean?" George slurred. "Mom said I could stay."

"Mom said you could stay for three days. That was a week ago. She wants you gone and we gotta move so let's go."

"I'm not going anywhere, this is my house! Daddy would have wanted me to have it!"

George's words sounded desperate. This was going down the hard way.

"George, just go," I pleaded as Matt quietly nodded. "You don't want to be here when Mark gets home."

"Why does this get to be Mark's home?" George yelled. "Why am I the one who has to leave?"

In the corner of my eye, I saw a fresh hole in the drywall I had just repaired days before. I didn't know which free loading 50-year-old was to blame but all reason was lost on me.

"Just get the fuck out!" I yelled. "Why do you even want to be here? No one wants you here, George! Nobody wants to walk through this door and have to smell your bum vodka!"

"No, you fucking leave!"

George barged my way, and my dad exercised a choke hold he'd been rehearsing his whole life. George was the more impressive specimen, but my father wasn't without his own imposing strength. He got my uncle outside, and the three of us blocked the entrance. Matt rang the police and gave the dispatcher the necessary details.

"I need to get my bag, let me go get my bag."

"Where's the bag, what does it look like?" my dad asked.

"It's green, in my room," he replied with arms crossed.

"You don't have a room," I snapped.

George wasn't my main nemesis in renovating the house but he'd still made a marvelous mess of things throughout my entire life and my breaking point was nigh.

"Hey Chris, shut your fuckin' mouth or I'll shut it for ya."

"Don't talk to my son like that, George." My dad retorted. "What else do you need from inside?"

"Let me go in and get my own stuff!"

"You're not going back in the house."

My dad's patience was waning, and he finally got George's cooperation for the time being.

As Matt and I ignored George's threats on the front porch, I lost sensation in all my fingers. The balmy weather of DC was a distant memory as I stood in the frigid New York air. Beside me, a puddle beneath the gutter was frozen solid. At some point I picked up a shovel and my knuckles were pure white around the handle. I blew into both hands and the hot breath actually hurt my frozen skin.

"George, this is all I could find, are you sure the bag isn't somewhere else?"

"Fuck you, I'm going inside."

The seconds that followed were a blur. I remember narrowly missing George's face with that shovel and wrestling him to the ground. Matt called the police again as I caught sight of my Fitbit: my heart rate soared to 180.

I could hear its frantic thumps in my ears throbbing for warmth.

"I'm gonna kill you all!" George bellowed as he fought back to his feet.

"Don't you threaten my son!" My dad's tone was menacing.

"The day you finally die will be the best night's sleep of my life," I said. "That way, I'll know once and for all you can't hurt my family."

I looked my godfather right in the eye, refusing to waver. Doing so gave me the moment's notice I needed for a shot at George's head as he lunged. I swung the shovel thinking I had everything I needed to plead self-defense but something odd flashed through my mind.

HEADLINE: *Local Intoxicated Madman Kills Recovering Uncle With Shovel.*

Cont. from cover: *George Veasey, 50 years old, was forced from his home by his nephew who would rather see him on the streets than under his own family's roof.*

At the last second I reeled, missing his head by inches, which at least sent the drunk into a cower.

"Ok, well now that the death threats are out in the open, let's give the police another ring, shall we?" I yelled to the entire neighborhood, arms wide open.

My stiff fingers could barely maneuver the three digits. Once I gave the address, the woman's demeanor confirmed what I already knew: we were on a list. Not a good NYPD list, the opposite of what that might look like. The cops had been called so many times to my grandmother's over the years that often a car wouldn't be dispatched at all. I imagined some pixelated note in their system that says *Wait, then dispatch upon third call.*

"Oh people are on the way?" I bellowed into the open air. "It's just that my cousin called you guys 20 minutes ago." I raised my voice, hoping to cause enough of a scene that our neighbors would also dial 911. "And my uncle HAS THREATENED TO KILL ME SEVERAL TIMES. And in between those threats, I HAVEN'T HEARD A SINGLE SIREN."

"Sir, please calm down. Help is on the way."

Matt and I returned inside as my dad made one final plea.

"The police are on their way, George," he began. "If you're still here when they arrive, they will take you to jail. Here's everything I could find, I suggest you go."

I heard the sound of the deadbolt and then more drunken laments.

"Good! I'll tell the cops you forced me out of my own house! You'll see who goes to jail!"

Every few minutes, I checked the window and found George still shivering on the stoop. I felt no remorse. I meant what I said about that good night's sleep.

Mark seemed to be allergic to mortgage payments but he was in fact a resident of my grandmother's home. A few months prior, George drunkenly attacked Mark while he was taking a nap on the couch. A speedy restraining order was filed by Mark which meant George didn't even have a right to be there, let alone claim ownership.

A quick 35 New York minutes later, New York's finest pulled up outside, and their lights filled the living room. I'd laid eyes on George two minutes before but was crestfallen to find an otherwise empty stoop when the officers knocked on the door. Gone again.

As I finished my final bite, I was surprised to find even more room in my belly. I contemplated seeking even more sustenance while a gentle drum solo brought the tempo to a crawl. The musicians nodded to one another and the singer grabbed the mic with eyes closed.

"Running over the same old ground, what have we fooooooow-ound? Same old fear.

"Wish you...were here."

Chapter Four

138 Miles Hiked, 2,051 Miles to Go
Days 12-17

4/25/17 – Peters Mountain Shelter, PA, 138 Miles Hiked – Day 12

At Clark Ferry Shelter, after cleaning the structure to the best of my ability, I felt well enough to hike onto Peters Mountain.

While strolling through Duncannon, PA two days prior, the infamous Doyle Hotel caught my eye. I'd heard horror stories of securing a room at the badly dilapidated establishment, but I saw no harm in swilling a Yuengling with the locals. The first among them was wearing several articles of alien memorabilia including an "I want to believe" shirt in an unironic, non-X-Files fan-girl kind of way.

"Yew can leave yer stuff there," she gestured while leading me into an adjacent room with endless alien trinkets and posters to be found behind the bar.

The tender of said bar had a pinky bent perfectly sideways. I noticed it regretfully submerged beneath the surface of my lager, and initially thought he was just trying to be fancy. Maybe at this time, I should have been inclined to say *no* rather than:

"No, don't close my tab, I'll have another. So when was your last alien encounter?"

Maybe then I wouldn't have been huddled in the woods outside Clark Ferry Shelter, in nothing but a shirt, shooting foul liquids out of both ends of my body simultaneously.

On my way out of Duncannon I found a gentleman snacking at an overlook.

"You stopped at the Doyle? You better pray, my friend," he said, taking a few steps back.

"Why? I left, what could possibly happen to me now?" I asked.

"I checked in there yesterday. Awful place, I could see into the bathroom above me from mine," he started. "I was supposed to stay tonight too but the entire place was barfing this morning. Norovirus outbreak."

Twelve hours after my greeter regretted to inform me of zero personal UFO sightings, I was scraping vomit out of Clarks Ferry Shelter only a couple miles north of that cursed hotel. Norovirus seemed to have abducted me in the night.

Later that evening I set up my hammock by the entrance to ensure minimal future biohazard cleanups. The night was a blur but I awoke with one vivid memory of going out into the woods, in pitch black, with nothing but a shirt on.

I crouched at an angle that would minimize splash back on my ankles and was alarmed to find that this wasn't the only expulsion my body demanded. Vomit exploded forward and I tried to avoid falling into either putrid pile. I returned to the shelter and slowly got into the hammock. The mild rocking kicked off another bout of nausea. Eventually the sensation passed and I fell into a purgatory between consciousness and slumber.

I stared at the lease agreement that was waiting for my signature. I couldn't bring myself to look Erica in the eye. If signed, it would lock us in at our current apartment through 2016 into early 2017. This was in direct conflict with our agreed upon plan to hike the Appalachian Trail starting April 2016.

"Please don't be mad," she said. "I'm just not ready to go yet."

"But we were supposed to leave in four months," I replied with frustration. "I can't work this fucking job any longer. I can't, babe."

"Then don't! You've got the job at the brewery, you could always get another job if you have to. You should still resign, this job is killing you."

"What am I going to do for another year?" I said with hands over my eyes. "We were supposed to hike this now, not in a year."

"I still want to hike the Appalachian Trail with you," Erica said while reaching out her hand. "I'm just not *ready*. If I work this job for another year, it could change my whole career. My whole life!"

"What about my life? I don't want to put the hike on hold for a year. I'm ready now."

"I'm sorry, Chris. Even taking the job out of it...I don't know, I'm not ready." Erica said with tears in her eyes. "If you want to go without me, I'll –"

"Nooooo," I said with a drawn out sigh. I took a deep breath and continued, "Once that bonus hits my bank account, I'm turning in my resignation the next day anyway. I can't work another day."

I grabbed Erica's hand, just like she grabbed mine in the Appalachian Trail Conservancy a year before, when I made the final decision to thru-hike.

"This is *our* adventure," I said through a forced smile. "We'll leave in April 2017, but no later, ok?"

"I promise," Erica said enthusiastically while squeezing my hand. "You won't go out there by yourself."

In the early morning, I opened my eyes to discover I wasn't alone. Loud, fatigued breaths could be heard but no source was within sight. I figured a person had set up a tent at a safe distance after smelling death itself emanating from the shelter where I was sprawled across the entrance in my hammock. When I left a short while later, there was no tent and no hiker to be found. Instead what I did find were signs everywhere warning about a bear who hangs out quite frequently near the shelter, when he's not making himself home properly inside of it. On my way to ensure my ghastly biohazard was adequately buried, I found a fresh looking array of bear scat.

Is vomit the best bear spray?

My entire body shivered once the realization properly set in that I more than likely napped alongside a bear. I audibly screamed when an image of him easily slashing through my hammock like a pinata made an unwelcome home in my mind.

I squirted all but one drop of hand sanitizer onto every surface of the shelter. I wanted to believe that I caught every last germ, and scrubbed like I was also trying to bleach out the horrid fantasies still lurking around.

I left the shelter feeling weak and sluggish. The intense sickness came at a terrible time. After Boiling Springs, I logged 17 miles and felt like I could've kept hiking. It felt like I finally earned my trail legs. Now, utterly dehydrated and sleep deprived, I knew I'd have to earn them all over again in the coming days.

4/27/17 – Rausch Gap Shelter, PA, 155 Miles Hiked - Day 14

I arrived at Rausch Gap Shelter, lied flat on the floorboards, and propped my feet up. The pain in my soles eradicated my appetite. Throbbing radiated up my legs and I cursed Rocksylvania's welcome wagon. As I took deep breaths, my body surrendered to sleep.

I jerked awake several hours later, disoriented and alone in the dark, unfamiliar shelter. I blew up my air mattress and hastily wiggled into my sleeping bag.

Waking to an empty shelter in the proper morning light brought little motivation with it.

I warmed myself and my sweaty belongings in the sun, banishing the chill still hanging in the air. Feeling calm and well rested, I felt no rush identifying a curious bird, an Eastern Phoebe, through an app I'd downloaded called *Merlin*. Ornithology was a hobby I never seemed to have time for. What excuse did I have now? The Eastern Phoebe fluttered around me as coffee brewed. I fixed gear that needed fixing.

I hadn't encountered another human in 16 hours, by far the longest I'd gone since my start. I'd hoped for more solitude as a thru-hiker but had started to give up on that wish on the rather busy footpath. The silence was welcomed.

After days of rumination on my breakup with Erica, and no distractions, my thoughts led me back there. Curiosity was the last feeling that burned inside me. I'd moved past anger, indignation, grief. I couldn't shake the curiosity.

What happened to her? What happened to us? *What revelations did hindsight afford her?*

It would've satisfied a lion's share of hypotheses to learn what caused such a dramatic transformation in just the nine months since she left me.

I'd gone through breakups before wondering whether my ex was an entirely different person than I'd come to love, but my conclusion each time was much simpler: that we just weren't right for each other. That and when a woman is done with a man, she is DONE. There was no crime of altered identity.

Upon this particular heartbreak, the person from whom I peeled my life away seemed entirely unfamiliar. Erica's goodness and open heart were what made me fall in love with her. Her refusal to find peace between us felt incongruous to an all around happy three and a half year relationship we shared.

The space that time carved made me realize the extent of my own transgressions. At first Erica's sharp responses rang true of an evil woman. Then a spurned female. And then a justifiably hurt human.

The first time I saw Erica after the breakup, I confessed that my old fears were bubbling up again. My old yet familiar critic, a long forgotten voice in my head, was using the breakup as evidence that I am indeed a bad person.

A major point of attraction for me was that Erica was unquestionably a good and pure soul. If she could love me, then I must be good too. Now that she no longer loved me, what was my verdict?

"You're not a bad person," Erica began while moving boxes out into the hallway nine months before my hike. "We're just not right for each other. This has nothing to do with your goodness as a human."

Six months earlier, Erica convinced me to sign a lease extension to keep us in our shared home. After blindsiding me with a breakup, she found a new tenant to take over the lease. We both had a couple of weeks to clear out.

Instead of helping with boxes, I blankly stared at her bed, which I occupied with another woman the night prior. Would she still think highly of me if she knew of that transgression?

"Thanks, Erica." I muttered. "Let me get out of your way for a while."

I wandered the neighborhood aimlessly, waiting for confirmation that she retrieved all her belongings.

A week before, Erica broke up with me while I was cleaning the apartment. I panicked and pleaded with her to stay with me, but the charade only went on for five minutes. At which point, I realized there was no will to fight for our relationship. I got no other explanation other than "I simply don't think we're right for each other." A voice in my head concurred. *She speaks the truth, we're not right for each other.* After that, a sterile calm came over me as I talked through breakup logistics with my hitherto life partner. Erica left that night, never to sleep in our home again.

On my third lap of our apartment building, a text told me that Erica was done gathering her belongings.

I returned to a sparse and unrecognizable home a couple hours later. A break-lease agreement was waiting for my signature on the counter, next to Erica's chalkboard. Bright pink leaders read *You are an AMAZING person.* The words haunted me like the empty bedroom and my subconscious set out to prove her wrong.

"I've continued to see Jen since we broke up..." I said with a sigh.

Erica waited, anticipating more to come.

"Oh, ok. Yeah I figured that'd happen," she said coolly, despite crossed arms. Apparently she expected me to continue seeing the woman we'd been inviting into our bedroom for several months. "Anything else?"

I nodded, unable to look Erica in the eye.

"Paula?" she asked.

I nodded again, inciting a cold laugh from Erica.

"I told you she was into you. Anyone else?"

I slowly moved my head up for another nod and she quickly threw up her hands.

"Wait, no! What am I doing?" she said, letting the silence haunt me. "What am I *doing??*" Erica began to sound manic. "I don't care. I don't fucking CARE!"

Erica headed for the door, looked at the chalkboard, and let out a small chuckle.

"Goodbye, Chris. I hope you find whatever it is that'll finally make you happy."

A slam of the door and I was left with nothing but dark thoughts. The unrecognizable home we shared and its stark, pale walls closed in on me. I found myself in front of the mirror. Defeated words escaped my mouth in an almost unfamiliar voice.

"No villain eyes a scoundrel in the mirror, after all."

Except I was eyeing a scoundrel. I finally saw right through myself.

The mind is a magnificent illusionist. Ego will do anything to preserve and mold the story to make someone a hero. Even if it means tearing down a loved one.

Such an intricate falsehood can only carry on for so long. The web of lies I had spun was too far gone to hold my weight.

I'd cultivated a seed of justification since Erica left me and the people I surrounded myself with watered it profusely.

"She broke up with you. *There are no rules."*

So every jab and cut felt righteous. There was no real obligation to share my sexual conquests of mutual friends but I convinced myself that it was "the right thing to do." A disguise for my own need to inflict emotional pain.

I halted right on the Appalachian Trail as the realization dragged over me like sandpaper. The full scope of it all had finally sunk in.

I deliberately hurt the woman I supposedly loved. I finally saw the grace she exhibited that day in not cutting me down like the rotten tree I was.

The lactic acid from the day's toughest climb paled in comparison to the regret I'd uncovered. There was no question that I'd been wronged and had a right to my hurt feelings, but I deluded myself into believing that I was obligated to share my sexcapades with my ex-girlfriend.

She deserves to know was more accurately *She deserves to be hurt, too.*

Amazing people do amazing things. Hateful people do hateful things.

4/28/17 – 501 Shelter, PA, 174 Miles Hiked – Day 15

A casual stroll turned into an intense cardiovascular workout as I rounded switchback after switchback. I was determined to rage the tall climb in one go under the unforgiving sun.

At the top I wrung out my buff, drenched from the unseasonable heat. I poured cool water back over it and rested the handful of salvation on my neck.

I felt the uncomfortable sensation of dog fur along my side. A friendly dog I'd seen several times on trail leaned up against me for more scratches as I complied.

"Scooby, leave him alone! It's way too hot for that," said her owner.

"It's all good!" I said. "Beautiful dog."

"Thanks, she loves it out here. I'm Scrappy, by the way."

"I'm Chris. At least for now, no trail name yet. Sorry I didn't introduce myself back there. I was determined to get to the top of this climb without stopping."

"No stoppy til the toppy!" an equally drenched male declared. "I'm Wonderboy. Nice to meetcha, man!"

"I'm Chris! 'No stoppy til the toppy,' I think I'm gonna have to steal that," I responded.

"By all means. Where ya headin'?" Wonderboy asked.

"I want to do another 10 miles but I'm not feeling my best today."

"Well we're stopping at 501 Shelter because a pizza place delivers there. Maybe we'll see ya," he said through a scraggly red beard.

"Sounds great, see you soon!" I waved and instantly decided that pizza was far too tantalizing to pass up.

Six miles later, I found my new friends scarfing down slices on a picnic table.

"You decided against pizza?" Scrappy inquired with a mouthful of melted cheese.

"What?! Fuck no, you guys said I could order pizza from the shelter!"

48

"Oops," Wonderboy said, preceding a swallow. "Yeah, not necessarily *from* the shelter. Technically the delivery guy meets you at the road a quarter-mile back."

"Gahhh, I guess I'll keep my shoes on then." I took out my phone to place an order.

"Sorry, mate. That's my bad. Here, to tide you over."

Wonderboy turned his pizza box towards me and may as well have opened a treasure chest. The smell of chicken, bacon, and ranch filled my nostrils and my stomach begged for it.

"It's ok, I'll just wait for mine to get here."

"Dude, take one, it's no big deal."

He clearly saw my intense unbroken eye contact with the slices before me and nudged the pie a few inches closer. I hesitated only briefly.

"Holy shit, thank you so much," I uttered. After inhaling the mouthwatering slice I strode away to call the pizzeria. When I got back my ears were burning.

"Oh yeah, he does," Scrappy said in agreement with whatever Wonderboy was saying.

"Uh oh, whatchu guys talking about?"

"With that hat, you kinda look like Indiana Jones," clarified Scrappy.

"That's kind of you to say that," I began with a smile. "Mr. Jones is a good man..."

Fractals vanished and reemerged among a bed of embers. The firepit was familiar, settled and moss-ridden after decades in the back of my family's trailer in the Poconos, Pennsylvania. Across the flames sat a friend away with me for the weekend. She found much less comfort in the blaze than I did.

A dozen yards off, a cricket perched on a weed beside a babbling brook. His leg was an impressive violin. The smell of damp pine filled my nose while dense smoke weaved in and out of my fingers like vaporous silk. My senses danced with each other, keenly aware of all of these things, and blurring the lines between them.

Ashley let out a heaving sigh as her LSD-induced anxiety waned. She looked up at the abundant stars, her posture indicating momentary ease. The acid was affecting me in a profoundly different way, inciting excitement and confidence along with my super senses.

The cricket continued, its clamor rippling along my cheeks. My awareness was pitch perfect while my mind was 800 miles away.

My feet took me over the Appalachian Trail's Franconia Notch. I saw sparrows. Wildflowers. A dark river slowly carving a green valley filled with life. New Hampshire's cold wind chilled my weathered face and I was smiling. Always smiling.

Above the fiddling cricket a raccoon climbed a tree. He was looking for those white gooey treats the humans tend to lose track of.

Another snap of my eyelids and I was beside a fire in the Great Smoky Mountains, very much like this one, beneath a full moon. A bear ambled a safe distance away. She needed to find some morsel for her young before she could return. A shooting star blazed across the sky and I gasped.

The stark vapor of my breath vanished in the Poconos mountain air.

My eyes dilated and the flames danced even more wildly, engulfing a large hunk of bark.

I'm ready.

I nodded in agreement with my thoughts, perplexing Ashley.

I'm ready, I will finish the Appalachian Trail.

The creekside cricket was gaining confidence in his performance, expecting to find a mate any moment now.

"You know with that hat and that bomber jacket you look just like Indiana Jones."

"That's kind of you to say that," I said without thinking. "Mr. Jones is a good man. An honorable man. I taught young Indiana everything he knows." My jaw found a hard to place manner of speech, a vague mashup of Daniel Craig and John Wayne.

"Is that so?" Ashley inquired through a smirk.

"I remember the first time he held a whip, young Indy. Looked a damn fool. But I knew he'd learn quickly. Stubborn as an ox. Had to be the best. Best in school, best with the leather."

"So you made Indiana Jones who he is?"

A smirk finally became a smile.

"Well I taught him a few things. More'n a few, I s'pose," I trailed off. "Damn kid wouldn't leave me alone. But he grew on me. Coulda charmed the hood off a nun with just a wink."

She laughed and I tapped into the John Wayne side with my gait, circling the fire.

"And what does a mentoring adventurer like yourself go by?"

Ashley asked.

The bit was improvised, yet somehow I knew the answer before my ridiculous claim to fictional fame. Before I took acid. The words formed in some nebulous time and space between me buying that ridiculous hat for $7.50 from Wal-Mart and setting foot on my favorite parcel of land in the entire world, the lot containing that mossy fire pit.

I looked down into the flames and grinned. I turned to my inquirer and tipped my hat just so. The cricket concluded his string solo.

"Well my friends call me Bones. Idaho Bones."

Chapter Five

4/29/17 – 501 Shelter, PA, 174 Miles Hiked – Day 16

"Idaho," a far off voice said as I slept. "Idaho Bones!" Scrappy blared with increased volume.

"Hmm?" I stirred.

"Idaho, we're doing laundry. You wanna get in on it?"

I sniffed my shirt, eyes still closed.

"Yeah I suppose I should. Thanks." I gathered my belongings and stepped out into the late morning sunshine. Wonderboy held a hose over a bucket in just his underwear.

"Idahoooo!" He said with a wave. "You might not need to do laundry, you haven't traveled that far, ya flip-floppa." A sinister grin came across his face and I reciprocated.

The night prior I divulged the origins of my alter ego, summarizing Idaho Bones as a 'less sexy, more drunk Indiana Jones.'

"That has to be your trail name," said Wonderboy as Scrappy nodded firmly once my full fireside spiel was completed.

After my name was established we continued getting to know one another by the fire. Wonderboy is from Atlanta. He decided on hiking the Appalachian Trail with similar reasons to my own and a familiar backstory.

"I worked a couple crappy jobs and was eventually fed up," Wonderboy said, shaking his head. "Had some money saved up and the AT seemed like the best way to squeeze every penny for the longest amount of time."

"I hiked Vermont's Long Trail last year," Scrappy shared. "I graduated college early. Ever since I set my mind on vet school I've been planning to hike the AT before veterinary classes start."

Three former strangers united by a new home in the woods.

The next morning would initiate my first day on trail where hiking wasn't a featured activity. My body appreciated the respite.

After laundry we reheated pizza over a fire and played Rummy. While picnicking in the sunshine I decided to whittle a little tiki head. Wonderboy's solar charger powered our phones and a Bluetooth speaker featuring reggae music.

"Wait, I forgot to ask," I began. "Where did *your* trail names come from?"

"Pokey here actually got her trail name before I did," Scrappy began, patting the enormous canine. "She wouldn't stop begging for snacks, so a hiker named her Scooby! She actually started responding to it immediately. Another hiker said 'Can't have Scooby without Scrappy' and that's how I got mine!"

"A guy literally couldn't read my signature in one of the trail logs," Wonderboy said. "As I was leaving the shelter he said, 'Wonderboy?? Sick trail name, bro!' and that was that!"

For the life of me I couldn't figure out what name could be mistaken for *Wonderboy* but I decided not to ask. It made me feel like a more legit thru-hiker to respect the alias.

Finally we reached a consensus that it wasn't too early to drink and we shared all my vodka with a pink lemonade mix. Kings was the drinking game of choice, which made short work of the cocktail. Luckily marshmallows outlasted the booze and we roasted them over the modest fire as the sun set.

A day spent on the trail without hiking is known as a Zero Day. And there were zero regrets to be found.

Any hiker who isn't going for a record will employ Zero Days, it's just a question of how many. It isn't sustainable to hike every day without rest. The average hiker will take at least one Zero Day per week.

I hadn't planned on taking one since the bout of norovirus slowed me down, but my newly healthy gut was telling me to stick with Wonderboy, Scrappy, and Scooby.

A shocking sound, the quintessential NFL jingle, rang from my phone back at my tent. With a sliver of cell service, an alert laying out the Giants draft picks at the close of the NFL draft popped up on my screen. I swiped the meaningless alert aside but sat in darkness recalling the disappointment from Mark's infamous brunch day. The last time I watched the Giants snap a pigskin.

After George fled from the cops, my father and I had disregarded our policy to avoid Mark when he's drinking to watch the Giants' wildcard playoff game. My aunt Michelle, whose policy was even stricter than ours, even made an exception. It was the first time all three siblings shared an evening together in over a decade. Everything had gone just a little too smoothly. That is, following the shared trauma of our confrontation with George.

My cousin Matt even insisted on documenting the evening with a photo. I looked at the damaged smiles on all their faces, thinking it couldn't be long before the other shoe dropped. Michelle wisely left at halftime, perhaps also sensing the bad voodoo in the air.

"Ooohhh, I'm very tempted...Mother fucker can't make a play!" my uncle began shortly into the third quarter. "I'm very tempted to say the n-word."

The last time he said yelled that word in front of me, I saw to it that he couldn't say it again for six whole weeks. After I broke his jawline that horrifying evening in the Poconos, he couldn't say anything at all, and had to sip beer through a straw.

It was largely disheartening but mostly infuriating to find that instead of learning his lesson two years ago, my uncle had just gotten - well I couldn't bring myself to use the word *clever*. Instead of yelling it at the top of his lungs, he'd taken to holding the mother of all racist slurs verbally hostage.

Mark's word games lit a fuse. There was no telling how long that fuse was. My heart began to race and I could sense my father and cousin succumbing to their own unique brands of fight or flight response. The air was thick with unease.

The shrill, amplified ring of the telephone rattled the walls and it only barely registered with my half-deaf grandmother as she answered. A long silence followed as she nodded her head.

"Okay, thanks for calling. Everything's fine now."

She hung up the receiver and the room boomed once more.

"FINE??" my dad's inquiry took us all by surprise. "You told the cops everything's FINE? That's a funny way of putting it."

The silence was cut by my father's rasping knuckles. The final tick in a series of habits that always preceded an Irish temper. The calm before the Gaelic storm.

"You send your grandsons into the den of a drunken beast and you think everything's fine now? You endangered my son!"

"I simply didn't want to come home to Mark and George fighting!" my grandmother moaned. She already sounded exhausted by the conversation, like she wished to sweep the incident underneath an already unkempt rug.

"Why did you ever let him come back here?" I yelled, the anger at my grandmother's negligence was boiling over before I could get a lid on it.

"Why don't you just let that man drown in his own shit?"

"Hey!" Mark yelled, eyes wide. "You think you can tawk to my muthuh like that? On my brunch day?"

"Do you hear yourself?" I whipped around to Mark. "You yell at grandma all the time! You yelled at her ten minutes ago! Is your precious brunch day ruined? Wasn't it already spoiled when you harassed your fiance's daughters? Why don't you go punch another fucking hole in the wall about it!"

Mark squared up to me and his eyes went even wider.

The fuse's spark was racing now, hungry for the blast.

"I'll do what I want," he began through gritted teeth. "This is my-fawck-ing-hoooouse."

"The house you were supposed to move out of five months ago?" my dad said, making his way over to Mark. "You think dad would be proud of you right now? He would've thrown your sorry ass on the street years ago."

Mark pushed my father and the tension finally erupted.

As if choreographed, my cousin and I withheld our respective uncles from one another.

Places, people! We're running Christmas fistfight circa 1999! Action!

Mark broke free from me and knocked over the dog's water bowl, casting water across the kitchen tile. I managed to gain another grapple on Mark mere feet away from my father's reach, who was still struggling against Matt's blockade of the kitchen. My grandmother remained in her recliner in the living room, either paralyzed by fear or smart enough to stay far away from the fray. Her strained pleas to stop fighting barely made it into the kitchen.

My arms effectively pinned Mark against the rear sliding door of the house and our eyes finally met. The same lunacy broke through his retinas that met my gaze that violent night in the Poconos. Fear melted down my spine as I wondered what end we'd meet under my grandma's roof, and whether all bones would be intact come morning.

Mark's maddening gaze shot around the room. He kicked off the sliding door and my feet slid along the wet kitchen tile. My right shoulder slammed against the floor but I instinctively righted my torso, prepared for more battle.

"I'm DONE!" I yelled from my knees, causing a unanimous pause.

"I'm DONE trying to help you people. All of you!" I continued as I got back on my feet.

Silence persisted in the room as relief rushed through me.

"Good!" my uncle yelled, eyes wide and crazed but not daring to cross me again. From a distance he settled on his scornful words. "Then get the fuck outta my house!"

"Oh fuck you all!" Matt wailed, storming out of the house.

"This is your fucking fault." I said as I followed, pointing at my grandmother, sobbing in her recliner.

She buried her tear-filled face in her hands as I resolutely left that awful house for the last time. I was still a long way from forgiving the woman who changed a dumpster's worth of my diapers. Her dangerous manipulations and alcoholic transgressions eclipsed the summer getaways she made possible in the Poconos mountains.

Snowflakes battered my flushed cheeks as I ran through Staten Island's slushy streets to find my cousin. My full and growing beer belly forced me into a power walk only a block later. Knowing that I'd soon be hiking all day everyday, I willingly indulged throughout the holiday season. I figured a layer of blubber may well save my life on the AT. And if I didn't need it for survival, it'd be gone in a flash.

What was I going to do for the next three months before my Appalachian Trail departure? My newly abandoned plan was to continue renovating my grandmother's house, hoping I could stay just barely ahead of my uncle's wrecking ball of a fist. Or that he'd find a stud instead of plaster.

The desire to help my family was genuine and pure. My grandmother dug quite a hole for my father and aunt burning through grandpa's settlement money after his untimely death. Then she fell prey to those sleazy reverse mortgage sharks. With my proposed plan, approved unanimously by the family (at least on paper), we could sell the house once I was done fixing it up and cover all the bases. There would even be enough for seven years of assisted living after every hand was properly filled.

One of those hands was my own. After spending my twenties scraping out savings from soul-sucking desk jobs, I was going to pay myself directly for my labor. At half the price of a licensed contractor, but still, it'd all be mine.

"Oh fuck," I panted, breath lingering long enough for anxious thoughts to swirl in my mind as I scanned the streets for any sign of my cousin.

I was relieved to abandon my plan, but this meant a substantially lower budget for my thru-hike. Not to mention the anxiety of having no purpose whatsoever for three months before I left. Peppered with fresh trauma of the day.

Filled with more doubt than peace of mind under the snow covered street lamps, I was able to make one clear decision.

Keep walking.

Wonderboy and Scrappy wisely tucked into their sleeping bags at 9:30, intending to get an early start and big miles the following day. Scrappy briefly rejoined me by the fire to brush her teeth and stare at the moon.

"I doo theesh evuhrynight," she sloshed out with a foamy smile. "Mayksh me sho happy."

My eyes couldn't seem to leave the moon's glow after that. I ambled the enormous campground, catching the lunar glow through a menagerie of stark canopies. A profound peace swelled within me, knowing that I was safe, where I was meant to be, with people who already exuded warmth and support.

I found my tent but decided I wasn't ready for bed yet. Eyes scanning the blurred line of the waxing crescent, I kept walking.

Chapter Six

202 Miles Hiked, 1,987 Miles to Go
Days 18-21

5/1/17 – Windsor Furnace Shelter, PA, 202 Miles Hiked - Day 18

From every ridgeline, blue mountains faded into nothing on both sides. It was as if Pennsylvania was the only place on Earth. Or at least, at the very edge of the world.

Once the magnificent views began to blur together, my mind drifted back to Erica.

I'd recently sent a text to her, the cringe of which still had me rolling in my sleeping bag that morning.

Finally on the trail. It's lovely. I hope you're doing well. I also hope that you come around to seeing that you owe me some kind of explanation for why you ended things.

The last text I sent her went unanswered. This response was immediate:

Dude, I don't owe you SHIT! Have a nice life!

For over three years I was convinced this woman was the purest and kindest soul to ever walk among us. Now she was unrecognizable to me. Mere days into my hike, Erica sent me a podcast on sex addiction with no explanation. She only said I might find it useful. Now it was clear Erica felt that I don't deserve *any* explanations.

The accusation of being a sex addict was quite the puzzle in and of itself, and one that uncovered even more questions. What would make her think that? It's not like Erica and I were having ridiculous amounts of sex, or that I was petitioning her to an unhealthy or harrowing degree. My educated guess was that her conclusion was related to our group sex dynamics.

Years before our breakup, Erica expressed a desire to delve deeper into her largely unexplored bisexuality. By chance, an old hookup turned friend of mine expressed a significant attraction to Erica. The three of us enjoyed a few romps before our special guest in the bedroom moved to another city. Erica enjoyed the trysts enough to seek more, and soon we were attending meetups for swingers. We met a woman, Jen, who began joining us in bed on a somewhat regular basis.

Having no reason to think it was a bad idea, anytime a woman expressed interest in the two of us, I'd present the prospect to Erica. She soon expressed feeling overwhelmed by that. I asked if we could keep going to the swinger meetups and she did not like that one bit; she felt like she wasn't enough. I backed off completely, Erica's security was my priority. Jen became a platonic friend.

I wasn't resentful of Erica, but a part of me was sad. That particular swinger community didn't feel like home, but the non-monogamous lifestyle felt ideal for me. I wanted to keep exploring it but my partner wanted to retreat. Ironically, I felt closer to Erica, more in love with Erica, when we were non-monogamous.

My hypothesis was that the sum of all these parts is what led Erica to conclude I was a sex addict. Unfortunately for me, Erica made it clear she wasn't in the business anymore of proving or disproving my hypotheses.

With no answers from my ex-girlfriend, I couldn't resist looking for them among the soundwaves cast my way. The subject of the podcast was a white male in his late 20s. He and I shared a promiscuous lifestyle. At least I knew why Erica believed I should listen. One of his sex partners recommended Sex and Love Addicts Anonymous and joining the group changed his life.

In her text recommending the episode, Erica shared that she too was finding peace in such a group, as she had self-diagnosed as a love addict. In other words, an inability to remain single. She concluded she had become what is colloquially known as a serial monogamist.

When she first shared it, I sent an unanswered text about the podcast I hadn't yet listened to:

Thanks for sending this, Erica. But may I ask why you felt compelled to do so? I've been upfront and respectful of every partner I've had and no one close to me has expressed any concern about my recent choices.

The lack of clarification opened up dark corners of my mind. *Was I* a sex addict? It was a question I'd asked myself and professionals in years past. Through therapy, research, and ample reflection, I ultimately decided the diagnosis didn't add up. The shrinks agreed.

Yet the person I'd been most honest with was treating it like a scientific fact. A fact without evidence! If it were merely a resolution, something with some meat on it, I could hold a debate. An opinion presented as fact left no room to properly oppose the resolution, or for me to render myself a new verdict.

I just wanted to know exactly *why* she felt I was a sex addict.

The podcast wrapped up with a heartwarming tale of how the sex addict abstained for a month. Two of his partners were vying for the privilege of taking his backload, and a threesome was agreed upon. Classic Disney ending.

I sat on a rock to switch to an audiobook as the sun left me in sudden darkness on the north side of the mountain. The shelter was still four miles ahead, where early birds Scrappy and Wonderboy waited for me to catch up.

I navigated the dimming woods without my headlamp, waiting as long as possible to switch it on. It was a habit I'd developed without fully understanding the why, but I'd begun to notice other hikers doing the same. My best guess was that our eyes are remarkably adaptable in low light, but once the headlamp is in use, all that goes out the window. The moment that LED is employed, one's vision is limited to that little tunnel of light and nothing more. Apparently I wasn't the only one who found the natural method to be surprisingly more comforting while alone in the forest.

Loud rustling cut through the bizarre dialogue of Kurt Vonnegut's *Cat's Cradle*. I paused the satirical tale of military overstepping and general human stupidity and tried to hear anything over my pounding chest. A crack of a branch and my headlamp was fired up, racing back and forth in the direction of the disturbance. A glimmer of euphoria passed through me when the Windsor Furnace Shelter sign was illuminated, but was dashed by the first visible signs of life. Branches snapped back into place about three feet above the ground. Something large had noticed me and thankfully seemed to be scurrying away from me.

Leaves continued to bounce and rustle but there were no eyes reflecting back at me. No white tail either which I knew to be very easy to spot on deer. All evidence pointed to a bear.

The sound of my heartbeat seemed to fill the air as every drop of sweat turned to ice. A quiet, shrill noise escaped my clenched jaw as I scurried up the path to any semblance of safety. I remembered that Wonderboy and Scrappy, but more importantly the faithful pup Scooby, awaited me at the end of the short side trail to the shelter.

That whole day I would've done anything for a distraction from Erica. A dusky bear encounter was not what I had in mind, but it was effective.

5/2/17–Allentown Hiking Club Shelter, PA, 219 Miles Hiked - Day 19

Claps of thunder kept sleep out of grasp much of the evening, making the snooze button irresistible. I finally mobilized around 12:30 and embarked on what turned out to be a pretty flat day with some gorgeous views along the ridgeline. I was struck by something odd along the way. Two rocks spray painted with "*Who Dis?*"

Part of this journey is answering the same questions people ask you about yourself over and over. "I'm Chris, I grew up in NY, lived in DC for 10 years, used to be a conference planner, me and the ex were supposed to hike together but here I am alone." *Jazz hands*

Basically an assortment of questions leading up to or implying, better yet, one inquiry:

Who are you?

Or alternatively:

Who Dis?

Despite being asked the same 20 questions for weeks, seeing this ridiculous graffiti prompt felt like truly pondering my identity for the first time.

Who Am I? Who have I brought to this trail and who will be leaving?

I meditated on it. I was pleased that the answer that initially kept ringing in my head was "*Idaho Bones. Dis be Idaho Bones.*"

A new "answer" presented itself to me:

"Who's asking?"

I grew up sporting multiple identities. To my family, I'm Chris. To my friends, I'm vz. To my fellow hikers, I'm Idaho Bones. So I can't tell you *who dis* until I'm aware of exactly who dispensin' the question!

Even then, I can't guarantee the same man with the same temperament will arrive at Mt. Katahdin, and eventually lay his hands at Springer Mountain.

In a middle school where whites were the minority and intelligence equated to a bullseye, I did everything to fit in. I tawked the tawk and my boxers could be seen between an oversized shirt and ill-fitting jeans as I blared Nelly from my Walkman. That didn't stop me from getting beat up or having things stolen, but I think it helped a little. I didn't like who I was, but it never really occurred to me to be anyone else.

It did occur to me to be someone with more money.

"I went over to his shitty ass apartment, and they eat glass when they run out of food," were the words a pitying friend revealed were being circulated about me.

I thought Craig was a good friend which made his insult cut as deep as the glass I supposedly subsisted on. I'd never spoken ill of him or his family. I was as confused as I was hurt when I heard about the nasty rumor. Eventually I confronted him directly. He said he was simply going along with the conversation, leaving me to trust no one.

For a year the other flavors of the week eclipsed the matter of my family's assets. Or lack thereof. Another friend whom I grew up playing baseball with was named as a source of the same old jabs.

"Chris Veasey is so poor, his family would call a dumpster fire 'free heating.'"

John waited on what was apparently hesitant laughter, which was a minor consolation.

"His family actually just bought a house."

"Oh," John replied. "Well I meant that he's poor in *comedy*."

I certainly had witnessed some bad standup acts, but *poor* was never the word that came to mind to describe the lackluster performance. It was a poor attempt at a save.

I remember being thoroughly perplexed. My family was nowhere close to the poverty line. We never ran out of food, and the radiator in my bedroom could've seared a steak. I mean sure, we rarely had steak, but even then I knew enough about socio-economics that we were still middle class. It's just that it took my parents a little longer to build equity, and that was enough for my so-called friends with their parents' cookie cutter houses to spread sinister rumors.

One afternoon five students were called out of their eighth grade classes. We were told that a specialized high school, Staten Island Tech, took a power score of our grades and state exams and handpicked us for their next incoming class. It was the most surreal moment of my life. I didn't even know such a school existed.

In my first high school class I ruined a perfect pastel rainbow of Aeropostale polos with a navy graphic tee. Second class plopped me down amidst a blurred line of emo and goth. Later, I walked the cafeteria of everything in between, finding each demographic at every table.

Everyone was different. And no one seemed to care.

The next day I wore a favorite Spongebob shirt I'd been afraid to wear out of the house and people loved it. So I bought more. My lunch money stayed right in my chain wallet where it belonged and nobody searched for the endless insults that rhyme with *Veasey*. No one wanted to see my family's income tax documents, either. There were cliques, but the territories weren't enforced. The student body as a whole just seemed happy to be somewhere they could unapologetically be themselves.

I had no idea Staten Island raised these kinds of kids. Granted, there were less than 800 of us in the entire school, but it still felt like an oasis. The institution had your run of the mill social conflicts but they were all watered down. Attending school in a bubble, I came to fully resent the island that birthed me.

Taking public transportation to school every day kept my finger on the pulse of the status quo. I couldn't blast my headphones loud enough to ignore the ignorance. By the time even two of my friends had a license to drive, we developed our own "high brow" white trash routines.

We'd take over Starbucks parking lots to discuss anything from masturbation to reparations. Then we'd air out dreads of existentialism between rounds of tag at the Miller Field Playground. After an angsty walk on the still trash ridden South Beach, us teenage prodigal hooligans would take over a corner booth at Mike's Diner to ingest still harmless complex carbohydrates until the sun teased morning.

My friends were always polite enough to resist pointing out that my "usual" was a toasted corn muffin with butter, even when I was starving. Setting me back a whole three dollars including tax and tip, only my less tactful companions would extend a hand my way when the bill was a few bucks short. They knew I myself had limited petty cash, but they weren't about to hold it against me as it had been in my past.

"Are you sure you want to spend the $60 on UPenn's application?"

It was Junior year, and personally I felt it was high time for a diploma. My college advisor was as subtle with her pants suits as she was with teenagers' dreams.

"I mean, it's a great reach school...but why not...?" She did this weird hunching back and forth shrug that movies told me was for losers aiming too far past the stars.

"You don't think I could make Penn?" I asked, head cocked.

Perhaps I should have been more realistic with a 1380 SAT, sporting the median score of my peers at Staten Island Tech. But what about the extracurriculars that were supposedly so important year after year? The principal practically shooed each of us along to some after school bullshit under the guise that it would shine brighter than any grade we could earn at a desk.

I was Class President. I ran track and field for a manipulative hardass every single semester. My inclination to do every term's theater production came from an even mix of respect for the craft and FOMO. After all, at 5' flat, the only chance I had for frenching girls was among a sea of theater guys fully at peace with their homosexuality.

By senior year, we were all discovering the distinguishing effects of each liquor at the same rich people's houses with no discernible prejudice towards one another. Goths filling beer bongs for jocks, cheerleaders holding hair for the nauseous debate team. Truly a sight to behold. Thank goodness there's a couple Staten Island parents sitting on a Florida beach during any given three day weekend.

We Techies were more immune to Senioritis than our friends at other schools. My routine at 17 years old was harrowing as ever:

5:10 am: wake up

6:00 am: catch bus

6:50 am: take advanced *College Now* courses

11:30 am: eat lunch while planning grade's events as Class President

2:20 pm: leave final class for theater. *Direct* said theater production

4:30 pm: Go consult with track coach to make up workout that I missed (that is, if I wasn't injured, which I often was)

6:00 pm: catch bus home

7:00 pm: Sleep two hours

9:00 pm: Eat reheated dinner and shower

9:30 pm: Begin homework

12:37 am: Turn on Conan O'Brien, put finishing touches on homework

1:00 am: Go to bed, but only if Conan's guests weren't fire so let's be honest, it was usually later

Once we all had our college applications sent off, Senioritis finally crept its way in. We were exhausted and free.

My crosshairs had shifted to Georgetown and I commuted into Manhattan for an alumnus interview. The Long Island trust fund man-child ran his fingers through his greasy dark hair, seeming to lead me with his eyes to every bit of accomplishment around his overkill office.

"So tell me," he began, putting a wet curl back over his brow. "Why Georgetown?"

"Well," I replied. "I want to be a politician. So DC's the place to be!"

"Ha!" He slapped a hand hard on his fancy desk. "I used to want to fuck with politics!"

I could sense where he was going. As I sweat into my dad's old suit, he leaned back in his chair with eyes narrowed, the soles of his shoes staring me in the face. Each following profanity sent me deeper into doubt and anxiety.

"You know," he muttered as he intertwined his white knuckles behind his head. "I'm not so sure I see you at Georgetown."

It felt like I was speaking with the institution directly. Like this cocky finance douche embodied everything about the school's culture that I was choosing to overlook.

"You know what," I responded, folding up my cheap little padfolio.

"I don't see it either."

I walked around the city, wondering what to make of it all. It felt like half my list of colleges had their own unique brand of preppy frat bro, ready to look down on me all over again. How could this Staten Island boy who could always count on a cinder block in his trailer's backyard ever fit in among them?

For the first time in years I felt truly proud of my upbringing. I was glad for Tech's influence on me. Yet something about growing up in the proper middle class, sitting upper upper deck at Shea Stadium and packing into my dad's ancient Plymouth Voyager didn't feel trashy anymore.

It just felt real.

Though I was only sporting the moniker for several days, Idaho Bones felt kismet. I couldn't return to civilization as Idaho Bones, and yet wearing that hat for a period of my life felt ineffably predestined.

The name Chris never bothered me, but its proclivity was maddening. I was once in a class with four other Chrises. It was hard to distinguish myself when we could've filled in half a Brady Bunch block. Hearing the hailing of other Chrises incessantly, I stopped bothering to turn my head at the grocery store in kindergarten. Chances are, I wasn't in trouble. If I were, patrons would've heard *Christopher Michael!* bouncing off the glass of the frozen food section.

It wasn't a scorn of the flagship name that made me so desperate to be given a trail name. It wasn't self-hatred, either. I was largely proud of the man I grew up to be but there were some tarnishes in the mirror. If I had to pin one one intrusive thought down to the mat, it would've been Chris's inability to finish endeavors he started.

This is why finishing the Appalachian Trail, an imposing, wild challenge, was so critical to Chris. It was a scary thought to think of leaving any of the path untraveled. Of admitting to myself and anyone watching that I had to leave it unfinished and be guilty once more of settling for less than I aimed for.

Good thing Idaho Bones was at the helm. His trail legs were getting stronger by the day. His successes were Chris's.

Chapter Seven

271 Miles Hiked, 1,918 Miles to Go

Days 22-26

5/5/17 – Church of the Mountain Hostel, Delaware Water Gap, PA, 271
Miles Hiked - Day 22

Foul whiffs of hot metal filled the room, fluorescent lights flickering
in time with a Maytag older than my sister. I entrusted the rusty dryer with
every bit of clothing I had, seeing no other option after yanking the sopping
load from a slightly younger Whirlpool washer. I wasn't staying at the motel
above me but laundry services were offered to thru-hikers. Donning
nothing more than my orange raincoat and a towel I snagged from a room
service rack, I ventured outside for a solo safety meeting. AKA time to
smoke a joint.

As I watched birds try to bone each other it truly hit me:

I'm fucking *out here.*

Nearly a month since those first steps, I was uncovering Trail Magic
everywhere in all its forms. I'd been vagabonding on trail for 22 days and
nothing about those first few weeks led me to believe I wouldn't see every
damn mile the AT had to offer.

This isn't to say I hadn't ever felt far from home before but
something about banging quarters into a slot in the basement of some
run-down motel in a town I never even heard of really drove it home. The
trail led me right into Delaware Water Gap, a town I knew nothing about. I
had no plans, no preconceived notions, no insights. Every trip I'd ever
taken in my life had been meticulously mapped out in advance. Bizarre
experiences like that are what beckoned me. Saying yes and ending up
somewhere unpredictable felt like the opposite of the autopilot I'd been
cruising on for as long as I could remember.

The things I thought I needed, all the things I was convinced were
essential to my happiness: they were an illusion. That life that I put on a
shelf because I thought it was too hard, too far out of reach, too much in
the hands of others. How wrong I was.

The world seemed to do everything to convince me that I needed
the job that filled me with dread Monday through Friday. That dread boiled
over every Sunday evening. I'd lie awake, exhausted but unable to sleep

knowing what the morning held.

My hierarchy of needs had been dismantled in Appalachia. Without a job, home, or partner, I was doing fine. Everything about my upbringing suggested that I'd crumble along with that dismantling. This wasn't the case.

It also wasn't the case for all the fathers, wives, and bachelors of all ages and backgrounds I'd already met on the trail. Anyone doing a thru-hike left something behind completely. Something they can't go back to. Maybe it'll be close to what it was but it will never be the same.

Thru-hikers take to the Appalachian Trail knowing they abandoned something forever. Yet they choose to deal, to cope, to survive. To see things they've never seen before. Things they *couldn't* see before.

Many thru-hikers return to civilization and opt for a new job. Often it pays less but fulfills more. Their paradigms have shifted.

For years I fought all that. I bought into the "work/life balance fallacy."

I live to work, I don't work to live. So I'll make sacrifices here, and I'll reap the benefits there.

But there is no balance anymore. I was always on call or under watch. Anytime I went anywhere I "represented the company."

My life wasn't truly mine.

The marijuana crackled and the industrial buzzing of the dryer beckoned me back inside. I tightened the towel around my waist and needed two hands to pry open the rusty door.

I pulled the heap of warm clothes to my face and breathed deeply. Lavender and metal filled my nostrils.

All the clothes I needed. All of them mine.

5/6/17 – Church of the Mountain Hostel, Delaware Water Gap, PA, 271 Miles Hiked - Day 23

"$4.50 each?" Johnny Quest interrogated. "Back in Connecticut these cost less than two bucks."

The owner of the pizzeria shrugged as Johnny returned The Steel Reserve Forties to the fridge, apparently never before experiencing a convenience up-charge. He found the 12% ABV Four Loko's market price to be more palatable and sat down.

Johnny and I met at Kirkridge Shelter and hiked into DWG together the day before. Us rowdy East Coast boys hit it off and ventured out to whet our whistles late into our Zero Day. I had been leapfrogging with Wonderboy and Scrappy, barely missing each other repeatedly over the previous handful of days. On the church hostel's WiFi, I told them I'd be waiting in Delaware Water Gap.

"Ok, so why on Earth are you hiking 40 miles tomorrow?" I asked Johnny.

"I'm training for the 24 Challenge," he replied, taking a swig of his malt beverage under the red neon glow of a pizza slice over the counter. Seeing the confusion on my face he continued, "It's simple, only three rules: 24 beers, 24 miles, 24 hours."

"Oh, that's easy," I said.

"You think so? I bet you 20 bucks you can't do it."

"Done. No problem. Then I'll take that twenty and buy a 30 rack, do my own 30 Challenge."

"You're crazy," said my new friend with the iron discipline.

"I'm Irish," I replied as I rose to purchase a six pack of Yuengling Black and Tan. "Oh, you know what. I'll take a Four Loko as well."

Johnny scoffed as I tipped the very patient business owner. As soon as I cracked the Robitussin-like poison I doubled down on my competitive nature.

"It's simple. Leave at noon, hike 14 miles. I can do that in six hours just about anywhere. 6 pm - 9 pm, drink 12 beers. That should put me right to sleep. Wake up at five with ten miles, seven hours, and 12 beers remaining. Drink a beer every mile, taking a lil nap if necessary, which I don't anticipate needing."

"Oh, I never thought of doing it that way," he began. "That's actually a really good plan. Let's do it in Connecticut, bro!"

An unease was welling up at the thought of taking on the 24 Challenge. My family's alcoholic history was at the forefront of my mind. Hiking and boozing had already intertwined past a point I was proud of. Without breaking a mental sweat, my brain devised a plan to combine the two in a problematic, if not dangerous way.

Johnny turned up the Lil Dicky song on his phone and started fist bumping at the table. A group of eight walked in and kept looking back at our table between glances at the menu. They muttered amongst themselves and left soon after.

"Oh, Johnny," I started. "You don't need it, but you should really keep drinking to make up for the business you just cost this place."

I couldn't help being keenly aware of the impact our patronage had on this small business. Three of my uncles had gotten themselves banned from a pub back home. All for different reasons. For the better part of my life, I'd perfected apologizing to strangers for the actions of my relatives.

"Matt!" I yelled, picking back up to a pathetic jog. He made no indication of hearing me. "Matt, c'mon, wait a second."

"No!" he said with a cracking voice. "I'm fucking done, I'm done with all of you!"

"Hey!" I threw myself in front of him on the slick sidewalk. "We have to be better. Remember? We can't be like them, we can't walk away from each other."

We embraced and I could feel his tension subside a little. *Be Better* had become the unofficial slogan between us. The words served as a promise to ourselves and one another to learn from our family's mistakes. We'll never be perfect, but we can and will be better.

I convinced Matt to join my dad and I at Legends Pub to watch the end of the Giants game.

"Give us a few minutes," I said to my dad at the bar. "I think a little time just the two of us will help Matt move on from tonight."

My dad's lack of response told me how hurt he was. Part of me was glad for it. He needed to see his part in this madness. From across the bar I could see tears at the corners of his eyes.

"He feels terrible," I told Matt. "I know he's sorry and he should be."

Matt stared at me intensely.

"*I'm* sorry," I relented.

"My dad's an asshole, no doubt about it," Matt also relented. "But when he's drinking like that...Do. Not. Engage."

"I'm not ok with that."

Matt let out a mocking guffaw.

"You think I'm ok with that? He's my *father*." Matt took a long swig of his beer. "But the man's gotten beaten to a pulp. Arrested. His own son wouldn't talk to him for two years. And he never learned from any of it. He's never gonna change."

I nodded, remembering that I wasn't the only one who had to get physical with Mark. His own son had to pin him to the ground whenever all other options were exhausted.

Matt's eyes carried the weight of the years I'd taken off from our family in DC. He was there for the fights and the restraining orders while I had the luxury of two hundred something miles and blissful ignorance.

It wasn't easy for me to finally cut off communication years prior. Mark was a complex man. In a family of Irishmen drinking away their feelings, he was generous with his love. Words of affirmation weaved together between misogynistic advances and outright anger in a bell curve of intoxication. When that bank of goodwill ran dry, there was still plenty of pity for the tortured soul. And goddammit if he wasn't cunningly charming shy of three beers.

Matt let out a fatigued sigh right before Eli Manning threw an interception. A slew of insults filled the air and my dad's bemoaning rose above the rest.

"Come oooon, who are you throwin' to?"

"All right," Matt began. "Let's go keep your dad company."

My father put an arm around each of us, seeming to will an apology through his shaking hands. Some semblance of normalcy was achieved but I could sense Matt's despondence.

An Asian man quietly entered the bar and surveyed the place beneath his wrinkled gray cap. Clutched under his flimsy windbreaker was a ratty old binder. He smiled at the bartender and made his rounds. It took a few patrons before someone's interest was piqued. DVD sleeves fluttered to reveal Hollywood's recent blockbuster hits with clunky faded stickers designating each one. He bowed his cap from dupe to rube, failing to close on anyone. As he neared my heart rate quickened.

My dad's hands, close to his sides, began to flail at the wrist as he tucked his tongue into his lower lip. It's a lifelong tick that haunts me to this day.

"You've gotta be fucking kidding me," escaped his sneering chops and I tried to distract with a jeer at the television.

The bootlegger appeared to deem us unworthy customers and kept shuffling down the bar. My father squared his shoulders directly in front of the feeble man who reeled before looking up.

"Hi. What do you have there?" my dad interrogated.

At first he waved a dismissing hand but my father's expecting palm was waiting. The binder was furnished and he quickly flipped through the collection.

"Dad, seriously? Come on, it's not worth it," I pleaded. "It's already been a rough night. Please."

"Where did you get this?" My father pointed at a page containing The Sopranos and awaited an answer. All he got was a nervous smile and weak hands grabbing for the discs. "I said, where did you get this? I work for HBO, this isn't authorized by HBO!"

His voice grew louder and I could hear the slight rasping of his knuckles against one another. The next stage of his tick. Flailing of the hands didn't coincide with coherent language. Thankfully he wasn't there yet. My dad was the last of his brothers allowed inside of this establishment, and it was looking like his residency was about to end.

"This is illegal, you are a criminal! I'm taking this to the police."

"Dad!" I yelled before lowering my voice. "Are you fucking kidding me? Haven't you had enough for one day? Let it go."

"This is why I can't afford a new roof." One set of knuckles got a break in exchange for a resolute point at the man who was eager to leave. "This motherfucker is why I can't afford to fix my car!"

"Ok, we're not doing this." I grabbed the binder and shoved it back at the traveling salesman. "Get outta here. Go!"

The man glacially moved for the exit while Matt stepped in front of my dad.

"Uncle Mike, come on. Please."

In a flash I uncovered a great deal of regrets in my life. The relentless stalking took me back to instances where I couldn't let sleeping dogs lie. Where alcohol tipped the scale so heavily toward rage that nothing could stop me. Not two of my friends. Not Buddha. Not even a 250 pound tight end. Anger had outweighed all of them my whole life.

Pristinely I saw myself in my father's irrational indignance. The angry apple that plopped right down on the dirt it plunged to. The red hot spitting image of Irish fury.

The old man pulled the door and my old man's foot stopped it.

"Give that to me."

I rushed over to pull the door and put a hand on my dad's shoulder. He swatted it away and grabbed for the binder.

"Enough!" I bellowed.

Again, all eyes were on us. I seized the momentary lapse in attention and kicked his foot out of the way. Finally the source of my father's misplaced madness was gone and I put my own foot in front of the door to prevent a pursuit. An eerie laugh followed as my dad returned to our spot at the bar. It should have been harder for Matt and I to act like nothing happened but turning a blind eye is in our blood.

The Giants inevitably blew it and we bade farewell to my cousin. Too drunk to drive, my dad and I began the chilly walk home. Still on edge, I hardly felt the icy wind hitting my cheeks. I couldn't believe how long we simply talked about football.

"I'm really done with trying to help grandma, you know. Done with renovating the house." I looked my dad in the eye and frowned. "I can't beat Mark. It's just too much to bear."

"Of course, buddy. It's not your fight. You tried your best."

I hated the thought of adding another failed project to my list but the relief was corporeal. My feet were even lighter realizing I wouldn't have to see my brutal uncles ever again, if I played my cards right.

"You know, you literally have the worst brothers imaginable." A chuckle I couldn't understand escaped me. "I mean, I've heard some family horror stories but your brothers are actually the worst."

"I know, man," my dad said before a long exhale, filling the winter air with thick vapor. "I just don't understand where it all went so wrong, what I could have–"

"No!" I declared. "No more of that. It's not your fault they're such fucking assholes."

I'd witnessed enough of him taking responsibility as the oldest for their tireless fuckery. I wished he could quit them the way I could. Maybe then he'd ignore bootleggers.

We sloshed speechless through the wintry mix for another block.

"So if you finish the trail -"

"*When* I finish the trail."

"When you finish the trail," my dad restarted. "What will you do next?"

It was my turn to fill the air with a ghastly sigh.

"I don't fucking know. I'm hoping any of these firefighter opportunities pan out." Realizing the slim odds of that, I continued, "I wish I majored in psychology. I regret not doing that, I think I could have been a great therapist."

"Monkeyman," my dad began, grabbing me by the shoulder. "I would sell my house to help you go back to school for that."

.I halted in the middle of the street and the tears came fast.

"Awwww, buddy." My dad pulled me into his chest and the levees broke. "Buddy, buddy, buddy. It's ok. You must have been holding that in all day."

Air rushed in but heavy sobs interjected before I could correct him. All my life, dad. All my fucking life.

"Yeah, lick it...lick it up."

As much as I wish I didn't hear them, lapping sounds did follow.

"No, don't bite it." Now my eyes were wide open. "Yeah, you like that don't you, girl?"

I rolled over to find Johnny Quest giving Scooby free reign over his mostly full jar of peanut butter. It was a relief to see him giving the dog a nutty treat and not the other way around. That being said, the allowance of a dog who eats poop into your main protein source disturbed me.

The return of the mighty mutt meant that Wonderboy and Scrappy had finally caught up to me.

"Johnny!" Scrappy said before giving him a big hug.

"Idaho, we gotcha!" Wonderboy exclaimed as he tossed his pack to the floor with a splash. "It poured all morning. Gonna start up again in a few hours. Zero?"

True NOBOs were quite vocal about the quicksand effect of trail towns, and how easy it is for them to suck hikers in with decadent foods, hot showers, and free-flowing booze. I pondered my willpower as the couch seemed to draw me deeper into its cushions, begging me to take two Zero Days in a row.

I felt guilty about taking another day off, but soon a clearer culprit revealed itself: I didn't like that I'd be drinking heavily yet again. Sure, I didn't have to, but Wonderboy and I just kind of had that effect on each other. I didn't think I'd drink so much alcohol on trail but sometime after leaving Harpers Ferry I got the impression that more drinking meant more comradery which meant more adventurous fun. It was like a way to ensure I was getting the most bang for my buck out of the hike.

As it turns out, the tiny town had a few stones I hadn't uncovered yet. A trail-famous spot selling pie and a hot dog for $2.50 was just down main street. On our way, a few wholesome looking men and boys took pause from building a gazebo outside the church to ask us about our stay. A tall man with a long beard offered his hand.

"Well if there's anything you need, even if it feels ridiculous, you let us know! My name's Kyle, I help run the church."

"Appreciate it, Kyle. That's a beautiful gazebo," said Wonderboy.

"Thanks, we're helping these boys earn a badge. We'll be done this afternoon, be sure to enjoy it before you leave."

After several rounds of dogs 'n' pie, we returned to the pizzeria to continue replacing lost business. A stone's throw away we sat under a much less impressive, dilapidated gazebo next to an abandoned inground pool.

"You really think you can shotgun an entire Four Loko, right now?" Wonderboy asked Johnny Quest.

"Bro, I used to do it all the time."

Johnny, who was supposed to be 40 miles north, was 40 ounces into his Steel Reserve.

"Yeah but you just drank a forty! And this sludge is so sweet, dude. There's no way," I egged him on.

"Buy me one right now."

"Ok," Wonderboy started, handing over $10. "But if you spill, you're buying me a six pack."

The three of us watched Johnny zig zag back to the lattice structure and we instinctively created some space from the show.

"Holy shit, he's actually gonna make it," I said.

Five seconds later syrupy mist was everywhere, especially from the nose.

"Why don't you get me that six pack in the next town?" Wonderboy offered to the human Jolly Rancher.

Johnny finished his Four Loko in the church's gazebo we relocated to. A thick joint lit up his face for every long drag as he wobbled to more mumble rap under the brand new shelter.

"Johnny, you're gonna fall. Why don't you put that out and sit down?" Scrappy's pleading tone played way better than anything Wonderboy or I could have said, and we all caught up while Johnny remained silent.

Thud.

The kid fell face first onto the floor and immediately christened the gazebo. We all tried to help but became aware that this was to be the scene of the crime, there was nothing we could do. When he was finally done vomiting, we rolled him away from the bile and collected the best cleanup supplies available.

After adding hand soap to a bucket of water and only finding toilet paper, Wonderboy and I returned to find Scrappy comforting Johnny over a whole new barf puddle.

"And this is why people call us Hiker Trash."

5/8/17 – Stealth Camp Site in Hardwick Township, NJ, 287 Miles Hiked - Day 25

I awakened to find $40 stolen amidst a smattering of belongings taken from my fellow hikers staying at the church hostel. Wonderboy and Scrappy, in full denial, turned their packs upside down to search for the missing items. Theft anywhere is a heinous crime, but to do so in a holy place generous enough to open its doors to weary travelers is on a new level.

Unrecognizable calm came over me as the three of us started hiking back up to the ridgeline in something of a daze. Even if I were $40 richer, I'd still have to walk those same steps. Perhaps just with more hot dogs and pie in my belly. Soon a soaked lower back tipped me off to a leak in my pack. Again serenity took over as I wrung my belongings and kept walking.

A month prior I'd been making 35,000 choices every day, toiling over many of them. Over 30 days, crisis or not, my dilemmas had essentially been whittled down to two:

Walk. Or Don't.

Things aren't so simple in the real world. Don't get me wrong, having infinite options and often infinite tools at our disposal has its perks. Though, there are times when that endless menu of possibilities debilitates you. You can do anything, and that paradox of choice can actually work against us.

In that moment of discovering cold water running down my back, I just had to put my pack back on to rage on. Or not.

I was finally learning to trust my gut, and in so doing, I realized how much I had come to make that a goal of my hike. I'd always insisted hiking the AT was as simple as yearning for adventure but I never denied wanting to come out of it a better person. I didn't realize til that day that reestablishing trust with *myself* was something of a hidden agenda.

The icy rain soon pushed my resolve to the limit and I decided I was ready for the "Don't" option on walking. I begged Wonderboy and Scrappy to call it. The consensus was that getting out of the trail town quicksand was a big enough win for the day.

Scrappy found some soft, lush grass thriving between large boulders. Once I found myself talking to no one, I started reading *The Martian*. The novel concept and exhaustive research drew me in immediately.

As my eyes grew heavy, the minor parallels between Mark Watney's life and my own charmed me. He and I were both many miles from home, rationing food, focused on surviving in an unfamiliar habitat, keeping a daily journal of our activities and thoughts. Hopefully I wouldn't have to use my own excrement as potato fertilizer.

Eat poop-powered potatoes. Or don't eat at all.

As the rain lightened up under the sagging canopy, I lifted my hood to a marvelous rush of cool air on my neck. I looked up to see steam vanish feet above me and something dawned on me.

I didn't get what I wanted from Erica, but I got what I needed. Her refusal to engage in a proper conversation after telling me that I need professional help rattled some convictions, but I came to feel that those troubles didn't belong to me anymore. They belong to Chris, and this trail bears the footprints of Idaho Bones.

"You know, I was hoping you'd propose to me," Erica shared the last time I ever saw her. "I wanted you to ask me to marry you so I could say no. Not in a spiteful way. It's just...I didn't have the courage to tell you that we're not right for each other. But I knew I'd be unable to say yes."

Idaho Bones didn't have time for someone who doesn't want the love he has to give. He didn't need reassurance from a good relationship with a nasty ending. He didn't want to spare any time trying to attach some logic to an abrupt parting of ways.

Unlike Chris, Idaho didn't seem to need reassurance on whether or not he was a good person. Chris spent over a decade chewing over that debate.

I caught my reflection in a pond as I kneeled down to retrieve water. My beard was positively unkempt and paired with that ridiculous hat, I looked a bit mad. But also happy.

"No villian..." I trailed off between the familiar words. I smacked the water, creating a dozen sadistic smiles in the ripples.

"No villian eyes a scoundrel in the mirror, after all."

Chapter Eight

5/10/17 – Jim Murray Secret Shelter, NY, 321 Miles Hiked - Day 27

I went to the woods because I wished to live deliberately, to front only the essential facts of life, and see if I could not learn what it had to teach, and not, when I came to die, discover that I had not lived.
-Henry David Thoreau, *Walden*

The complex vernacular rang in my ears, as I felt the temperate air against my bare skin for the first time in days. Though threatening rain, the skies held their water all day long. Thoreau's imagery compelled me to stop and marvel at every turn of my own.

I felt like I was finally hearing the gentle rasping of every leaf against one another. It became apparent that certain flowers were following the sun's daily course. I could smell upcoming fir groves from downwind.

This natural attunement brought on a surge of enthusiasm and vigor. I was in the big leagues now. I was averaging nearly 20 miles a day since meeting Wonderboy and Scrappy. The daily tasks of nomad life grew easier by the day, even in the persistent rain.

Every morning was a cheerful invitation to make my life of equal simplicity, and I may say innocence, with Nature herself.

Henry and I found ourselves discontented with the society that society itself demands conformity within. It bemused and saddened me to think of our parallel lives, eyeing the pines for years before each taking up a sack and residing there. Listening to his incredible self reliance and ingenuity brought pangs of guilt for not sewing my own clothes and sleeping bag.

The fault-finder will find fault even in paradise.

All day long the book spoke to me directly, bringing perspective and precedent. Thoreau's essays reminded me that all along my path was leading here.

Trees cleared and my jaw dropped. Piercing the gray overcast before me in a sea of rolling green was an obelisk that could rip the whole sky clean in half if it nudged just enough. The sight was more familiar than spectacular.

One of my earliest memories in life itself is of seeing this landmark.

It was the pinnacle of High Point State Park, very much resembling the famous Washington Monument in DC. I first caught sight of it in the back of my grandparents' Chrysler, thinking that surely something this spectacular was held in regards with the likes of the Eiffel Tower or Big Ben.

"That's the highest point where New York, New Jersey, and Pennsylvania all meet," my grandfather confidently declared.

Each subsequent time I'd pass it, I'd stop whatever else I was doing to gaze at it as long as I could. The memorial caught my eye less than a month before I left for the AT. I was on my way to snowboard Camelback, driving from the very trailer where I imagined myself the first time I read *Walden*. The same trailer where the moniker Idaho Bones was born. I had no idea how close the trail would lead me to that sharp constant in my life.

After unsuccessfully trying to call Wonderboy and Scrappy a few miles ahead, I checked my phone's map to make sure they were one and the same. Deep down I knew it was the exact tower I'd stared at wondrously as a child. It felt very cosmic to think that I had been drawn to this one seemingly insignificant point all my life, and that choosing to hike the Appalachian Trail took me back there. Still in that nostalgic stupor, I stepped north out of New Jersey and into my home state.

Soon after, by the virtue of my own feet I found myself back to the place where my dad's friend Jeff told me about the Appalachian Trail all those years ago. As I continued to listen to the sentiments of Henry David Thoreau, in the familiar and monumental setting, I knew I was exactly where I was meant to be.

Simplicity, simplicity, simplicity! I say, let your affairs be as two or three, and not a hundred or a thousand... In the midst of this chopping sea of civilized life, such are the clouds and storms and quicksands and thousand-and-one items to be allowed for, that a man has to live, if he would not founder and go to the bottom and not make his port at all, by dead reckoning, and he must be a great calculator indeed who succeeds.

I knew what my affairs were, in this most uncivilized life.

Walk. Or don't.

5/13/17 – Wildcat Shelter, NY, 352 Miles Hiked - Day 30

Before leaving for the Appalachian Trail, I was warned of the nefarious days spent being poured on at 40°. It took a month to find that wrath.

After obtaining whiskey in town, Wonderboy and I held debate:

Walk. Or don't.

Don't. It was a compelling case. One worth drinking over.

Problems out on the trail can be solved, and out of necessity they will be. The quickest, most efficient options for every single problem will come to you faster every day. The white space your mind creates in this environment can often make attainment of perfect clarity a bit jarring. As if your body is waiting for those hardwired doubts of a former self to burst through the stage curtain in flames. They don't. Because you're too exhausted, invigorated, starving, present, and smart to let those thoughts in.

Several times a day you'll think to yourself, *everything I need to live is on my back. And I could easily drop 10% of it right now if I truly had to.*

You went from deciding that a uHaul couldn't fit all your needs to cramming it all into one singular bag and sleeping better than you have in your entire life.

Every day poses infinite problems but they're all fixable. "Fire together wire together" kicks in very quickly. You progress every day.

Many hikers shared that this was the first time in their lives they're challenged every single day and gradually mastering a craft. Many areas of the brain take over that have been silenced by lizard brains (or lizard brains silenced by others, as one could make a compelling argument for).

So quickly does one forget not just the now trivial problems of the real world, but more accurately that *this* world even exists. Without warning, I felt incapable of missing *anyone*. It was a strange and selfish realization to have come to, but I couldn't talk myself out of it. It's not that I didn't remember or appreciate people from my past, it's just that I came to know they could never possibly understand who Idaho Bones is.

5/15/17 – Fingerboard Shelter, NY, 366 Miles Hiked - Day 21

"Bear. BEAR! Black bear! SHOO! SHOO, BEAR! SHOO, BLACK BEAR!"

A panicked voice filled my ears and I jolted awake. I unzipped my sleeping bag and grabbed my phone. It was the best of circumstances to properly lay eyes on my first bear. There was a dog, roughly six other people, and a safe distance between the beast and myself. I was amazed by how harmless the bear looked and holy shit was that bear *black*. I assumed they'd look more dark brown. I'd only recently crossed into NY, but was already close to NYC being in the tri-state area. I couldn't believe a bear was roaming about an hour drive from home.

Once I'd gotten my fill and a decent video, I returned to my tent. My head was throbbing from a midnight nose bleed. Without even realizing it, I zipped my bag closed, making myself a bear burrito. Which I like to call Bearito. I hope he enjoys the burrito that I myself consumed yesterday. Two for one!

I'll have the burrito stuffed burrito, please.

Excellent choice, Mr. Bearenstain. Excellent choice. Can I interest you in any appetizers this evening?

"Idaho! Idaho Bones!"

"I'm up! I'm up!"

With a clearer head a couple hours later, I packed up and joined Johnny Quest and his friend Patrick heading for New York's Bear Mountain.

Along the way we got to see the many phases of the Manhattan skyline. As day turned to dusk, buildings alternated between themselves, reflecting the gold against the gentle pink background. Lights gradually filled the sky scrapers as the backdrop itself shifted to a perfect navy haze. We were comfortably nestled in our hammocks for the night when the sight finally accepted its destined brilliance of a shining metropolis that truly never sleeps.

Johnny and I passed Jack Daniels back and forth in its glow. A month's worth of hiking left me staring at my hometown from a mountaintop.

I began to slip away from consciousness as my mind flooded with memories of New York from my six month interim residency there. These mountains came to feel more like home than The Big Apple ever had.

5/18/17 – Canopus Lake Beach, NY, 398 Miles Hiked - Day 35

In a group of half naked hiker trash, I strolled back to the lake where we enjoyed a moonlight swim the night before. Large boughs riddled the closed off road and a ranger pulled up to turn us around.

"Oh, your colleague just said it was fine and to stay on this side of the street," Eagle confidently replied with a thumb over his sunburnt shoulder.

"Oh, well if Frank said it's fine, then just be careful!"

I didn't know who Frank was but hoped Eagle's white lie wouldn't get him in too much trouble.

Eagle, Starshine, and Sharkbait were all hikers I'd grown accustomed to seeing on a nearly daily basis. Johnny Quest was often in their company but still marching to the beat of his own drum. Though our parties got along well, they moved independently. This little lake getaway was the first time I camped with them without Wonderboy and Scrappy. The duo put in big miles the day before and were somewhere north.

My lakeside crew had recently watched *Fight Club* at a hostel. Just like my trail family AKA tramily, they had grown weary of seeing so many tourists on the trail day to day. In the movie, Edward Norton's character grabs a woman forcefully and shouts in her face, "You're a *tourist*, Marla!!" Well that settled it. They started calling day hikers "Marlas." Wonderboy and Scrappy loved the ring of it and I found it positively tickling. The nickname spread up and down the trail for the AT Class of '17 as we all resented Marlas taking up space in our shelters and failing to abide by *Leave No Trace*. It was largely all in good fun, though. After all, we all knew we'd turn into a Marla ourselves once every mile was behind us.

We arrived at an empty beach that should have been packed with Marlas on this 96° day. Lush pines encapsulated the sparkling water. I plopped down on a dock to watch little fish dart around my feet in the warm water, hungry and curious. Starshine's husky pup Sasha did zoomies along the shore line, taking breaks to chomp her infinite beverage.

"Screw York is showing some serious love right now," I said to my fellow beach inhabitants. "Nice to see its good side."

My home state was largely filled with grumpy day hikers, eager to escape the highly populous Manhattan, disappointed to find a whole population of smelly residents, all in a straight line north to south.

I thought back to all the natural wonders I'd seen in every state I would have previously thought myself familiar with. Each one had so many secrets to share along this trail. Evidently Benton and Mackaye, the founders of the AT, knew what they were doing.

A suspicion grew that perhaps I don't have to settle down near a city after my hike. So long as there's even one mere acre of wilderness, with a body of water, I'll find plenty of splendor to ramble on through. I didn't get the sense from Thoreau that he tired of Walden after two years there.

Chapter Nine

407 Miles Hiked, 1,782 to Go
Days 36-48

5/19/17 – RPH Shelter, NY, 407 Miles Hiked - Day 36

What should have been a casual check in with my planned timeline brought on a small panic attack. I double checked my mileage on Guthook, the handy thru-hiker companion app for all things Appalachian Trail. I'd hiked 407 miles. Not a bad way to start this, that's a back and forth trip between NYC and DC. It also meant that I was roughly 20% of the way complete. That didn't immediately feel panic inducing, but then I realized I was nine days behind schedule.

I largely figured this plan was going to get thrown off one way or another. I found myself looking down the barrel of a trail completion in late October at best, early to mid November at worst.

Anxious sweat rolled down my back realizing the need to defer student loans at least one more time, maybe twice, with a whole lot of interest accumulated. Already I was feeling rushed and unable to smell the roses.

Directly opposing sensibilities nagged at me.

Did I really want to be on the trail that long? Did I really want to be on the trail for only six months? Was it possible to remain mindful on the trail without knowing what was coming after the final miles?

5/23/17 – Pine Swamp Brook Shelter, CT, 462 Miles Hiked - Day 40

I had to find a way to Kent, CT. I was hoping to do so quickly, as I'd fallen behind Wonderboy and Scrappy for a few days, and was beginning to miss their stench.

A forest fire caused an eight mile section of the AT to close. I looked for cardboard to make a sign for hitching. Finding nothing, I cursed the local Adopt-A-Highway program. A good 50 cars passed before I made breakfast and coffee right there next to the road.

A car pulled up right as I had given up. A newlywed couple looking for some excitement on their Sunday drive dropped me off at the ice cream parlor in Kent, CT. Eagle was making himself comfortable there with a case of beer.

I found myself once again unable to say no to Eagle's weight shedding sales pitch.

"This 30 of PBR was basically the same price as an 18 of Bud!" he said proudly in the parking lot of the outfitter featuring an ice cream parlor. "My pack's too heavy, want a beer?"

More hikers enjoyed the same welcome wagon until Eagle was light as a feather.

Amidst helping Eagle lighten his load, 20 iron horses galloped into the parking lot.

"You guys hikin' the AT?" asked a woman who looked like a high powered business woman once she dismounted her trike. Eagle and I nodded with beers held high. "Want some ice cream? What's your flavor?"

The three of us continued to chat over a cone as her far more grizzled colleagues melted over a puppy out front. The only thing more precious than watching a burly tough guy baby talk to a dog is watching him wipe ice cream from his buddy's beard.

For days I'd been warned about Kent, the rich, snooty, MAGA ridden Connecticut town with a distaste for hiker trash. After parking lot PBRs, I walked the length of the town to stock up for my next section. I experienced nothing but friendliness from a town where everyone seemed to be a neighbor. The data doesn't lie, this town did vote for Trump. I began to see that *people* were behind those votes and that which box we checked off on a ballot didn't have to leave anger between us.

I sat with this realization while crossing the Housatonic River, watching its ripples catch dusky pink sky with each undulation.

On the west side of the river, my bowels spoke up with fervor:

Warning, gotta take a shit. OH MY. OK, getting pretty urgent down here. Prairie doggin...never mind! The consistency is NOT, I repeat, NOT...equipped for prairie doggin. Halt ALL farting-related activity!

I didn't know what to do, standing between the river and a road Robert Frost wouldn't have exactly called less traveled. With such limited options I undid my pack anyway. Tragically the waist strap caught on my fanny pack, leaving me unable to remove my pants.

Final countdown, you better hurry – 10-no, 6...NO, 2! --yeah you're shitting myself.

When I should have been crying or cursing I was laughing at the intriguing Buddhi-an slip.

You're shitting myself.

Separation of ego and physical self. It only took Pabst Blue Ribbon, a pistachio ice cream cone, and 90 degree heat to embrace *The Four Noble Truths* through the majesty of sharting.

5/24/17 – Riga Shelter, CT, 481 Miles Hiked - Day 41

The next morning Scrappy, Wonderboy, and I woke up in adjacent tents for the first time in nearly a week. We celebrated the reunion with Irish coffees in a swinging chair overlooking the forests beyond. The familiar banter and inside jokes filled me with excited anticipation of having hiking companions again.

Shortly after our departure we ran into familiar fellow hikers Sharkbait and Starshine.

"Idaho, I think this is the first time I've seen you hike!" Sharkbait remarked.

"Holy shit, I think you're right," I confirmed as Scrappy cackled. Sharkbait had banged his poles on my tent half a dozen late mornings but was always comfortably enjoying camp by the time I'd roll up.

Connecticut, a supposedly easy state on the AT, disappointed us all with its constant elevation changes. After burying a footlong with a six pack of beer in Salisbury, we begrudgingly tackled Lion's and Bear Mountains in one go. The 2,400 altitude change seemed to bear a chip on its shoulder, challenging every account of this section as "easy peasy."

At least the exhausting ritual provided some very spectacular views I never expected. It was a necessary reminder that the vistas I came for don't just happen. They don't call it a vantage point because you can drive a van up there (looking at you, Mount Washington). Each time the climb sapped me of my good nature, it was immediately followed by gratitude for the sights before me.

I rolled up to camp finding three PBRs sitting in a perfect spot for a tent.

"Where did these come from?" I asked Scrappy.

"One of the shelters had a trail magic 30 rack. Enjoy!"

Connecticut was full of surprises.

5/28/17 – Trail Angel Levardi's House – Dalton, MA, 549 Miles Hiked - Day 45

I went to bed drunk on the trail angel Tom Levardi's porch, but not nearly as drunk as I planned to be. I decided to make my hike into Dalton the illustrious stage for the completion of my 24 Challenge. As Johnny Quest explained it, it's 24 beers, 24 miles, in 24 hours. I did 27 miles in 12 hours, planning to drink 12 upon arrival, wake up at 8, and have 3 hours to drink the remaining 12.

Wonderboy only bought me 12 of the 24 I requested of him. Tom told me when I arrived that liquor stores wouldn't open until noon the next day. When I mentioned going to any of the three bars Dalton has to offer that night, they were due to close in ten minutes at midnight.

My desperate and exhausted mind searched for other alternatives but found none.

The day before was largely a nightmare. I continued to hold out hope for the easy conditions of Massachusetts we'd all heard about but only found sharp, wet roots with nearly every step. Where there weren't roots, there was mud. Where there wasn't mud, there were scores of slippery rocks covered in wet leaves.

My daylight spills paled in comparison to my last fall, in the dark: a nasty spill that sent all of my body weight onto my right forearm. Before pain could set in, I resumed my hike, doing my best to ignore the tingly, numbing sensation in my fingertips and the red hot throbbing at the source.

Why didn't I quit? There was a shelter three miles before town that on any other day I would have called an audible for. Yet I hardly even slowed down to read its sign. I needed to get to Dalton. Maybe it was the smorgasbord of food Wonderboy conveyed to me. Maybe it was the fact that he and Scrappy had both pushed themselves to their limits in the previous 48 hours. Maybe it was the desire to finally reach into a dry pack.

That said, would you ask a marathoner why she didn't quit? Because that's how important the 24 Challenge was to me. The gash my soggy wet sole developed couldn't be for nothing. It could only be avenged with a belly full of beer.

The night before I was caught in a downpour. I pitched my tent and tossed in all my wet belongings. There was nothing comfortable to change into because everything was wet. I divided up my soaking belongings in a way that seemed sensible and began to drift off after cooking dinner from my wet sleeping bag which was housing my cold, wet body and threads.

The condensation from dinner dripped down as I surrendered to bed. Before I could sleep I noticed that water was leaking rapidly from the tent's highest point. My rolled up socks served as a makeshift solution until I discovered they simply redirected the drops to my face.

In the morning, I calculated that the closest landmarks and hot showers were 28 miles ahead. Not to mention the beer.

Pulling on wet socks in the 49° brisk morning air nearly brought me to tears. Once on, I marched in the only direction I could.

Slipping became normal, tripping customary, and falling was no longer negotiable after a while. I operated on autopilot before checking my progress. Then I cruised for eight more miles before allowing myself to stop, six miles out, to eat the mashed taters I'd prepared earlier along with some other snacks.

Soon after the headlamp was turned on, I suffered a face first mudslide. I hiked parallel to a river which left thick fog hanging in the air, blocking my vision. The mist miraculously faded, but my own breath started to blind me. I figured out how to breathe without costing me my vision only to find that the steam from my body filling the surrounding air. Then it rained.

I got lost several times in the damp stillness of the night and what made my disorientation ever more unnerving was the total silence of the forest. Dark woods are creepy but silent, foggy, dark forests are the very fibers of terror and nightmares. No crickets, no critters, no wind to keep me eerie company through pitch black unknown lands.

Finally I limped up to Levardi's house. This marvelous saint gave me soda and water, salad and pasta salad, pasta and rolls, and seconds of whatever I desired. I staved off my desire to keep eating for the sake of the 24 Challenge.

My gracious host led me to the porch and pointed out the now futile beers Wonderboy got for me and I immediately decided to drink Wonderboy's five remaining pilsners out of spite.

The next morning, I wasted no time interrogating Wonderboy.

"They only let me buy 24!" Wonderboy explained.

"Why didn't you go back?" I asked.

I was still angry about my 24 Challenge going up in smoke.

"I was tired too, man! Sorry I didn't hike 28 miles but I was pooped. Get off my ass!"

Our spat remained in Dalton as we hiked on to Wilbur Clearing Shelter. Wonderboy and I enjoyed the mildly improved trail conditions under gray skies selfishly hiding the sun.

After a marijuana fueled safety meeting, I allowed my eyes to wander the swampy surroundings. A moment's distraction halted my momentum. For yet another day, the earth sucked my shoe clean off.

Setting up my tent cost me the sensation in my hands. Down jacket on, I still shivered in spasms on Memorial Day, the unofficial first day of the summer. I could see my breath clear as day from my sleeping bag

My first week on trail it was 80 every day and I spent my nights shirtless. How did I go from that to nothing I own being dry and putting on makeshift ear muffs every morning?

New England was proving to be a greater challenge than I could've ever imagined.

5/31/17 – Melville Nauheim Shelter, VT, 591 Miles Hiked - Day 48

My optimism burned on fumes. It's not that I was getting wet. It was that I could never get dry. It wasn't that I couldn't get on Facebook. It's that I couldn't even get a weather report to plan strategically around the rain. Then I finally accepted the rain, but I couldn't get over the puddles that formed with each and every step. Each day I'd eventually give up the charade of hopping from rock to rock until inevitably slipping down into the river formerly known as The Appalachian Trail.

Massachusetts.

Massive-Tree-Roots.

Vermont.

Vermud.

"FUCK YOU, trail maintenance!" I yelled at the mud I'd plunged into, just inches from my filthy chin. "This is the poorest excuse of upkeep I've ever seen. Pure fucking bullshit. Fuck you all!"

I felt immediately guilty for verbally damning and cursing volunteers. No good deed goes unpunished. If I at least kept it to myself I had plausible deniability.

My coffee tasted extra bitter, tepid after the constant massacre of black flies.

The bites weren't nearly as powerful as a horsefly's, but the pests made up for that shortcoming with frequency and distraction. For every kill, two more arrived at the epidermis buffet. My legs took turns kicking like a stag on a burning Texas hilltop.

Every few minutes I had to swat away groups of flies from the netting covering my face since I couldn't see what I was doing. I kept them at bay long enough to discover that my shoes, jacket, and trekking poles all attracted slugs seeking refuge from the cold rain.

The constant mud filled bubbles beneath my feet made me wonder whether I have the resolve to actually finish this trail. People tried to warn me, hiking in the rain and having a bag full of wet belongings are staples of the AT. Finishing it entails morning rituals like flicking slugs off my insoles in disgust.

Later that afternoon, thunder rolled from all sides after a blinding burst paralyzed me.

Flash. One. Two. Three. Thunder.

Flash. One. T-Thunder

Flash. On-Thunder.

For several seconds the world was a hot blue silhouette all around me. When blackness returned the thunder shook me to my core. A

87

hundred yards to my right, I watched lightning set a hopeless patch of earth ablaze. Smelling ozone, my hairs stood on end as I stomped in a straight line determined to get away from this terror.

Hail peppered the ground beneath me as if some giant were sprinkling me with sea salt before dropping me into boiling water.

Adrenaline prevented me from noticing the transition back to rain, or the halt in precipitation altogether. Steam escaped my raincoat as I tore it off, finding the hood full of ice. I scooped out a palmful of hail and had deja vu back to a travel edition of Yahtzee I had in elementary school. I never knew that hail came cube shaped.

I looked up to find the source of the freshest smelling pine I'd ever whiffed. The orange glow of tree bark caught my eye and I found myself tugging on the plucky green needles of a downed tree over the footpath. I inspected the disrupted soil on both sides and smelled fresh earth. I was so distracted by the possibility of being struck by lightning that I forgot the danger of death by timber.

A mile onward, the shelter had moss creeping up its three sides, seeming to lean over as if to receive a secret. Water continued to run down the shingles long after the rain stopped.

I plopped my pack down into the mostly dry 40 year old lean-to and squished around the perimeter.

Stillness prevailed as I explored beyond the shelter, priming me for a stunning view up a hill.

The white candor of the sun's rays filling the storm's rising mist made it hard to believe there was ever a squall to begin with.

Chapter Ten

6/1/17 – Story Spring Shelter, VT, 609 Miles Hiked - Day 49

It was forecast to be the first rainless day in a week but of course it poured. Vermont had been unpleasant, unsafe, and undry every step of the way. I trudged along the trail doing its best swamp impersonation, every mile feeling like two or three. Each logbook entry echoed the same sentiment, with lots of shoes being sucked down into muck. I wasn't the only one contemplating surrender.

I first smelled fire leading up to Kid Gore Shelter and it took every bit of discipline to keep walking. Five miles later, I couldn't resist the same allure at Story Spring, already giving up on catching Wonderboy and Scrappy. Yet again, their ambitions outweighed my own.

The shelter had a bizarre layout, with several structures flanking what seemed like a courtyard with a fireplace centering it all. One hiker was all tucked in, headphones pumping through a show on his phone.

I found a gruff man in a Rob Gronkowski jersey, aptly named Beast, stoking the fire's flames.

"Is that whiskey?" I asked while unpacking, pointing at a plastic bottle.

"Sure is."

"That's really funny. I've been shipping myself Poland Spring bottles of Jameson. It's weird to see another one."

"It's called Jefferson," Beast said, bottle mid-air. "Try some."

I felt no need to flinch, wince, or contort my face, even after he divulged that the spirit was 114 proof. After a deep inhale, the flavor improved.

The trail provides, even in the form of a sticky water bottle housing brown. It was resplendent to have a fire warm my damp clothes and whiskey warm my damp heart.

I watched Beast fight to keep the fire alive, realizing I was basically a New York counterpoint to this New England lumberjack. He recognized the same white trash upbringings in me when he tossed the Jefferson.

"Cereal? Fuh dinnuh?" my childhood friend Nicholas inquired. They were his first words since watching little yellow pebbles clink inside his bowl.

My dad, on the other hand, had milk dripping down his chin, halfway finished with his Corn Pops. My bowl was just hitting that golden consistency where the outside is soft and a little mushy but the inside still crunchy. I wasn't gonna stop during this crucial window to convince my best friend that this was normal.

No, for Nicholas, this was eons outside of his world, where you simply never ran out of homemade tomatuh sawce. Even when back from Flahruhduh, you just -

"Pawp out one from the freezuh, putitinthe microwave."

Nicholas ate cereal but only before school or once in a while as a snack. Had his mother ever served him Rice Krispies for dinner, generations of Italian women driven to the ground by guilt and agita would have rolled in their graves.

"Oh...well, what else can I make for ya buddy?" my father asked. "You want some French toast?"

Of all the meals I'd seen Dad cook, roughly 92% of them were dunking Wonderbread in milky eggs and tossing them on a pan. He was quite good at making them but the affair had as many steps as Shake and Bake.

He opened the freezer and sighed with relief upon discovering freezer burned chicken nuggets. His relief may have been premature because he did achieve that burny on the outside cold on the inside dynamic.

Nevertheless, Nicholas realized this was the best he was going to get. Cereal wasn't my first choice, but with Mom traveling for work I'd come to expect to be staring cartoon friends in the face for my last meal of the day.

Rice Krispies with bananas and a little sugar was often my go to, but man do you have to eat quickly before those turn. Captain Crunch on the other hand: I gave up trying to figure out how long to let them float before they'd stop cutting the roof of your mouth. Lucky Charms and I had a thing for a while, but the sound, yes *sound* of the marshmallows squeezing between your teeth like styrofoam...once I noticed it couldn't be forgotten. Even when I didn't want Cocoa Puffs I'd have 'em because I still haven't found a more delicious chocolate milk than the chocolatey remains in the bowl.

You might say I became something of a sommelier in terms of cereal. I even determined the ideal amount of time to let each soak in milk.

Apple Cinnamon Cheerios: 2 minutes, 10 seconds

Kix: 2 minutes, 30 seconds

Life Cereal: 45 seconds

Rice Krispies: 1 minute

Captain Crunch: 0 secs - 4 minutes: mouth bleeding. 4 minutes: Perfect. 4 minutes one sec - infinity: Soup.

My mom picked up some interesting kinda thrifty I guess habits from a sprawling Brooklyn family. Don't think I've ever seen her throw away a "Pathmark bag," even when there were some bursting out from under the sink. When I wanted to throw away something remotely useful, I had to toss it in the dumpster behind the Chinese restaurant across the street. If it found its way into our trash bins, they'd be rescued and brought down to a basement that would look like *Raiders of the Lost Ark* if it weren't for the miles of clothes hanging from rope.

I wouldn't consider the places I grew up in to be *trashy*. They were a generation removed. The hoarding and meal preferences remained, but the decor was more evolved.

The house where the white trash stank most was my dad's family's house. There was typically a bologna sandwich waiting for me there. I'd watch my grandma spread butter over the white bread, then peel off a pink slice and administer more butter upon that. There were three slabs of Oscar Mayer ready to slide off each other at any given moment.

I still remember the unique way those sandwiches would get stuck to the roof of my mouth: bread thoroughly lodged at the top, then having to slither away each buttery portion with my tongue until it was time to pick saliva ridden dough from my molars with grimey fingernails.

Like many things in my life, one day I just realized how ill-fitting this sustenance was and refused it for good. I think that's when she started making me Spaghettios.

As if Latchkey wasn't stereotypical enough for my socio-economic class, I often had to go to my grandmother's house afterwards since my mom couldn't get out of work on time. There I'd bear witness to an endless stream of riff raff in their late teens or older, all bringing their skunky musk into the living room as they kissed my grandmother on the cheek one by one.

Grandma Mary Lou was loved by all and could have easily

procured a loan for an orphanage. People brought her anything she ever asked for and never dared try to slink away from the drawn out heart to hearts that ensued. Every bastard on that island would find their way to her doorstep for some amount of time.

In the dank basement, my uncle would hold court with all types, toking away indiscriminately under a sea of black lights. This behavior wasn't egregious enough for my grandparents to kick him out, nor was it bad enough to prohibit my cousin and I from entering the basement ourselves. There we'd watch rated R movies and sometimes win a few bucks playing poker before blowing it at 711 down the street.

Each wall depicted some sort of spray painted message that would singe through the darkness if even one dark light remained on. *Tara Loves Pat* remained long after the tramp stamped burnout had stamped out for the last time, hurling profanities at my uncle after a breakup. The blurry outline of an evil clown looked me in the face when I tried to renovate the basement a decade later.

The seating options were a sun faded array of wheelchairs, barstools, and cracking faux leather recliners that could break the skin if angled just so. Beer cans stewing with cigarette butts for far too long were everywhere.

One could tell when the weather got good by the amount of beer cans thrown about the yard. Every week or so they'd disappear after my grandpa blew a gasket. After he died, their presence was far more imposing but remained hidden by unkempt weeds. Sometimes my cousin and I would get ambitious and clean up a trash bag's worth, then grab another to fill with dog poop. Since there was often a broken down uninsured car in the backyard, we'd usually play wiffle ball in the street, grabbing the least repugnant trash can to use as a strike zone. Before games we'd take batting practice in the yard where the above ground pool used to be, hitting itchy balls over the house.

When I got to high school, though I was no longer ridiculed for my living situation, I still found myself wanting to create distance from it all. My new friends would invite me over and I'd gawk at the art and pianos that apparently didn't justify mention. Their pantries were organized and their plates all matched each other. Their plasma screens dazzled. Best of all, the pools were inground and the water wasn't green.

Those visits would incite more wonder than envy: why did my family choose to live the way they did? Without question many of those other families found more secure footing in life, but the margin seemed too great. For a while I thought a deficit in space was the issue. Our second Christmas in the new house proved that was incidental, as I unpacked things from the eighth Christmas decoration box that I had no memory of.

One hot high school afternoon I decided to do my grandmother a favor and clean all the dog waste in the yard. As I scooped fossilized pile after pile with an old shovel, I noticed a brilliant five petaled purple flower ascending through marijuana leaves. I parsed the weeds away to find an understory of violet petals fit to burst. I walked the length of the garden to my right to find that these persistent beauties were patiently waiting their turn for a good 40 feet.

I brought a flower inside for my grandmother.

"Hey grandma," I began, holding out a little purple assortment of petals between her and *Wheel of Fortune.* "When did you plant these?"

"Ya found that," she began as I nodded. "In *my* yard?"

I gently rotated the flower, focusing on the bits of pollen that had gathered all about.

"I never planted those," she said, followed by a snort and a gulp of her vahkatahnik. "Mustuh been theh all these yeeuhz."

I'd grown up planting and picking and weeding but for some reason these little slices of lavender really caught my eye. I snuck away to the backyard that night. There I peeled away the cannabis, flashlight clenched between my teeth. Carefully I removed four feet's worth of flowers and put them in a shoebox by the road. I sprinkled a little water on them and went back inside.

My dad lingered to chat when he came to pick my sister and I up later and I snatched his keys. I set aside the junk from his '95 saturn and placed the box beneath a cluster of it all. Later that evening, I silently turned the key of the trunk and extracted my smuggled goods.

Throughout the night I was sleuthing the internet to properly label my discovery.

I'd found a bed of native Phlox divaricata, or Wild Blue Phlox, finding rays of sunshine to rise through in a mess of weeds. It turns out that Phloxes are native to Staten Island, never needing a hand to drive them into the ground or pull them up into the light. They long outlived my family, or even America. As history drifted by they found a way to blossom.

Wild Blue Phlox couldn't help where it came from, but that didn't stop it from rising above. And in the process, it wasn't trying to be something else.

In those first weeks on the Appalachian Trail, a thought couldn't help finding light amidst the many hours of silence.

Had I grown up in some house with commissioned art, or an antique cello tying together a rumpus room, I wouldn't be here right now.

Nature served as an escape for my entire life. The clutter, Judge Judy, and family spats drove me outside. The rustling of the trees always made sense when my family's lifestyles didn't.

Good or bad, nurturing or stifling, I owed my incessant curiosity to the people and places that shaped me.

The night I discovered the Phlox, I let murky topsoil fill each fingernail as I cleared room in my parents' front yard. My shovel picked up each little root cluster and plopped them into earth between misshapen bushes. The water from the tea kettle seemed to comfort each flower into the tilled ground.

Those flowers would have never seen the light of day under the careful supervision of a contracted landscaper. Each protruding leaf would have been cast aside to make way for something flashier.

Instead, under steady irreverence and neglect, a native flower blossomed. It then found itself propagating miles away from its unapologetic brethren; forgetting their roots could prove to be fatal.

6/2/17 – Palmer House, Manchester Center, VT, 626 Miles Hiked - Day 50

After slithering on wet socks every morning for weeks, I still found myself hopping among roots and boulders in vain attempts to achieve any semblance of dryness. Vermont didn't seem to empathize with my futile efforts as I stared down a trail devoid of any reprieve. As if I tossed my own heart into the mud, my spirits sank into a murky helplessness.

Dead end. There were no rocks left to hop amongst. I extended my leg as if dangling off a plank and braced for the ick.

A few steps in my foot disappeared into mud. My leg jerked reflexively as I felt a tickle up my leg.

Squirming on my calf were two tadpoles wondering why the hell they couldn't breathe. I nudged the younglings back to their muddy home and raged on.

Both shoes managed to stay on until I plopped down my pack next to the road. A green Subaru sedan pulled over immediately.

The driver rolled her window down and with a smile asked, "Y'need a ride?"

"Sure that'd be great!"

"Where to?"

"Oh, Manchester Center," I replied, thinking that would be obvious.

"Hmm, I'm actually heading in the other direction," the woman began while eyeing the other side of the road. She quickly honked at an oncoming car with a hand out the window and asked, "Hey can you take this hiker to Manchester Center?"

"Sure I can, hop in!" My new driver pulled over and beamed as I joined him.

I'd probably spent over 24 hours with my thumb out in the previous three states of my hike and here I was 2/2 without even extending my arm.

Vermont seemed to hand my muddy heart back to me after giving it a small polish. Things were looking up.

The driver took me all the way to Palmer House, a quaint little resort. I cautiously asked how much it'd set me back to spend the night, eyeing the marble statues adorning the concierge desk. I caught sight of the welcome mat, covered heavily with earth from my morning's march and winced.

"How much ya got?" asked the third friendly face I'd encountered. The woman's eyes exuded friendliness, practically glowing with helpfulness. She cocked her head gently to the side as I contemplated my answer.

"Fifty?" I said sheepishly, expecting to be laughed out of Manchester Center entirely.

"Sold! Let's get you a room key."

I couldn't believe it. For $50 I bought myself hot water, cable, and breakfast. This was no free church hostel. Everything about the place screamed triple digits for the run of the mill traveler.

Vermont had arranged one helluva welcome wagon.

I tossed aside my muck ridden boots and socks outside the door. I wanted to forget the swampy torments of my recent treks. I was leaving every bit of the trail behind. Even if just for one night.

6/3/17 – Palmer House, Manchester Center, VT, 626 Miles Hiked - Day 51

I schmeared my fourth mini bagel and stood at the edge of the sunroom, taking in the nine hole pitch and putt course of The Palmer House. Continental breakfast is a term with a dangerously wide range but this place delivered.

"Do you want a bag for those bagels?" asked the girl clearing tables. She was wearing a Class of 2020 shirt.

There's something particularly humiliating about being caught with a pocket overflowing with mini bagels by a human being in just her second year of "teen-hood."

"No, thanks..." I muttered bashfully, already thinking of a Plan B for all the other contraband.

"My brother and I want to hike the AT someday!" she shared with a smile.

"That's amazing! Can't recommend it enough."

My mind wandered to a future version of the girl, stuffing muffins into her backpack somewhere in Virginia.

After breakfast, I mosied down to the outfitter where a package would be waiting for me.

"I'm sorry, sir," the store's manager began. "I have thoroughly checked everywhere and we definitely don't have your package."

A nervous sweat pooled in the small of my back.

"I've seen this message before, I'm pretty sure USPS has completely lost your package," he continued with pity. "Here's a number you can call to confirm, I'm so sorry I can't be more help to you."

Pacing the pitch and putt course, I finally reached a representative to tell me USPS lost any trace of the package days ago. The box was mostly full of food that I was thoroughly sick of, so no love lost there. The real problem was losing a month's worth of Lexapro. I'd mostly forgotten about my plan to wean off the drug in Vermont's daily monsoons, but it appeared that a detox was being thrust upon me. I panicked for a few minutes longer before I was overtaken by a profound calm.

I wanted this. I can do this. I trust the universe.

I pushed the late checkout as far as it would go in the hot tub across the courtyard. Once my eyes could no longer stand the chlorine, I returned to my room to pick up my pack. In desperation the night before, I washed my whole pack in the shower with Dr. Bronner's soap. I was pleased to find the pack was perfectly dry, and renewed like myself. I dropped off the keys and sat by the resort's pond, listening to a baseball game's cheers on the other side of the meadow.

"I didn't know life could be this good," I said aloud, surprising myself. "I didn't know it was possible. I didn't know it was within my *grasp*."

It was hard to believe my spirits sank so low only days, even hours, before that moment. My mind was made up to look at the lost Lexapro as a divine opportunity for my mental health. Though the comforts of civilization rejuvenated me, I was feasting on the life the AT injected into my soul. With the dizzying obstacles in my wake, optimism blossomed. I knew there would be more but I felt capable after my restorative stay at Palmer House. I was ready to walk again. I was ready to see what my mind was capable of all on its own.

I was also ready to see Scrappy and Wonderboy after my little multi-day respite from company.

On the pond's dock, I wondered what I might have done differently after college, had I known what I'd just discovered. The beauty of the simple life. The existence narrowed down to two choices.

Then I chewed on the dangers of making any alterations to my past. Following my instincts got me to the trail and to that very magical moment. Any side trail could have led me astray from that epiphany. In Appalachia I came to trust the greater oneness of our existence and to stop settling. I couldn't risk losing that by eradicating any mistakes made along the way.

Three months before I was standing over a fire, certain that I was more prepared for the Appalachian Trail than I'd ever been for anything in my life. It was satisfying to vindicate that conviction.

Chapter Eleven

678 Miles Hiked, 1,511 to Go

Days 55-58

6/7/17 – The Yellow Deli Hostel, Rutland, VT, 678 Miles Hiked - Day 55

The trail provides.

Time and time again I'd heard that sentiment for 600 miles but it never felt more true than when I arrived in Rutland, VT.

The pendulum seemed to fully swing in the other direction after my Palmer House stay. A few days removed from Manchester Center, I got separated from Wonderboy and Scrappy yet again. My unreliable phone made it impossible to find out where they were and plan accordingly.

Three days after checking out of Palmer house, I left the shelter in particularly low spirits, trying and failing to accept that my phone was broken. It only added six ounces to my pack, but the weight carried far beyond that.

Upon departing the sanctuary of the lean-to, the rain wasn't bad. Cold, yes. But not much more than a smattering. I was pleasantly surprised that the trail, within feet of picturesque Little Rock Pond, wasn't a complete mud pit. Naturally my shoes were soaked within minutes, but still conditions were decent. I was even making great time.

Then the temperature dropped. Rain mounted and poured steadily, flatlining at "Cats and Dogs." A manageable mucky trail became a stream. At its most recognizable the trail was a healthy assortment of rocks, roots, and leaves being held together by all-consuming mud. A white blaze marked the center of a 200 foot slick rock angled at 45°. A block of ice would have been safer to traverse. I couldn't imagine anyone considering this to be an acceptable bit of footpath. But there I was sliding down it with surprising grace. The rock led to a steep mud laden hill of conifer roots. I fell hard. It was inevitable, I knew I wasn't going to make it to the end without falling. Thankfully I fell onto my cushy pack. The worst pain was the strain on my knee as I tried to muscle my way up using my trekking poles.

I hitched the second car coming my way and I couldn't be more elated. 48° on the dashboard.

"Probably damn near freezing at the summit," Bob remarked.

"Can confirm," I replied through thawing lips. I spent the drive fantasizing about the shower that couldn't come soon enough. Not to mention that forgotten season: summer.

Bob waved me off with a smile at the curb in front of the Yellow Deli. The employees buzzing between tables looked unusual and it took me a few moments to comprehend why. It was as if Amish folk were dropped off at a thrift store and told "ok, now go dress like the people you see in this outdated magazine."

They appeared out of place but none seemed to mind. Smiles and humming and good old fashioned elbow grease abound. The food smelled heavenly and the patrons' expressions matched. Murals on the walls smacked of dirty hippies but the undertones were distinctly Judeo-Christian.

"Here, let me take that for you!" A fit gentleman with dark brown hair tied in a short ponytail assisted in my pack removal and gestured to a comfy chair.

"Can I get you a drink? When Aysh is done getting the other hikers settled he'll come down for you." The man offering me a beverage was standing with perfect posture behind a dark wooden counter, drying a glass and grinning the same exact smile I'd seen a moment before. He also had the same hair and beard, albeit with more salt and pepper, and wore a very similar plaid short sleeved button down.

"Yes!" I clapped my hands on the counter. "What do you recommend?"

"We're famous for our Yerba Mattes!" Another rehearsed gesture towards the wall. "We've got Mango, Hibiscus, and Peach." Back to the smile.

"I'm gonna have to try all of those but for now I'll have the peach, please."

As he prepared the drink I vaguely heard him describe how they grow and cultivate everything, down to the mate leaves from Brazil I'd be imbibing momentarily. It was hard to focus on anything but the incessantly cozy decor of the place. Dark wood, which I rightly assumed they also cultivated themselves, comprised everything. The polished chairs and tables, the floor, the stairs. Only a tasteful brick wall broke up the stained knotted pine. Wicker baskets hung over each booth as adorable lamp shades and appropriately aged doily curtains adorned the windows.

"Ok," I gasped after my first sip. "That is my new favorite drink."

"Fantastic!" My bartender clapped his calloused hands. "Enjoy."

Upon my next gulp of the unbelievably refreshing brew I felt tingly with gratitude. I couldn't be more pleased to escape the elements. I was hurt, I was tired, and I'd forgotten what warmth felt like. It was coming back to me now.

Vermont radiated beauty in those brief moments of sunshine, but in between, I oscillated between utter despair and resounding hope.

"Does that large green pack belong to you, friend?"

To my right stood yet another plaid man with the requisite hair and beard.

"Idaho." I mirrored his smile and held out my hand.

"A pleasure to meet you, Idaho. I'm Aysh." He clasped my hand in both of his.

We walked upstairs to a whole new flurry of activity. Girls with hair conservatively tucked beneath bonnets were zipping in and out of rooms with sheets, all of them smiling and humming. Neatly made bunk beds all matched one another and a variety of goods could be found on each adjacent nightstand. Posters featured the same hippie but Godly theme with varying degrees of subtlety. I saw more than one Beatles reference, including their famous "Yellow Submarine" sandwich and did not have the mental capacity to start piecing together that puzzle.

"Beast!" I exclaimed upon seeing my burly friend in one of the newly made bunks.

"Idaho!"

I embraced the large man extra tight, as seeing a familiar face was icing on the cake of this already extravagant stay.

"Ah, you know each other! This young man has a pack even larger than yours!"

"Yeah, by only 20 pounds." I slapped him on the shoulder and Aysh continued laying down the ground rules.

We found ourselves back at the top of the staircase once every base was covered and Aysh clapped his hands once more.

"That's about it! The rate is $17 a night, unless of course you're open to working for your stay. We have a strict ban on drugs and alcohol and the front door will close promptly at 10."

I wasn't thrilled to hear this last disclosure but it should have been expected.

"Hi there, I'm looking for Aysh?" said a man so tall that he had to hunch in the archway just to peek his head inside. At no less than 6'4", he was strikingly handsome with a well manicured beard. I felt like I knew his name before his introduction.

"Yes Man." He held out his enormous fist.

"Holy shit, *you're* Yes Man? I can't believe I'm finally meeting you!"

This guy was a legend, the most notorious thru-hiker I'd heard about. There were half a dozen stories about how he got his trail name.

100

Anywhere from having no plan and seeing where the trail takes him to wearing women down with repetitive inquiries to go on a date with him. Meeting him in person made it difficult to believe the latter. He was a tall drink of water with a calming and confident presence.

"Idaho Bones." My puny fist met his massive hammer and I tried to make up for it with a confident smile.

"Ah, so you're the man they call Bones." He pointed his other finger and looked just as thrilled to meet me.

"Yes...I am? I am!" Confusion intertwined with a slight sense of being star-struck.

"Well, I'm sure this big guy is aching to get those boots off," Aysh remarked. "Let me show you around!"

I wandered into the bunkroom across from my own.

"Idahooooo!" Johnny Quest was sitting on a bed looking positively refreshed. Familiar faces lined the rest of the room. Eagle gave me a lazy salute. Nala and Allspice, two teenage hikers I'd recently been leapfrogging with, greeted me with smiles.

"I can't believe how many of us are here!" I exclaimed.

"There's more on the way, bro," said Eagle before a trademark burp, which told me their paper cups were filled with beer. "Everyone had to get the *fuck* outta this rain. We were swapping stories of Vermont faceplants."

Back in my own room, I rigged up my phone next to a hair dryer. Then I let hot water run over me for quite some time in the shower. While drying off I was happy to find my phone stirring back to life.

Outside the window, I saw some other thru-hikers in Center Street Alley across the street from The Yellow Deli. When I joined them, we smoked a blunt that never felt particularly risky. Rutland struck me as a crunchy party town with a shared affinity of reefer. I went upstairs to prepare for an evening out. At the top of the stairs, I saw a familiar figure dripping onto the wood floor.

"No fucking way! Wonderboy!" I said with outstretched arms, though unwilling to hug my drenched friend.

"Ohhh shit, Idaho! Heard you finally met Yes Man." Wonderboy said while carefully peeling away his raincoat.

"Wait, how do *you* know Yes Man?" I asked.

"Met him at Goose Pond Shelter. So I get there and they've got a fire going. I'd hiked 42.5 miles. I stop in to warm up and I finally meet the famed Yes Man."

"Dude, how did you not collapse right in front of that fire?"

"Well, funny you should say that." He laughed while unpacking his belongings. "Yes Man goes to me: 'Well, Wonderboy...It seems to me you have two options. You smoke a bowl and you keep going. Or you hang out by this fire, and we smoke...*all* the bowls.'"

"Fucking legend."

"Fucking *legend*. The dude is *so* chill. He just makes you-"

"Want to say yes to everything," I finished his sentence. "Lived up to the hype."

"I can't believe I was gonna keep hiking." Wonderboy headed for the bathroom. "Brutal."

"When you're finished washing that stank off you, come meet us at The Venue. It's gonna be wild."

A parade of nearly 20 thru-hikers trodded the two blocks to a beloved local bar.

We hiker trash slammed our empty shot glasses on the bar to a discord of approving whoops. The tab was on a red faced woman named Wendy, who promptly wrapped her arms around Allspice after we drank up her whiskey.

"I *like* you guys. You sure you can't stay a few days? Mmmmhmmhmm hahaaa." Wendy bit her bottom lip and feasted her eyes on the other marvelously fit men in her perimeter. "Impolite to make a lady drink alone."

Allspice tried to slither away before another round was ordered as I retreated to the karaoke DJ. I gave him five bucks along with a slip of paper.

"Alllll right, everybody! Let's give it up for Idaho! He'll be singiiiiing... Ignition... Remix."

I wish I cherished that performance more, knowing that my days of shocking crowds with my R. Kelly impression were numbered.

After the seamless intro the bar collectively started moving. Every thru-hiker had a drink in the air and it was a sight I'll never forget. Hiker trash and locals were completely intermingled, arms over shoulders, hands on butts. Everybody was living in the moment, appreciating a gathering that was as random as it was genuine.

I returned the microphone and opted for a game I've always had a penchant for: billiards.

I put a dollar down.

"Anyone got next?"

"All yours. We'll be done in a moment." My greeter had a face a bit too large for his 5'6" frame that looked a lot like J.K. Simmons, except topped with long, white locks pulled tightly into a ponytail. He was featuring an outfit from the 2017 Mr. Clean collection and winked all too often. I could feel a friendship just sips away.

His counterpart couldn't seem to shake a sour puss and smelled as such. He was wearing Wal-Mart plaid with badly contrasting New Balances. An *Orange County Choppers* trucker hat tied together the whole ensemble as he scoffed repeatedly for the remainder of their match. His wife looked the thru-hikers up and down like a hungry cougar. I was grateful that her spouse was too distracted with other displeasures to notice.

"Can I get you gentlemen anything?" I pointed back and forth between the two men who each waved me off with a hand. I'd spotted Wonderboy entering the bar and wanted to fill his empty hand with a drink.

"You any good at pool?" I inquired while hailing the bartender.

"Yeah, I'm all right." Wonderboy answered.

"Good enough." I said while trading cash for whiskey gingers. "One of our opponents is a crusty old geezer and I wanna kick his ass."

I racked. Ponytail coolly chalked his cue and introduced himself to us as Randy. Chopper continued to scowl.

"Yer not from around here," he slurred.

"No, sir. New York."

"Ha!" He twirled around looking for agreeable laughter. "Of course you are."

I kept my eyes resolutely on the break and knew this would be an easy match. A few turns later, we had a comfortable lead. I missed an easy shot.

"Big Apple? More like big asshole!"

I tried not to show it but I was boiling inside.

"Sorry about my husband," said his wife as she shuffled up next to me. "He can be a bit of a loser, especially when he's drinking."

Her hand ran from my neck down to my waist while her nicotine scented lips lingered for entirely too long near my ear.

"But he's all *bark*. And no *bite.*"

The clatter from her teeth caught me by surprise and I hurried to Wonderboy to talk fake strategy. I didn't want to test Chopper's bite. Who knows if that hat came with a free gun.

As the game progressed he grew increasingly belligerent. Johnny Quest came to watch the game and Chopper's wife wasted no time getting to know him better. It was impossible for Chopper not to notice and he turned his aggravation towards me.

"What're you doing?" I asked as he picked up the cue ball and paced the table.

"Table scratch." He placed the ball down and prepared for his shot.

"Buuuut...it wasn't." I shrugged to Randy for support but all he did was cock his head with a skeptical look. "Bud, I hit the nine at the beginning of the shot and the cue went for a ride." I grabbed the white ball before he could strike.

"What the *hell* do you think you're doing?" He pushed me and a silence fell.

"Don't touch me, man."

"Or what?" He pushed me lightly and I regained the ground lost between us.

"I said don't touch me." I stared him down and remained completely still. I could see fear in his eyes.

A moment preceded his nervous laugh.

"I'm just kidding around!" He did a 360 with his arms out. "I come here all the time, this is where I come to kid around, come on..."

I shook my head.

"Don't touch me again. We gonna finish this game?"

He nodded and was silent for the rest of the match. Upon our victory, Wonderboy decided he'd had enough and Chopper wasn't done sulking. His wife on the other hand was in relentless pursuit of Johnny Quest for *Build Me Up Buttercup.*

"How about we make the next one interesting?" I asked Randy, as it became clear a two player game was our only option. "Winner buys shots?"

"You're on." Randy said with a smile. He gave me his impression of the town as I made short work of him. We did a shot and I suggested we go double or nothin.

"But we just did a shot!" he said incredulously.

"I was never good at math, Randy!"

We laughed, arms around each other and he racked up the next showdown.

"Heyyy, I'm real sorry for before." Humbled, hat literally in hand, Chopper came over to apologize.

"It's all right, I appreciate that." I responded.

"I've had a bit too much, I didn't mean to offend you."

I looked him in the eye and held out my hand. It felt good to come to such a nonviolent resolution. I stood my ground but found peace. A year earlier a shove would have been license for my right hook. I wasn't around a whole lot of peaceful conflict resolution in my adolescence. Getting physical was familiar. Somewhere along the way it became congruous to having a Y chromosome.

I took down Randy in a gentlemanly fashion and we knocked back two doubles at the bar.

All right Randy, this one's for all the marbles. The poor guy couldn't stand up straight as I negotiated another three shots on the line for the man who sunk the eight ball.

Randy sank the eight ball. But he still had three stripes on the felt.

"Time to pay the piper, Randy."

"No way, man! I bought your shots!" He waved me off and looked for an open chair.

"Raaaandy! We shook on it!" He sat and shook his head fiercely. "Claaassic Randy! Hey guys, Randy won't make good on his bet!" Drunk hiker trash booed Randy who was pretty close to clueless of the goings-on.

"All right, Randy. How about just *one* last shot?"

He nodded unenthusiastically and we put one more down. By this point several other hikers had made great pals with Randy and I got an idea.

"Ok everyone," I began back on the karaoke stage, microphone in hand. "I want to first thank all the Rutland locals for welcoming us into this bar with open arms!"

The bar boomed. All around me there were dirty homeless cheersing with Venue regulars. And it was a lot harder than you'd think to decipher between them. The air was electric, good vibes were palpable.

"But I'd like to dedicate one song to someone special," I said as I paced the wooden floor.

Strangeloves blasted through the speakers and there was distinct confusion for a few seconds.

"I know a guy who's tough but sweet!" I bobbed my head from side to side, nervous for a moment that I'd overextended. "He's so fine, he can't be beat!"

Two more long lines until finally the chorus:

"Weeeee love Randy!"

The rest of the chorus was unanimous. Randy lit up like a Christmas tree and he was swarmed. A couple female thru-hikers wrapped their arms around him and repeatedly kissed his red cheeks.

Eventually hiker trash began its mass exodus. Diffusing Chopper on the billiards table felt like a great leap. Years before I learned that my fists could get me out of any situation my mouth couldn't. Since then it was a constant battle to refrain from delivering my own brand of justice to the deserving villains of the world. Had a fight broken out at The Venue, it would have broken a three year streak of not punching anyone.

I set out to find what The Buddha called *The Middle Way* after indulging my most brutal inclinations years before at the trailer. *That* indulgence nearly cost me my soul.

Embers lingered longer than usual on that July evening by the fire. I watched every one of them fade on the nearby forest floor, ensuring none brought about any unwanted combustion in the summery Poconos air. Some would remain red for nearly half a minute, burning on in vain with no fuel to be found. Fading to black, a forgotten and broken cinder.

"You hear that?" my friend Dan asked.

"Yeah, what the fuck is that?" Brian inquired.

A car horn was growing louder and soon its source could be seen through neighboring yards and trees. An SUV was careening down the 10 MPH gravel roads at nearly 50 and brights were flashing in sync with the blaring shrill cutting through the quiet summer night. My heart raced as the car skidded into the driveway, narrowly missing Dan's prized sports car. A man fell out of the driver's seat onto the stony ground, laughing maniacally. He got to his feet for a moment before falling beneath a tree. Rolled onto his back he resumed his hysteria.

"If you want to ruin a car, then buy your own, asshole," I said with contempt, snatching my grandma's keys from my uncle Mark.

"Hey!" he yelled, trying to get up. "Hey!"

I ignored the drunk and discombobulated loser and returned to the fire pit. We tried to resume some semblance of normal conversation as Mark finally made his way into the trailer. Muffled conversation could be heard of him arguing with my grandmother, also intoxicated, until a clear refrain could be heard from the trailer.

"All niggers must die!" He bellowed, almost singing it. "All niggers must *die*."

I knew then that there was no chance of lowering my heart rate for the foreseeable future. My eyes wide and my knuckles white, I got up and walked slowly to the window.

"Veasey, don't. It's fine," Brian called after me. Half black, he must've thought that a pass from him would halt the sequence of events.

"No, it is not fine," I started quietly, feeling my voice rise with every word. "It's not fine now, and it's never been fine. He's a racist, he's a sponge, and he's verbally abused every girlfriend I've ever brought up here. And he's going to *finally* shut his fucking mouth!"

Upon this last declaration, Mark paused his repetition for a moment.

"Hey!" he said while approaching the window. "Did you hear? All niggers must die!"

"Why?" I screamed before lowering to a reasonable volume. "Why are you yelling that?"

He brought his face up to the screen and grinned his yellowing, cracked teeth. His eyes were honest and horrifying and without realizing it I brought my own face to the window.

"Because it's *true*."

In a flash my fist was punching through the mesh that separated us. The barrier impeded enough for my strike to be nothing more than a glancing blow but the beast had awakened. Mark looked at me, shocked, and grabbed a chair before running outside.

"What's going on?" Brian asked.

I calmly walked over to the cooler and put two beers in my pockets, two more clenched in my fists. Silently I planned my defense: throw two beers at him, and hope that would get him to drop the chair. Then I'd pounce.

"Oh shit!" Dan said with hands in the air. He and Brian put themselves between us and Mark weakly threw the chair over them, missing me by a large margin.

"Who the fuck do you think you are?" he screamed, spit flying everywhere.

"Guys, let him free," I said.

"You're shit, just like your *father*."

"Let him go."

"Enough!" Dan yelled. The uncharacteristic volume was enough to stop all parties in their tracks. "Everyone needs to calm down! Now!"

My heart sank as Mark walked away. I wanted nothing more than to dig my knuckles into my uncle but my best excuse to do so was fading fast.

"At least my father *raised* me," I paused. "Mark. Everyone *but* you raised *your* son."

In complete adrenaline driven cliche, seconds lurched like a freight train coming to life. A traffic cone flew by my left ear as I dug my left foot into the ground. My right fist was cocked and raged forward once my right foot anchored my hook. A crack you'd hear at a baseball game hung in the humid air and Mark's feet were airborne.

A sickening thud followed as the ground knocked the wind out of him. I grabbed him by the shirt and wound up my right fist again. Brian's protests sounded far, far away but I could already see death in Mark's bright blue eyes.

At the very last moment I reeled in my fist, making its landing nothing more than a goodnight kiss.

I stood over those eyes wide shut, waiting for something, anything. I could see every offense behind that punch play out in his ghastly pupils and I found no regret.

A breath.

Brian's. Not Mark's.

Crickets. So many crickets.

My lungs burned as I myself forgot to breathe. My inhalation was all tremors and panic began to rise.

Blood spewed from his black teeth and he closed his eyes with a great sigh.

I rolled Mark onto his side and spat on his shirt. The traffic cone he hurled at me was covering the sharp tip of a hitch attached to the trailer, rusted and perfectly capable of impaling flesh. His head landed inches away from it. He was that close to orchestrating his own death. At least that's what I had to tell myself to sleep that night.

"We all get what we deserve, don't we? You piece of shit."

"Veasey, come on," Brian said with disappointment.

"Come inside," I told my friends. "We need to get the police here before he wakes up."

An hour later, a conflict could be heard from the ambulance at the end of the driveway, flanked by a cop car.

"Yeah? Well you're a goddamned disgrace and I can't wait to see what they do to you in jail!" spat the police officer as he exited the ambulance.

The cop walked up the driveway muttering more profanities, no doubt a result of making Mark's great acquaintance for himself.

"Well, I can take him in if you want," he began, notepad out. "But that would mean taking you in too."

"Me?" I exclaimed. "Why? It was self-defense, I have witnesses, you met him you--"

"Look, I know! I believe everything you're telling me. But there is no way I can take him to the station alone. I'm sorry. In fact his jaw's broken. He's going to the hospital either way."

As he kept talking, my mind drifted to a fantasy of Mark with his jaw wired shut for six weeks. Unable to say anything, having to keep his racist tripe all to himself.

"A hospital won't hold him. He'll find a way back here!" I sounded crazy even to myself but meant every word. "He'll walk here if he has to for revenge."

"Well we can't get the police involved on our end unless he's explicitly banned from the community," chimed in the security officer on call of the community the trailer resided in. "So Mary Lou, that's your decision as the property owner. But once he's banned, there's no undoing that. The Property Owners Association won't allow a reversal."

"Can't you just...keep him out for a little while?" my grandma muttered between sobs.

"You can't be serious right now!" I yelled.

"He was living here, Chris. We can't just--"

"He could kill us!" I pleaded. "Tonight! My friends! You have to tell them."

"All right," she said with tears. This was not her first time banning a son from her happy place. George got himself exiled years earlier.

"Mark Veasey is not welcome here anymore."

6/8/17 – The Yellow Deli Hostel, Rutland, VT, 678 Miles Hiked - Day 56

I replayed the fuzzy exchanges with Chopper in my mind, seeing if there was any particular place I could've diffused the situation better or earlier. Some Buddhist texts found their way into my audiobook rotation, and I wanted to apply my newfound ideals to the exchange. There were many opportunities for improvement, of course. Even the Dalai Lama himself identifies as a *practicing* Buddhist.

More than wanting to eradicate my violent tendencies, I wanted to become a beacon of peace and serenity.

In my sophomore year of college I saw the Dalai Lama speak. I was on staff for the event and quite far from his holiness. Even from 200 feet away I could *feel* his kindness. He calmed me dearly. Too much, in fact. I dozed off for a couple minutes during his words of wisdom delivered at 6 am.

I wanted to have that effect on a room. I'd never be one in a line of Buddhas but perhaps I could be more like Yes Man. Or Aysh.

"It was worth it!" exclaimed Aysh as he stepped outside into the radiant splendor, not a cloud in the sky. "It was worth all that rain for *this.*"

I could see it in his eyes and his outstretched arms, catching every possible bit of sun. The complete gratitude. I immediately wanted it for myself. Which is distinctly un-Buddhist.

I was as grateful as can be, but this man's capacity for thankfulness was so far above mine. The trickles of understanding began as I realized the sudden appeal to this "cult," as it had been described to me for hundreds of miles. I wondered why none of them had offered us the ~~Kool-Aid~~ Yerba Mate.

It was because they didn't have to! These people just radiated joy. Among the shrine-like folk music there was palpable *happiness*. The Yellow Deli was another slice of life the trail brought me to that I otherwise never would have encountered.

Some distance away from the AT and the static nature of this 36 hour respite made me wonder: what is it I love *most* about this experience? What am I most grateful for?

When you walk every day, 15+ miles away from where you woke up that morning, you are bound to live singularly unreplicable experiences. Even if the trees all look the same, even if you're trudging for what feels like eternity, it will be new. You will smell new flowers. New people will come into your life. You will leave fresh footprints.

Tomorrow can never be today.

Granted, this to some extent rings true in everyday reality. You will smell new pollution. Unfamiliar people will cut you off on your commute. You will step in fresh dog shit.

That pure and unadulterated cynicism was beyond what I actually felt. I knew I couldn't live out on the trail forever and would in some fashion return to society. That kind of negative mentality would lead me to the same rut that I crawled out of. To avoid it, I should find a way to cultivate novel experiences every single day, even if it must be in workaday suburbia. Just as some campsites with no view at all have been equally special to one with an unencumbered valley vista, one must find natural beauty everywhere the light touches.

Surely, Aysh has days where he doesn't love his role in this group. Not every thru-hiker would appreciate this hospitality and respect their rules, and it's his job to ensure the guidelines are followed. I'm confident he misses working at their farm on a perfect spring day. Yet something in his core nature takes 10 straight days of rain and says, "It was all worth it for *this*."

"Today's parents...they too easily lose their children's hearts," our new friend, Isachar lamented while rolling dough.

Wonderboy was earning his keep learning to make fresh bread (so naturally I started calling him Wonder*bread*). I'd been assigned to do the same but it ended up being a two person job so I remained with them and cleaned up when needed, which was embarrassingly little work.

"I struggle each day to remain active in the lives of my children. It is all too rare that I read to them." The look in his spectacled eyes was remorseful and even having just met the man I knew he was splitting hairs.

"My fellow tribesmen, they tell me to *make* time. They are right to say it, I need to shift my priorities," he said with a sigh.

"I think you're being a little hard on yourself," I observed cautiously. "Every time I see you, you've had a chore to do. And a lot of times you've been teaching the kids important stuff!"

"That's very kind of you, Mr. Bones."

Oh, you better believe I liked the ring of that. A lot.

"But in today's world we let our children grow up too fast. When they ask to hold a hammer, we should be patient and instead furnish a ball."

Isachar appeared to be rather in tune with the modern world. I wondered where that knowledge began and ended.

"What do you know about Center Street Alley, right across the road?" I asked.

Directly facing the Yellow Deli entrance was an inviting archway, luring passersby in with live music and lively spirits. There seemed to always be a sinful buzz and the juxtaposition intrigued me since my arrival. Isachar shook his head with a smile.

"Not much, honestly. I've never been. No desire to," he said while preparing a pan for doughy piles that would soon be mouthwatering jalapeño cheddar loaves. The Yellow Deli is famous for these unbelievably savory breads, and I'd been lucky to find one in the day-old bin for a dollar. If it were that fresh a day later, I couldn't imagine it fresh out of the oven. Hopefully I wouldn't have to.

I thought I detected a tinge of longing in his answer, but perhaps I imagined it. After all, every parent has moments of yearning for life before a family. His sentiments soon returned to his children, either way.

Initially it was a shock to me that anyone could live across the street from a never-ending good time and not once so much as pop his head in to investigate. A years-long mystery could be solved with an afternoon stroll no longer than five minutes. My curiosity is much too pesky to leave that box unopened.

That feeling transitioned into a different kind of shock. A shock that so many of us live the *other* life. The one of incessantly seeking something better. Something bigger or faster. Isachar must have so much more energy as a result of his complete contentment with things as they are. With the children maybe he from time to time could take or leave.

More pieces fell into place for the acclaimed detective, Mr. Bones.

He began to understand the inviting cultish danger that allegedly lay beneath the surface of this delicious deli respite. Hikers are lost wanderers, by nature. Seeking meaning and purpose...and bread for their grumbling bellies. P.I. Bones just had to keep his eyes on the crumbs of the jalapeño cheddar loaf...leading to the center of it all. Without losing *himself*...

6/9/17 – The Yellow Deli Hostel, Rutland, VT, 690 Miles Hiked - Day 57

Wonderboy had become a slackpacking mastermind, it felt like we might be able to hike without our packs all the way to Katahdin in Maine. He furnished a crude but effective sketch, showing how we could slack pack around Rutland as base camp. Vermont proved to be by far the easiest state for hitch hiking and we resolved to take full advantage of it. Rutland was primed for a whopping 83 miles of slackpacking should we choose that approach.

Hiking without a pack was beginning to truly spoil me. It was hard to ignore how much more pleasant walking the trail was when one didn't have 40 pounds gnawing at your shoulders' and waist's tender skin. Slackpacking, hiking without your pack, was objectively a faster endeavor, but time also flew on lighter feet. The day was a pleasant blur of the rolling green mountains that had been hiding beneath relentless rain clouds for nearly two weeks. Vermont was a fantastical shade of green, and the leaves shone brighter as the mud gradually turned back to dirt.

Par for the course in Vermont: Wonderboy and I barely had to stick out our thumb for a ride back to Rutland. After my post-hike nap back at the Yellow Deli, I rallied back to life to join Eagle at The Hide-a-Way, toking his tin foil one hitter on the way. Lingering after last call, we caught the eyes of two mature regulars.

"And who do we have here?" said a woman trying to look 20 years younger.

She looked straight out of a Claire's catalog and struggled to stand up straight. A push up bra was keeping a purple *I Woke Up Like This* shirt fairly tightly wound. Once I saw the bedazzling on the jeans I realized that my estimate was conservative: she was trying to look 30 years younger. It wasn't working but to my dismay, something was.

"Annette Fucking Rider," she said with a cigarette hanging backwards between her wrinkled lips.

"Idaho Fuckin Bones," I said with a smile. I've always had a thing for older women and the weeks of backup weighed my testes down like a lead balloon. Was I really going to settle for someone who 100% did not wake up like this?

"Who's yer friend?" Eagle asked. He bit his lower lip and laughed giddily, and I was shocked to see his interest mirrored entirely.

"Name's Janine, don't mind the ring." She laughed and winked and suddenly the absurdity of it all hit me.

What comprises the water in this town? The night before we basically had to fend off a horde of middle-aged women and here we were doing it again? This shit only happens in the movies. Granted, none of these ladies were bound for Hollywood but still the eagerness was out of place.

"So what were you talking about?" I inquired under the harsh awning light of the Hide-a-Way bar.

"Whores. Every night fuckin' whores. Had to punch one in the face tonight," Annette said while trying to light the filter of her cigarette. I turned it around for her.

"No shit?" I said with a wink.

"Bitch was talkin' shit, as usual. It's not my fault her son is so hot," she said while finally torching her dart, nearly at the expense of her fake eyelashes.

"You're fucking her son?"

"Sometimes, yeah." She inhaled. "I don't see the big deal, he's of age."

The fact that she had to clarify that definitely concerned me but I was still thinking with the wrong head.

"Annette's friends with the owner so they kicked *her* out instead," Janine clarified as Annette held up a cigarette for her.

"I'd love to fuck *your* brains out," AFR began. "But my roommate's husband's a bit of a killjoy."

"Try being married to him," Janine chimed in without missing a beat.

The two women laughed hysterically and I was certain I'd see at least one faceplant but was luckily mistaken.

"So you're roommates?" I hadn't yet processed the brains part. "Interesting."

"We got weed! We're walkin! Let's all walk together!" Eagle exclaimed dramatically, trying to work past the husband at home issue.

"Idaho Fuckin Bones, I wish," said Annette with cigarette pursed lips. "I woulda ridden you into the sunset."

Unexpectedly Annette Fuckin Rider firmly grabbed my ass and kissed me repeatedly on the mouth. She stopped and looked down.

"You've got yerself a *woody*!"

"No I don't!" I said as I regressed back to middle school, hiding my stark shame with a thick binder.

I looked down and there was no denying the obvious: I was harder than Chinese algebra. My severe backlog left me completely unaware of my own body.

Three pecks and a spank on the BE-hind, that's all Idaho needs!

"Wow...yes...yes I do have a woody."

Eagle nearly had an aneurism laughing and the smokers headed back home to Mr. Cockblock. The Yellow Deli was in the other direction and we walked while smoking more brick weed and aluminum.

"Maaaaaaaann, Woody! I was so ready for a blowjob from the fat one! She looks like she gives a good one...The husband screwed it all up!"

It had been a bizarre evening but watching a 52 year old man with a permanent sunburn mourn a blowjob he just learned about might have taken the cake.

6/10/17 – The Yellow Deli Hostel, Rutland, VT, 711 Miles Hiked - Day 58

"We can't run out of ice cream!" said the barista with hands in the air.

I sipped my mate and rotated my stool.

"I'm the only one who knows how to make it but I've got my hands full up here. Is anyone listening to me?"

I thought it might have been a relief to see these people act like something besides shiny, happy robots but it was distinctly eerie to watch them come undone about frozen milk. Aysh volunteered his assistance and the barista boiled over inaccuracies of the recipe and the instructions. I had to leave to hitchhike before anything came to a head.

"I feel like many of them have a wicked temper," Wonderboy theorized after I recounted the morning scene. "It sounds like a lot of these people came in from 'normal' lives. No one can shed their bad emotions forever, I'm sure there are lots of times where their old selves creep in."

"That's fair," I agreed. Even so, the illusion was already shattered.

Not that I was ever thinking of growing a modest ponytail to forever don a plaid shirt, but I did find this community of good hearted folks to be rather captivating. Yet now it was much harder to imagine them holding the key to salvation.

"Made me rethink the Scrappy kitchen incident," I started. "That was really shitty."

Scrappy finally caught up with us the day before intending to join us for our last night at the Yellow Deli. In exchange for Scrappy's lodging, she was asked to assist in the kitchen. Upon arrival for her shift, no one

114

would talk to Scrappy, even those she'd met earlier. Eventually diplomat Aysh had to come in, take my friend to the side, and explain that she couldn't work in her current attire. It turns out men with old Hebrew names are wildly unproductive when an irresistible shoulder is within sight. Once Scrappy's weapons of tan seduction were safely housed, everyone working the kitchen warmed up to her.

Luckily the salacious sidetrack didn't delay breakfast, and the meal's great orchestrator sat with her son at a table full of thru-hikers. Thankfully, Scrappy was finished with her breakfast and away for the soapbox.

"God, Jesus, Men, Women, Children," she laid out, counting her fingers. "That is the order of things. I know the women's movement has good intentions, but it's terribly misguided. It's natural and good for women to submit to men and to embrace their security in return."

This forward thinking feminist used up her last strike earlier in the kitchen, after expressing relief that Scrappy's mom does not work.

"Women belong in the home," she said with a light pat on Scrappy's now covered shoulder.

After breakfast, Scrappy retrieved her pup Scooby and met Wonderboy and I outside. We quickly hitched a ride and before long we were ascending a mountain.

The day entailed Killington and Pico, formidable peaks that made me grateful for another slackpack. I did not miss my pack. I did miss the trail, however. Sure, we were still hiking the Appalachian Trail, but our lifestyles had made a hard left turn in Rutland. I missed campfires, waking up in my tent, vistas lacking anything man made. Amidst the unraveling of the Yellow Deli's oasis, I came to miss my home, the AT.

From the top of Pico, I could see a change in the landscape far to the north. Impressive white mountains beyond the rolling greens of Vermud. The time was nigh to take on the famous peaks of New Hampshire in only a few days' time. The sight thrilled me and a full fledged yearning to go back to living out of my pack had emerged.

My feet were throbbing when we finally got a ride at dusk after more than thirty miles traversed. I shuddered to think of what my feet would've felt like under my pack. Nonetheless, I was excited at the thought of doing things the old fashioned way again.

I nestled extra tight in the sheets of my bunk, cherishing their softness for one last time.

Chapter Twelve

711 Miles Hiked, 1,478 to Go

Days 59-69

6/11/17 – Trail Angel Kate's House, Hanover, NH, 711 Miles Hiked - Day 59

In a snap decision, I grabbed my pack and sprinted out of the Yellow Deli. Scrappy and Wonderboy were eager to plow on the old fashioned way and give our thumbs a rest. I concurred, enthusiastically even, until I caught sight of the miserable three day forecast. I desperately wanted to go back to proper thru-hiking but scrolling through rows and rows of rain on the hourly forecast changed my mind. I'd try my luck with hitchin' 'n' slackin' the muddy ground between Rutland, VT and Hanover, NH. That plan was contingent on first getting to Hanover, so I sprinted to the bus idling in the parking lot outside my window.

The bus slugged through the small Dartmouth town, lurching to a halt every half a block for a gaggle of students in graduation gowns, or a sloppy group of teenagers taking bottles of wine to the face.

I dismounted the bus to find myself more out of place than I'd been in weeks. Families of seer-sucker and sun hats strolled past me in the blazing sun as fresh cut flowers contrasted my stench. It was graduation weekend. Any swagger I'd accumulated as a rugged mountain man vanished in the perfumes of radiant college students celebrating an end to homework, whether it be for a summer or for a lifetime.

My poles clicked along side streets until I found Trail Angel Kate's house, right where the app Guthook told me I could find it. I let my friends know where I'd gone and swiped faces on Tinder. Annette Fuckin Rider's nicotine kisses lit me up like a cigarette. I went from hardly thinking about sex to fantasizing about it at every idle moment.

I swiped a few more lady suitors while waiting for a hitch and then managed to crush 12 miles in just a few hours without my pack. The rolling hills seemed to be taking it easy on me under the lightest drizzle I'd experienced in a while.

I easily got a ride back to the scene of rampant partying I'd witnessed earlier and was shocked to find no evidence of it at all. My phone buzzed and I was surprised to see a Tinder match messaged me first.

Cat waving GIF

*Whale with *WHALE Hello There!* GIF*

LOL

"Tonight is possibly my only night in Hanover,
where should I be going for some trouble??"

"Go home! There's nothing in Hanover."

"My tent is here! Besides, you're here ;)"

"I have an interview on Monday morning that I really
need to study for, but I sat and watched South Park
ALLLLL day, so now I'm kinda dying."

"Let me help you study."

"That's so cool you live in a tent, I've never been
inside a tent EVER."

"Come on over, I'll give you a tour."
Kenny from South Park GIF

"I need to study!"

"You told me and I just refuse to believe it because
you're too damn beautiful to abandon hope on.
Where are you interviewing?"

Many death emojis
"You called me beautiful...you're making
me blush! You're cute too, why did you have
to choose tonight as your only night in
Hanover?? :("

"Come on, I'll actually help you study."

"Do you know SQL or Tableau?"

"No, I'll provide moral support."

"Noooo shhhh you're gonna be terribly
distracting, I know it.
Do you have your laptop? Do you have your
phone? What would happen if you get eaten
by a bear? Where do you shower?"

"Your place."

"You have the WORST timing! Yesterday I totally
would have helped you shower."

*GIF of Will Ferrell in Elf showering
with tiny showerhead*

"Oh fine, I guess I can study early tomorrow morning.
WAIT A SECOND. Are you a psycho serial killer who's
gonna rape my ear hole and leave me for dead in the forest?"

"I prefer the eye socket."

"Oh yeah the eye socket. That's perfectly fine then."

We met at Murphy's, which Namita deemed the least murder-y bar in Hanover. I wasn't expecting such a thick Indian accent, or to be drinking alone. She was staying sober for her interview prep. After a few failed attempts at making her laugh I asked whether she'd like to do anything else.

"Yeah. The river's pretty, let's go walk there."

When we arrived at the Connecticut River there were a dozen people swimming across.

"They're probably skinny dipping," I said. And hoped.

The naked swimmers soon sprinted past us, sending us both into hysterics.

I seized the opportunity, leaning in for a kiss and she collapsed into me. Her lips and tongue were fierce. She reached into my pants and squeezed my cock.

"Uhhh...do you wanna just go to your place?" I asked, gesturing to the door she pointed out a block away.

"Noooo, my roommate eez so nosy! She hates when I bring any guys home. I have never brought anyone home. She eez bad, I do not like

118

her," she replied with one breath.

Namita took me by the hand as I crossed the bridge back into Vermont. She sat on an empty picnic table and opened her legs wide. I could see lace glistening under the far away street lamps. I teased the clit through fabric before pressing down firmly and biting her neck. She pulled down my pants completely.

"Holy SHEET! There is no way DAT is feetteeng inside of ME!"

Namita pointed at my throbbing penis as if it wrongly accused her of murder.

"What're you talking about?" I asked.

"That's the beeggest deeck I've ever seen!"

"Oh come on, it's not that big."

"Really? Let's see you put a con-dome over tat teeng."

I tried to make the application look as easy as possible. The charade was convincing enough as she grabbed the challenge firsthand. I felt a good bit of resistance and then the welcoming envelopment that had eluded me for more than two months. The tightness of my tiny partner brought on the realization that I hadn't even *ejaculated* in weeks. How many weeks? Four? Five? Six? Six sounded right. I was floored. Maybe I wasn't a sex addict after all.

My grand return was on course for a hasty closing ceremony. I couldn't hold back a month and a half's worth of restraint in this finger trap.

"Owwwww! Eet *hurts*!"

"Don't yell *that*!" I scream-whispered as my finish line fell out of sight. "We're not alone, I'd rather not be interrogated by cops this evening."

As if that distraction weren't enough, I could suddenly see Namita's dark nipples clearly as she lay on the table. I noticed my silhouette stretching on a hundred feet past the table and heard several cars honking. I turned around and found myself blinded, only seeing my starchy white butt cheeks before turning back around. People were hollering and whooping by this point.

Right when Namita seemed well adjusted to the new diameter of her vagina, I felt a bite on my ass. Then another. At once, my exposed buttocks accumulated seven bites from hungry mosquitoes.

"Yeeehawwww!" someone yelled at the street. To distract myself I looked at the full moon as I mooned a caravan of voyeurs.

"What the hell eez tat?" Namita panted.

"They're just geese," I sighed, all but giving up on my orgasm.

"They sound like tey're going to attack!"

"They are not going to attack us, I promise."

"Ok, vell eet's starting to hurt again."

Namita yanked off the rubber and started enthusiastically gagging on my cock. The satisfaction of remembering the distinctly lovely sensation of oral sex set me back on track. I began convulsing and gave my fellator a fair warning.

"I really don't know what his problem is," said a man approaching us from the street.

They were heading straight for our table. I cleared my throat and my dick cleared Namita's. Then another car illuminated my posterior.

"Oh," said the intruder and all I heard next were the clinks of his six pack.

Another moment passed.

"Hey...do y'all mind company?"

"YES?" I said, bewildered.

"Ohhh," he began. "Y'all are fucking. Good for y'all!"

"There's another table over there!" I yelled, surprised to find that I felt bad for them.

"Nah, y'all got the best one," he yelled back.

"I seriously think they might have been trying to swap," I whispered to Namita.

"I mean, if he was tall, I might have done eet."

"Odds are he has a smaller dick, right? That could work to our advantage."

I walked her home as she apologized for the messy evening.

"Relax, it's not a big deal. I had a good time," I assured her, kissing her cheek.

"Ok, fuck eet, let's just go eenside."

Namita opened the door and dropped her jacket on the floor.

"Oh, sheet! Dat's right, my roommate eez out of town for the weekend."

I immediately cast aside my outrage to make room for animalistic lust.

In the comfort of her bed I welcomed the long awaited sheer ecstacy. After basking in the throbbing glow of it I smothered her clit with my tongue until Namita left deep scratches on my neck.

"Owww, eet huuuurts," were words I woke up to in Namita's bed the next morning.

"I'm REALLY sorry. How can I make it up to you?"

"Distract me."

Namita opened her robe to reveal two fingers deep inside her already. She rode till she squirted all over my belly. I turned her over and managed a simultaneous orgasm for both of us with fingers on her clitoris and teeth in her shoulder.

On my blissful walk of shame to my tent, I stuffed a free muffin into my mouth to free up a hand for my phone. Namita's words bubbled up before me.

Now I'm horny and I blame you. I hope you come over later.

With a big doofy smile on my face, I found Wonderboy and Scrappy ready to hitch out of town for another slack pack. My happy disposition was immediately compromised when I remembered that staking my tent in New Hampshire didn't mean I was done with Vermud just yet.

The high regard I held for Vermont's rolling hills were long forgotten as I got itchy to cross another state off my list. Besides, I'd been hearing about New Hampshire's epic Presidential White Mountains since my first day. I was ready to see them for myself.

Another day of mucky deception and slurping ended with us crossing that same fateful bridge under cover of darkness.

As if my horny ghost were still haunting that bridge, I found a fire burning in my chest and my phone was ringing Namita.

"Why you call so laaaate? Eet eez crunch time, for real!"

"I need a shower."

"Go jump een dah reever," Namita said. " I'm too stressed."

"Did you forget how many times I helped you destress this morning?" I asked.

"Coming to getchoo."

The fact that I was still hiking the trail nearly every day was staving off my guilt about indulging in civilized and carnal pleasures in between the treks. Plus ironically, though my tent was two blocks from fresh pizza, I was technically camping right alongside the actual trail!

The desire to get back to proper immersion, to having my pack with me at all times, was still there. I was consciously tipping the scales in favor of ease knowing that my ability to slack pack would soon run out.

6/12/17 – Trail Angel Kate's House, Hanover, NH, 727 Miles Hiked - Day 60

"You have a Batman tattoo?? Stop it, I'm gonna fall in love with you!"

"How is this the first time you're seeing it," I asked before the red flag could fly. "We've fucked half a dozen times."

"Ya, vell how many of doze times deed I geeve eet to *you* from behind?"

"Well in that pant suit, it'd be a crime to not let you in my backdoor."

She fell onto the bed laughing and stroked my hair.

"I can't imagine any woman on earth breaking up veeth you," she began with adoring eyes. "You're so funny and cute, loving and affectionate. Vut eez wrong veeth-her?"

Namita's words hung heavy in my head as I thought back to all the times with Erica I'd been un-loving, with no affection after the breakup. Yet in my mind, I still had no proper idea why she broke up with me, or what was wrong *veeth-me*!

"All right," Wonderboy declared later that afternoon. "Where can we get some beer?"

The weather was simply too perfect. As the less ambitious hikers like to say, it was too nice a day to NOT zero. We stopped at Ramunto's Brick and Brew, known for giving thru-hikers a free slice and they added a free gelato too. Our gratitude and dough drops in the tip jar must've really left an impression. Fifteen minutes later the owner came out with an enormous pizza box.

"You guys still hungry? It's a little burnt, but still completely edible."

At Free.99, the five of us would have eaten a charcoal pie.

We asked where we could get a handle of whiskey, but it turns out that Hanover has the same number of liquor stores as it does black residents: zero. Not counting the students, of course. I left the convenience store with a 30 rack of PBR and lugged it to the Connecticut River.

"Hey, guys!" a thru-hiker named Trail Domme yelled, waving us over to a dock she was sitting on with a visiting friend.

Trail Domme was a thru-hiker we made friends with during a safety meeting at a lookout in Vermont. We all got along swimmingly, and she likely would have joined our tramily if she didn't have so many friends meeting up with her in New England.

Trail Domme was not shy, as the trail name might imply. Beneath her pink tinted hair lurked hungry eyes, unashamed of surging sexual positivity. It was her favorite conversation topic and she carried a two person tent on her back with the intent to use its full capacity. We were in agreement: what a shame it was to get hotter by the day with no one to appreciate it.

I tossed a beer to everyone and put the rest in a plastic bag tied to the dock. Hiker trash cooler.

Bit by bit the other hikers disbanded and it was just Wonderboy and I. I decided to give in to Namita's demands for celebratory sex, as she was moving on to the next round of interviews.

"Ok less dock jumping, more cock humping," I said, clapping.

"Wow," Wonderboy muttered through the hand in his face.

"It's time to leave the Connecticut River," I started as I hopped onto solid ground. "For cunnilingus wiv-her."

"Please stop."

"She wants my dart-" I let it hang in the air.

"Don't," Wonderboy said with a raised voice.

"In her mouth."

"You're a disgrace."

I showered while Namita called her mom and then collapsed naked on her bed.

I slept off Milwaukee pilsners and sunburn in her bed and dreamt of a woman sucking my dick. It turned out to come true. I kept my eyes closed for a few minutes, wondering how I got so lucky going from a stinky born again hiker virgin to a clean tantric savante with a beautiful mouth for an alarm clock.

I surprised her with a hand around her throat, tossing her back onto the bed with welcomed force. My fingers gripped her black hair as I thrust into her, teeth clamped around her perfect nipples. Now familiar moans gave me a countdown so I brought my lips to her ear.

"Are you gonna be my good little slut? Don't you want to cum for me?" She nodded as I felt her soak my balls. "Or can you only cum when I rip off your clothes in a crowded park?"

Namita arched her back over and over, screaming into the humid air, squirting onto my torso as I filled the condom in one final thrust.

As Namita showered alone, I reflected on the previous bit of a trail in a blissful haze. In that moment, I felt satisfied and energized to a point of deep longing for proper thru-hiking. Sipping beer after beer in the clear river water, retreating to a beautiful woman's homestead for more trysts and comfort, my cup had runneth over.

I tried to find the words for Namita as I knew I'd be moving on for good the next morning. It was hard to pinpoint why, but my sexcapades with Namita made me feel better about my relationship with sex.

I'd gone six weeks without an orgasm and here they were for the taking for as long as I wanted. Yet all I desired was to walk into the woods and stay there.

6/14/17 – Hexacuba Shelter, NH, 755 Miles Hiked - Day 62

Scrappy was slowly filtering her water when I arrived at the stream a bit up the trail.

"How are ya, champ?"

"Been better. Not sure how far I'm gonna make it today," she confessed through squinty, hungover eyes.

"Can't blame ya there."

We were all pleasantly surprised with the improved condition of the trail. Vermud left a bad taste in our mouths but whatever flavor wasn't washed out with free food in Hanover was fading away on solid ground under lush evergreens. Before I knew it, the day was done and we stopped at a shelter shaped like a hexagon.

I found myself acutely aware of how detached I'd become from the trail in Rutland and Hanover. Hiking without the weight of my pack and a little too certain of where my next plumbing situation might be.

Carrying that weight for two days made the lightness of gathering wood a distinctly satisfying experience. Sensing the sharp snap of each branch against my dirty hands, I felt home again.

6/15/17 – Southern Base of Mount Moosilauke, NH, 771 Miles Hiked – Day 63

"There's a surprise coming," Wonderboy said, teeth visible through his viking-like beard.

"A *big* surprise," Scrappy added.

For ten miles I pondered and guessed and never came close. Finally I caught a sign through the lush green tunnel.

"The *Omelette* Guy?" I said, thinking how fucking good a bunch of eggs sounded.

"You folks hungry?" a gentle looking man asked behind a sizzling skillet.

The Omelette Guy was a content looking fellow with a real quiet distinction about him. He was dressed for fishing and it was hard to picture him wearing anything else. Gray locks and humble spectacles tied it all together. His boxer Wilmer whined any time we weren't petting her, much to Scooby's chagrin.

80s on 8 blared 30 year old classics as course after course fell under my nose. Banana bread, coffee, pancakes, potatoes, then of course the omelette.

"How many eggs you want?" he asked.

"Two?"

"Oh, come on! Live a little!"

"Four?" I asked.

"How about eight?"

I nodded enthusiastically and watched him throw in ham, onions, peppers, and a fistful of shredded cheese. He told us about the guy who ate 21 eggs.

"I thought he was gonna throw up but he hung out for some time and kept it all down."

"What made you start doing this?" Scrappy asked between chomps.

"Well I retired from the military and figured I could travel the world. That sounded pretty nice, but also exhausting. Then I thought I could instead stay in one place and be perfectly happy."

"This way, you kinda *are* traveling the world!" I offered as he nodded.

We learned about his nifty and secure system, complete with pulleys for hikers who stumble onto the stand after "business" hours. He couldn't be more pleased to have us and offered us a cup of coffee for the road.

The trail's return to a muddy stream got to me a lot less with a belly full of deliciousness. For the first time in a while, I began to think about life after the trail. I told myself I wouldn't end up back in Washington, DC, but I never actually believed it. Now fairly certain that I'd finish the Appalachian Trail, and in so doing see pretty much the whole East Coast, I felt far more prepared to leave and start a new life elsewhere.

Colorado immediately popped into my head.

I'd been twice, once on a road trip and another time for work, and the Rocky Mountains positively seduced me both times. After the work trip to Denver, Erica couldn't believe my report card.

"The place just...honestly? Made my heart sing!" I said while pacing our living room. "The people just seemed happy to be there! I've never lived somewhere like that and I think I'd love it."

As dusk approached, I couldn't think of any reason *not* to move to Denver once I summited Springer Mountain.

While rock hopping a stream at the base of Mount Moosilauke, Scrappy spotted an unopened Heineken chilling below the surface.

"*Two* trail magics in one day? New Hampshire is amazing!" Wonderboy exclaimed.

That sealed it, we were done for the day. I hadn't actually enjoyed a Heineken in years but that evening, in the glistening sunset over our little water feature, it was verifiably the nectar of the gods.

Chapter Thirteen

778 Miles Hiked, 1,411 to Go

Days 64-75

6/16/17 – EconoLodge, Lincoln, NH, 778 Miles Hiked - Day 64

Failing again to conjure up Scrappy and Wonderboy's discipline the day after our decadent feast, I climbed Mount Moosilauke alone. The cold rain that kept me in my sleeping bag had only gained more strength. Icy pellets pounded my bare skin for every false summit. Finally, when there was nowhere but down to go, I stopped to put on my raincoat.

As I fiddled the cold nylon onto my damp skin, I was already fantasizing about the civilization I wanted to leave behind a few days prior. The thought of a warm shower stirred my loins hotter than the memory of Namita's brown skin awakening my own.

For two miles I descended alongside raging torrents. 24 hours before I would have enjoyed a dip in any of the many wading pools and tested out what seemed like ideal natural water slides. I kept my raincoat pulled tight and my boots moving. The slick rocks and mangled rebar made the 3,300 foot descent a far longer chore than the climb.

I stood in the parking lot turned puddle with my thumb out. When the nonexistent sun should have been setting, I gave up and called a cab. Wonderboy said they'd gotten a motel room in the next town.

"EconoLodge in Lincoln, please," I told the driver.

Two days, that's how long we all made it without plumbing and electricity. All it took was a summer Nor'easter to have us shelling out cash for four walls.

6/17/17 – Chet's Hostel, Lincoln, NH, 797 Miles Hiked - Day 65

I returned from breakfast at the EconoLodge to find Wonderboy masterminding a web of hitchhiking yet again, finding rain more palatable without a pack on. He had a crazy look in his eyes, looming over a hand drawn map on the motel room's desk, but goddammit if he didn't get us this far.

"What happened to *really* getting back on the trail?" I asked.

"This happened," Scrappy piped in without looking at me, continuing to wave an ancient hair dryer at her myriad of wet belongings hanging throughout the room.

126

"Dude. I think we can slackpack 70 miles from Lincoln," Wonderboy said. "And it turns out there's a super cheap hostel, Chet's, a few blocks from here. A few comments in Guthook indicated that he's very open to work for stay so it could be free."

I found myself nodding. I didn't like how far I felt from the trail yet again, but one look at Scrappy's still soaked shorts persuaded me.

As we packed up, I found myself evaluating my mental health. It had been two weeks since I quit my SSRI cold turkey. I didn't notice any side effects, but that could've been from the pure distraction of fighting the constant rain. Though my mood was up and down, everything felt manageable. I didn't find myself yearning for the mood boost that Lexapro had been providing, or the numbing of negative feelings. Even stuffing wet clothes into my bag, I was happy to be feeling the full spectrum of emotions in all their glory.

A fantasy of New Jersey's sandy shores filled my mind. Once Katahdin was mounted, I'd be swimming in the Atlantic Ocean for two weeks before hiking south. The midway beach vacation was part of my initial plan when I was preparing for my thru-hike. There were moments where I feared the repercussions of this intention, of losing my trail legs and momentum. Yet the thought of wiggling my toes in sand was enough to propel me over some of my most dangerous ascents as lightning crashed around me. Whether or not it was a net positive, I'd be beach bumming it in a little over a month and couldn't wait to get there.

We soon headed to Chet's hostel to drop off our packs. They'd be waiting for us there later that night. The slack packing bug was still coursing through our veins. Not having to carry our packs was a modest consolation in light of a 10 day forecast riddled with thunderstorms.

Back near the main road, we got the old bait and switch ready. It had recently become clear to us that hitching is a lot easier when Wonderboy and I hide as Scrappy sticks her thumb out holding Scooby in tow. It worked yet again and this guy didn't even seem to mind. The gruff gentleman pulled over to leave us on a puddle filled shoulder near the trail.

"Hey, you guys toke?" he asked, passenger door still open.

"Oh yeah," Wonderboy replied.

"Here," he said, handing a hefty eighth of marijuana over to my buddy. "Hopefully this cheers you up after another rainy day."

We hiked up another mountain, wondering if we'd even be able to light the weed under steady downpours.

We woke up to torrential downpours and debated what to do with the day. It was clearly an ideal zero day.

"The other day was awful, I finally got everything dry. Let's just take another zero," Scrappy pleaded.

Wonderboy and I stared, wondering what this imposter had done with Scrappy the overachiever.

"What?" she squeaked out. "I hardly took any zero days in the south intending to use some up here!" We remained silent. "I'm tired!"

"Bad weather coming in," said Chet, rolling in on his wheelchair. He was back again to play the devil on our shoulder, as he did the day prior when we were holding court on the same crime. It looked like this time he was going to get his way. Chet continued, "Downright dangerous if you ask me."

"I'm fine with staying," Wonderboy added.

"I guess that settles it," I said, shocked to be the only one desirous of hiking out.

"Hey, we should watch a movie! I'll see if there's popcorn." Chet tried to back himself up but got caught on a chair. "Hey, you move that chair for me, I'll consider that a work for stay."

It was pretty clear in my mind that Chet was lonely. He'd made over a dozen jokes about minor tasks that absolved us of the responsibility of paying for his hospitality. And yet again he successfully kept us around. I held no resentment or ill will, opposite if anything. The guy suffered a freak accident with some camping equipment, leaving him paralyzed from the waist down. Whatever the settlement's sum was, it enabled the house and a modest lifestyle. Most importantly though, it left him with the opportunity to host thru-hikers for years to come. The hostel left him with a tenuous hold on the trail he never got to finish.

Rain washed over Chet's roof for hours until finally letting up in the early afternoon. We seized the opportunity to resupply, purchase some items in need for Chet's, and pick up a 4L jug of Carlo Rossi's...ambiguous red blend. We enshrouded the monstrosity in our other items as Chet's was a dry hostel.

We covertly sipped wine and didn't bother fastforwarding the outdated DVD previews. After all, we had nowhere to be.

6/20/17 – Chet's Hostel, Lincoln, NH, 825 Miles Hiked - Day 68

Much to everyone's surprise, I got out of bed immediately when

Scrappy poked me gently at 4:10 am. I quietly put on my outfit, laid out next to me, and stifled groans and bitching since I had a stranger for a bunk mate. As humans are wont to do, we remained silent for the car ride while the sun teased dawn on the way to the trailhead.

The trail wasted no time getting up the mountain, and we were grateful for another pack-free day of hiking at the higher altitudes. Mere minutes after bidding our chauffeur a gratitude filled farewell, I was huffing and puffing, groggy and tired from the Carlo Rossi the day before.

Views became more and more breathtaking as more and more breaths were required for the traverse. My stomach lurched atop the 5,300 foot giant at the center of the most beautiful trail I'd ever hiked in my life.

"Someone in Guthook compared it to the Great Wall of China," Scrappy shared.

Having the distinct privilege of seeing both sights in my life, I found the resemblance to be extremely appropriate. However, the views from Franconia Ridge were indeed superior to its analogous wonder of the world. I had to bundle up tight to enjoy the panoramic beauty.

Gliding along a 5,000 foot ridgeline for five miles on a groomed path, we were afforded 360 degrees of views, all completely filled with mountain ranges stretching into oblivion. Each range got paler and a little fuzzier until eventually soaked up by the horizon's sky.

A menacing storm crawled over the furthest range like a spider.

"You can see exactly where the rain is," Wonderboy observed, handing over a joint.

The distinct edges of the sun's rays piercing through made the patches of downpours even easier to spot. The wet stripes cleansed the ranges before steaming above. Between the spotlights of evergreen and oak, lightning began to strike. Their illuminations flashed silhouettes of blue figures climbing the same ascent we'd suffered hours before.

The many safety meetings of the day came back to bite us. The sun vanished behind a thunderhead with eight miles remaining in our 28 mile day. A pack mentality set in as we entered a death march. The downside of hiking four miles an hour manifested in my soles.

"Idaho, we're almost there," Scrappy encouraged me after I stifled a scream into my buff.

I heard Wonderboy's victorious howl ahead and knew the conclusion was imminent.

The gravel ground against my knees as I dry heaved. My feet felt like balloon animals pulsing within my boots. Life is Suffering, all right.

I turned over on my back and opened my eyes to a warm smile beneath a thick beard.

"Scrappy finally got us a ride, let's go sleep this off."

6/21/17 – Mizpah Hut, NH, 829 Miles Hiked - Day 69

The morning after Franconia's trial I awoke to Wonderboy's cackle. "Idaho! Where are your clothes, man?"

My hand ran along a luxurious surface that shattered in my waking sights. I found myself cuddling an old spring mattress, peppered with questionable stains.

"Ohhhhhh no," I blurted. "Why?"

"I dunno, man! We put you in your sleeping bag 12 hours ago!"

Across the room was my dirty sleeping bag draped out of my former bunk. It was funky, but funky with *my* funk. This mystery mattress was stained with the sins of hundreds of strangers, and in my sleepwalking state apparently clothes were optional.

"How many drinks did I have last night?" I asked, oddly hoping for a high number.

"You? Nada," Wonderboy answered.

I looked down at the bespeckled surface with horror and bolted for the shower.

A generous Trail Angel dropped us off at the first terminus of proper backpacking that we'd experienced in some time. Once the sulking period was over, the three of us found great delight in returning to happy vagabonding in the forest. Wonderboy and I took an extra long safety meeting as Scrappy hustled ahead to the Appalachian Mountain Club hut we doubted we'd be admitted to. In the White Mountain Range, thru-hikers are subject to cruel and unusual punishment. They must lodge in AMC Huts for a fee, among the numerous tourists, which we'd all been calling Marlas, traversing these popular mountains.

Wonderboy and I happened upon exquisite breasts in golden hour. The woman laughed as we searched our peripheries for any promising diversions. Finding none, we acknowledged our passersby, regretting the absence of sunglasses.

"Did you not get the memo?" asked our topless acquaintance. "It's Hike Naked Day!"

"Riiiight," I began sheepishly. "Dude, I *said* we should hike naked!"

"It's not too late," replied the brave exhibitionist, grabbing her boyfriend by the hand before bouncing past us.

"All right! Let's do it," I said, without a trace of sheepishness. "We have to!"

"Do iiiiiiit!" she yelled from out of sight.

Wonderboy and I debated how to initiate our initiation into the hiker trash holiday.

"Well," I said, unlooping a handful of the belt's sections. "We can use our shorts as loincloths, no?"

Wonderboy and I were soon apologizing to an entire group of middle-aged women who were all unaware that they'd find our testes pinballing our thighs if a 180 was employed.

I lost sight of my companion when I stopped to conceal my genitalia after some tiny hail pellets assaulted my nether regions. Soon the destination was in sight.

"Idaho!" Scrappy shouted as she ran towards the trail from the hut. "Don't come inside!"

Feeling most indignant in my loincloth, I was a little offended that my friends thought I'd enter the family-filled Mizpah Hut in my birthday suit. I hope to have my own kids someday, so being banned from playgrounds would have been most inconvenient. Hike Naked Day officially came to an end as I got fully dressed behind a tree.

6/23/17 – Campsite by the Peabody River, NH, 848 Miles Hiked – Day 71

For days, the air never settled. Gusts seem to erode our very souls. Rain came and went, often peppering in hail. An ominous gray lorded over us predominantly in the White Mountains, yet every so often the sun broke through brilliantly.

Those rays kept us going, as did the views. Our legs were being pushed to the limit and the daily elevation changes should have sapped our spirits. They didn't. As unlikely as it was, The Whites were my favorite part of the trail.

Everywhere I looked there were impressive peaks. We'd climb all day to find a false summit, a lookout we thought was the top of the mountain, and we'd have to keep going. I didn't even mind, I wanted to keep climbing. I wanted to see it all.

I strapped Scooby's leash to the front of my pack. She excitedly pulled me up Mount Washington, the most tumultuous peak on Earth in terms of weather. Scooby's tug was amazingly helpful and I found myself hiking twice as fast with her assistance. Wonderboy and Scrappy soon insisted on taking turns with Scooby none the worse for wear.

We all braved the 70 MPH winds for a photo opp and were surprised to find no line for the Kodak moment. The queue for the cafeteria bordered on ridiculous.

"Don't forget muh curly fries!" shouted a woman from her knees.

She struggled to get up after adhering a fresh *THIS VAN HIKED MT. WASHINGTON!* bumper sticker to her Honda Odyssey.

The Marlas, in full force, were content to take in the sights of Mount Washington behind fortified glass inside the welcome center. It made our group decision all the easier.

Keep walking.

6/26/17 – Descent of Mount Success, NH, 884 Miles Hiked – Day 74

Wonderboy and Scrappy had every right to give up on getting me out of bed at a reasonable hour, but they continued to try. After the third attempt that morning, they left me to cross into Maine. Once I did get moving, I trekked with resolve and vigor. The Whites were exhilarating, but I was exhausted. No matter what Maine had in store, I was ready to move on from the massive peaks of New Hampshire.

I bitched and moaned alone all day, shocked that I hadn't caught my friends. Mount Success was one last "fuck you" from New Hampshire Moose Dampshit and thoroughly kicked my ass. Atop the massive peak I looked back at The Whites, which despite my moosey term of endearment had been by far my favorite section of the AT.

Purple mountains cascaded into infinite blues at each lookout of the White Mountains. Living among the clouds for several days left a steady haze over the world we'd all left behind. I was too exhausted to properly appreciate or recall its favor then.

Suddenly, every rugged peak of The White Mountains fell into shadow. Like a kiss on the cheek, the presidential range bade me farewell with a sunset that took my breath away. It reminded me that every memorable view on the trail had come on the heels of an arduous hike. Nothing ventured, nothing gained.

The setting sun ushered in the final chapter of my First Act: Maine.

I walked several miles down a narrow pathway along a cliff, begging the mountain for a flat spot for my tent. A spring gushed out clear water from a collection of rocks, and adjacent to it was barely enough room for my one person tent. It wasn't flat but it was good enough.

Wondering how Wonderboy and Scrappy had any energy to go further than I had, my eyes grew heavy. I slept deeply to the sound of the lively spring.

6/27/17 – Speck Pond Shelter, ME, 896 Miles Hiked - Day 75

There was no rhyme or reason for where the glorious Appalachian

Mountain Club, responsible for maintaining this section of trail, might offer some assistance. One moment a meaningless footbridge would greet me, providing safe harbor over perfectly dry land, only to leave me to my own devices in ankle deep mud as I stepped off of it. Around the next bend I'd find rebar to hoist me up a rock I could have easily handled, to then discover the next boulder wet and covered in lichen.

I was barely across the Maine border, and finally laid eyes on the new state in the early hours. I was enamored by the wild yet welcoming ambiance of Maine.

New Hampshire is only a few inches from Maine at any shared border, but the two states couldn't be more contrasting. New Hampshire was carved and molded for ordinary man to behold. For any breathtaking view one can employ a train or a gondola and spare the sole to feed the soul.

I reveled in New Hampshire's beauty. Every single day I was humbled by the rugged landscape and hidden glory. But then I met Maine.

Maine makes no concessions. Maine laughs in your face and feeds on your suffering. Maine is like the high school prom crush you never even bothered to try getting turned down by. She knows she's hot, she knows she's better than you, and she isn't gonna pull any punches when you try to put a corsage on it.

Maine is for the bold, the strong-willed. It's fitting that a state where nature is playing dangerously coy is the final test for most thru-hikers. One can feel the warning to stay away with its rugged trail and shin deep mud puddles. But we cannot resist the allure of untouched splashes of green and sweet smells of conifers lording over budding flowers.

Maine. Is Pain.

No doubt about it.

My plan was to rise at 6 and get to Full Goose Shelter early, where I estimated Wonderboy and Scrappy spent the night. After my delayed start a few days prior, I still hadn't caught up or heard a peep from them. I couldn't imagine them tackling the Mahoosuc Notch, known for being the AT's "hardest mile," the day before. The terrain of the miles leading up to it was too aggressive.

The walk between Mount Carlo and Goose Eye Peak was exposed and unpleasant. The constant strain to keep my balance compelled me to take off my jacket, but I was repeatedly struck soundly by cold, hard gusts. The contrasting climates between the baking interior of my coat and the frigid ridge line gave me a terrible headache.

I stepped onto what looked like an ordinary plank. Perhaps it was in a past life, but now it served as a booby trap. I stomped confidently onto it to find no integrity at all. The plank disappeared beneath the muck and somehow neither boot found the bottom of the morass. It all happened very quickly. In my escape I managed to soak my left leg in soft earth all the way up to my mid thigh.

I was astonished to find, from the safety of a nearby rock, that the plank returned to its innocent looking state after nearly sucking me in whole. Welcoming all passersby to come and lay a foot on good ole Woody II.

Thunder filled the air like laughter, Maine mocking me in all her natural grandeur.

I made it to Full Goose Shelter. My original destination from the day before. It took me more than three hours to go the meager distance from where I set up my tent.

At Full Goose I found Nala and Allspice, the two ceaselessly penny-less teenagers. I can only imagine having that much independence (and booze and weed) at the tender age of 18. They assured me that I should catch my tramily by the end of my day, specifically at the campsite just after Mahoosuc Notch. Allspice also revealed that Wonderboy was stingily rationing our Black Velvet whiskey. This was especially important because after the many violent spills in Maine, whiskey had become my most powerful motivator to put in miles. I couldn't tell whether I was fixated on getting my fill of the whiskey ration because I needed it or because I bought it. I hoped it was the latter.

I took my leave of Full Goose after lunch beneath clear blue skies. My phone indicated that starting at 4:30, two hours of clear weather would lead up to some light rain. Three miles from the entrance to Mahoosuc Notch, all seemed well.

The beginning of the AT's hardest mile was surprisingly enjoyable at first. It felt like a natural obstacle course. Then the increasingly gray sky let out its fury.

The next 30 minutes were filled with pain, rain, and agony navigating a maze of slick rock. I fixated on the boulder field ahead. It was distracting enough to nearly cost me my life.

My left foot slid and my whole body followed. Only a moment to react, I managed to turn my torso sideways. I was stuck between two rocks at the expense of my right shin. 20 feet below my dangling boots were more rocks. Luckily there was a groove into which I could put a foot and hastily recover from this close call. The gravity of the incident shook me deeply and I resolved to keep my eyes no further than five feet in front of me.

Mercifully I found a reasonable path by which to walk and steeled myself for the Mahoosuc Arm climb that followed. I found more rocks and no clear way out. Apparently I wasn't done with the Notch yet.

Lightning painted a clear picture of the crevices before me and the thunder to follow was a callous guffaw.

I came to a narrow opening that required the removal of my pack. This prospect gave me great anxiety, and I scurried back and forth looking for an alternate route. I found higher ground to the right and began bouldering a heavily moss-ridden ledge. Shortly thereafter, realizing I was being a complete moron, I doubled back and approached it again. I remember vaguely feeling like I had re-spawned in a video game, back at the checkpoint following a grim descent into a valley of rocks.

I threw my poles carelessly into the cavity. I thrust my pack forward and climbed over it. Struggling to get through what can only be referred to as trail by the wicked and stupid, I tore holes in my pack cover and the rain jacket tied around my waist. My breaking point was near. Tears were at the ready, waiting for any excuse to be released.

Finally pointy bullshit gave way to stony trail and I found the campsite that Wonderboy and Scrappy mentioned to Allspice they'd be stopping at. Under the roar of yet more thunder, I pleaded that I'd find them there with whiskey in hand to drown my sorrows.

I carefully tread the side trail towards two tents. Upon closer inspection they were the wrong brand. I couldn't believe my eyes, since they were the proper color and shape. Alas, no *Big Agnes* seals to be found anywhere.

"But I can hear them," I said in what must have been a whisper compared to the clouds' symphony. I was devastated and disoriented. To make matters worse, my phone decided to go back on the fritz.

"What is happening?" I asked no one, unable to focus on any sight or sound.

Another lightning strike forced me to brush off my wishful thinking and face my fate. Since my friends were nowhere to be found, I made up my mind to push past the modest campsite. A little more than three miles ahead was a proper shelter, and hopefully whiskey and friendship. I reluctantly began my ascent as rain turned to steady waves of icy typhoon.

No part of the Mahoosuc Climb was easy, but especially difficult was a 40 foot stretch of lichen-laiden boulder. The slab was angled somewhere between 50 and 60 degrees. I tested the surface and was impressed to find my slippery boots agreeable to it. I inched carefully upward, consciously keeping my weight evenly distributed. The shuffles, six inches at a time, seemed entirely ridiculous. But after nearly falling into a giant hole just an hour before, my conservative nature was in control.

Finally I was within one step of trail. Not rock, but muddy, reliable earth. I planted both poles in the muck and stomped onto it with my left boot. Everything stopped for an instant and what remained of my body weight sent my other foot downward.

My body raced down the boulder and my right foot caught between a fallen tree and the giant rock. The momentum spun my torso hard into the tree, turning my whole world on its head.

Upside down against the rock face, I struggled for air. Lightning bounced off the icy cracks in the boulder. My ankle, pinned between spruce and stone, writhed under the downed tree that had plucked me from my descent and undoubtedly saved my life.

I reached up to free myself but didn't didn't get far, fighting the weight of my pack. Fumbling with the straps, I managed to free the waist. The heft of the bag lurched down the wet rock, and the chest harness choked my throat. Not better. Blood pooled in my ears as stiff hands finally freed the pack to tumble out of sight, carrying all of my possessions into oblivion.

My bloody fingers found a splintered branch two inches above the calf. A spear that would have turned my leg into hamburger meat.

Behind me was the hardest mile on the entire Appalachian Trail. Ahead lay two miles of hail covered footpath to Maine's next shelter, grade as steep as it gets. I was without a working cell phone and thoroughly alone, save for the one question I'd brushed off for months, now finally demanding answers:

What the hell am I doing out here and why did I think carrying 50 pounds on my back for 2,200 miles would be the easiest way to fix my broken life?

Dangling off that boulder under the wrath of a Nor'easter, I was more than a thousand miles short of my destination, and a whole world away from truly understanding where my feet were taking me. At least by then I'd come to learn the journey was much deeper than fulfilling a long forgotten nevertheless lifelong dream, as I'd initially told every curious well-wisher.

"I've always wanted to hike the Appalachian Trail, it's as simple as that."

The carefully crafted persona of a carefree, free-loving wanderer was built on sand. The innocent restlessness of a romantic cowboy was a myth.

Right there on that boulder my illusions were caving in.

I could've eaten bland rice and prayed my way through some cushy ashram to love myself for a few months. Instead of flying somewhere with a favorable exchange rate for existential answers, I stomped right into the wilderness in my own backyard. To the footpath that always beckoned. To uncertainty and the whims of nature.

I realized then that to make an honest and lasting peace within, I'd always intended to stare death in the face.

Just maybe not upside down.

Eventually, I yanked my leg free. My pack caught a lower branch of the same fallen tree that stopped me from greater harm, so at least something was going my way. I carefully yanked the pack up the hill and walked away with only a couple bruises. I took a long way around the boulder and pressed my way through the storm.

Mercifully I reached the next lakeside shelter right as the storm cleared. The thick mist rising off the mile-high pond was actually of considerable consolation. It was a beautiful sight, a tender counterpoint to the fury I'd encountered on my way up to it. I dropped my pack in the brand new lean-to shelter and wandered weakly through the campsites looking for my friends. Having come up blank in my search, I sought out the AMC Caretaker who had turned in for the evening.

"Be right out!" were the words I heard through canvas among the shuffling of belongings.

"I'm so sorry to bother you!" I said while shaking my head and backing away from her camp. "Please don't worry about it, it's not a big deal."

"Oh my god, you're bleeding!" The caretaker's job demanded she take care and the woman retreated back behind canvas.

"Oh, so I am..." The words sounded so defeated in my own ears.

"Here, do you need help?" she asked with a fistful of first aid items.

"Nope, I've got it but thank you so much. Sorry again for disturbing you."

"It's not a disturbance! But I am sorry to say there are no thru-hikers here."

Where were my friends? It didn't make much sense to me but I concluded they must've been at the stealth spot near the summit of Old Speck Mountain, another two treacherous miles ahead featuring another 600 foot climb.

In a most dejected state I crawled into my sleeping bag without even attempting to nourish myself. Closing my eyes just replayed the horror of my journey over and over.

Chapter Fourteen

896 Miles Hiked, 1,293 to Go

Days 76-92

6/28/17 - Speck Pond Shelter, ME, 896 Miles Hiked - Day 76

I sipped coffee and watched a duck squire her little ducklings across the pond. The sun made a brief appearance, lifting my spirits. I was grateful for a new day. It wasn't exactly a new lease on life, but in the morning light I was able to recognize my near death experiences with clearer eyes and be grateful for making it to Speck Pond intact.

"Idahooooo!"

I turned my head to find the source only to have Scooby nearly knock me on my ass a second later. Wonderboy and Scrappy ambled up the side trail along with Trail Domme, all looking as happy as I was to feel the sun beating down.

"You guys were behind me?? How the..." I trailed off, head shaking.

"Didn't Allspice tell you where we were?" Scrappy asked as she gave me a hug.

"Yeah! I checked! There were even tents that looked *identical* to yours but –"

"Dude, it was the wildest thing! There were tents so, so similar to ours," Wonderboy said. "I think they were REI brand, they were already set up when we got there. It was like the Twilight Zone."

"So did you camp somewhere else?" I asked, trying to remember any flat spots since Mahoosuc Notch.

"There was another campsite down the hill from those tents. We set up there yesterday afternoon before the storm rolled in," Trail Domme answered.

"I *knew* I heard you guys! I stopped at those other tents! I was so confused, so desperate for whiskey," I bemoaned.

"You mean...this whiskey?"

Wonderboy snatched a bottle out from the top of his pack and tossed it to me.

"OhmygodIrishcoffee," I muttered out in one breath before pouring a bit into my bean water. I sipped and beamed. The notion of telling my friends that I nearly died for the hooch was not appealing but the familiar warm tingles pushed that regret aside.

"We were thinking," Scrappy began. "We had a good run of roughing it. We can get a proper meal and stay for free –"

"YES!" I interrupted as Scrappy laughed.

"--In Bethel," she finished. "There's a church we can camp behind and we can be there tonight with a hitch."

I downed my coffee and clapped my hands. We were soon on our way.

The four of us made record time, all heads full of town-food fantasies.

6/29/17 - Bethel Methodist Church Backyard, ME, 901 Miles Hiked - Day 77

The rain slowed to a drizzle. Moments later the heavy construction across Bethel's main street lulled to a stop. Filling the air around our tents was the unmistakable sound of humping.

15 feet from my head, Trail Domme's tent was a-rockin'. Moaning picked up gradually with overlays of slapping and sucking. Laughter joined the chorus to the fap fap fap beat of P in the V. Soon after were the satisfied gasps of horny tent-mates.

Trail Domme brought her new friend to her church-adjacent tent only 20 minutes before. Awkward giggles gave way to muffled exasperation and resumed fappage.

It surprised me to feel so bashful and uncomfortable feet away from the deed. There was no trace of judgment about it, not even about the 20 minute orientation session. Maybe it was lying down in the shadow of a church. After all, I'd grown accustomed to group sex while living in the nation's capital. A month prior, with a grad student on a riverside picnic table, I had my ass out and my dick in. Everyone prepares for interviews differently.

Turning my attention inward as round two picked up, I was surprised by how little strife it caused me to go this long without sex yet again. It was comforting to know that I can exist happily in such a celibate state. I searched my mind for any clue of being fulfilled by monogamy long term, or whether I was close to being ready to settle down.

"Could you imagine if this was switched?" Trail Domme's guest uttered in a hushed tone. "'Hey lady, I promise I'm not dangerous, but I don't really have a home. Want to try to read me briefly in a public location and then squire me back to my *tent?*'"

He neglected to mention Jesus in the stained glass window lording above our four tents.

Our new setup had a multitude of issues, including where to relieve ourselves. The trail provides. Next door, a new Bed and Breakfast was days away from a grand opening. The enthusiastic owners, Jeanette and John, loved the idea of a soft opening with us. They were thrilled to wait on someone, anyone.

"Please, feel free to use our bathroom!" Jeanette offered us.

"And make yourself a cup of coffee!" John added. "We're excited to test out our new Keurig."

"Luckily, we booked up completely next week!" Jeanette said while handing Wonderboy and I mugs of breakfast blend in the Bed and Breakfast's common room.

"You are all our test subjects!" John added with a wink.

That evening, the coffee's effect was undone by half a gallon of ice cream and six PBRs. I slowly moved my bloated body out to my sad looking tent.

I stood in the unpleasant downpour, despising my disgraceful structure. Moving the stakes made a slight improvement. I yanked one of the sides to make the shelter taut and heard what couldn't possibly be what it sounded like. Because it sounded like the bottom of the tent split clean, and that split sounded like it went over a foot.

Reaching under the tent, I found my hand on the wrong side of the netting inches away from my nose. I could hear my heart beat like a drum beneath the rain's relentless percussion.

I ducked into my tent and stuffed the hole with whatever I could find but the damage was already done. Prickles of no-see-um bites ran up and down my sweaty neck. They proved to be most challenging to eradicate from my home.

Once horizontal I realized my butt was firmly on the ground. I blew up my broken air mattress to kick off what would become a ritual throughout that night and miraculously fell asleep.

6/30/17 – Holidae House, Bethel, ME, 901 Miles Hiked - Day 78

"Idahooooo," Scrappy began. "It's time to wake up! Jeanette made crepes!"

The smell of fresh coffee brought me out of my ill disposition, leaving me full of compliments for the chef.

"I'm shocked you two overachievers aren't itching to get back out there!" I said to Wonderboy and Scrappy before sipping the brew. Trail Domme nodded in agreement.

"Dude..." Wonderboy trailed off as Scrappy shook her head. They both had a spooked look in their eyes. "This rain...It's *really* getting to me."

"It wasn't like this in the south!" Scrappy cried before burying her face in her hands. "I'm losing my freaking *mind*!"

"And Trail Domme," I began. "I assume you're staying a bit longer for Romp Round 2?"

"Round 3, actually. Maybe even four."

I gave her a hearty cheers with my coffee mug.

I explored the bed and breakfast's grounds once the rain slowed down to a drizzle. There was a beautiful network of gentle trails with flowers smiling down upon me. It struck me as bizarre to be among nature that I wasn't waging war against. Instead of challenging me, these grounds welcomed my eyes for without them its beauty would be for naught.

Back at the B&B and feeling the digestive benefits of my stroll, I found myself in the pristine resplendence of a Victorian style bathroom. I smiled at the fancy trims and frames as I deposited the byproduct of the previous night's questionable dietary choices into my porcelain throne.

It was easy to smile after hearing the story of Holidae House's transfer of ownership.

"Jeanette and I both got home from work late one night. Eating a lousy meal we started questioning what we were working so hard for. Were our paychecks really worth the 'busy busy busy' culture of the desk jockey?" he asked. "We thought we'd test out our southern hospitality up here with the Yankees!"

It became clear throughout the day that this new life was just the right amount of challenging for the pair from Dixie. They clearly enjoyed learning all the new skills that came with their natural instincts of taking care of travelers.

Hearing about two daring but utterly ordinary people cast off the shackles that bound them to a desk filled me with great optimism. I hoped that I'd remain steadfast in my determination to avoid desk jobs after the trail.

It's never easy to leave behind the creature comforts of civilization, but it was extra challenging to leave behind this slice of carefree bliss at the Holidae House.

7/1/17 - Frye Notch Shelter, ME, 909 Miles Hiked - Day 79

Tent still damaged, I crawled into another crowded shelter after another rainy day. Wonderboy and Scrappy sought out high ground to stake their tents. My late arrival relegated me to the leaky corner of the lean-to. When I tried to move away from the water torture, I was devastated to find that my attempt at fixing my air mattress failed. Water filter still functioning improperly, that left me 0-3 on the day's gear repairs, and utterly despondent.

While inspecting the air leak, an enormous moth repeatedly smacked me between the eyes. I panicked and grabbed the creature, feeling a wing snap. A tiny scream rang in my ears and in my frightened state I only squeezed harder. The insect writhed and I could feel its tiny heart racing. The shrill pleas for mercy haunted me as I closed my eyes for the fatal crunch between my fingers. Legs kicked involuntarily as I tossed the corpse aside and reached for the hand sanitizer.

This was far different from killing tiny black flies too stupid to stay away from my skin or clasping endless mosquitoes in a fist. This felt like definitive murder.

I wasn't sure where the line was for voluntary bugslaughter. In feeling the last moments of panic, in actually hearing the blaring terror, I knew I'd crossed it.

An early childhood friend taught me how to smear fireflies along twigs to make our own glow sticks. It only took me one subsequent rave session to deduce on my own that it was an awful practice to never be repeated.

That realization made me rethink pests found in the home, though I didn't always spare spiders. Never silverfish.

In the shelter, I cast the corpse out into the downpour and returned to my leaky corner. Sleep eluded me as I wasn't yet aware of how many clueless moths I'd come to rescue from fire pits to atone for my sin that night.

The drops raining from above soaked me in empathy and dread as I begged my own mind for slumber.

7/4/17 – Campsite Behind The Little Red Hen, Andover, ME, 924 Miles Hiked - Day 82

The Fourth of July brought perfect hiking weather, which helped me move past my first bout of true homesickness. Perhaps that isn't the right word because it is not home that I felt a yearning for. It was the Poconos. 2017 marked the first time in memory that I wasn't at the trailer with great friends and family.

I'm an Independence Day purist in that it needs to include fireworks. Luckily we caught some dazzling explosions below us on the vast shores of Upper Richardson Lake on July 3rd, so that need was technically satisfied.

142

After our hike, Wonderboy surprised me with the six dollar wiffle ball set I couldn't bring myself to buy the day before. The familiar white trash sport made the holiday a little more authentic. Once it was too dark to play, sparklers in hand, we danced with Scrappy to Wonderboy's undeniable trail theme song: *Welcome to New York*.

I wondered why I'd been so ready for this half to end. Mounting Katahdin meant the end of Wonderboy, Scrappy, and Idaho.

There was a growing urge within me to lone wolf it, but still I knew I wasn't ready for our tramily to bid farewell. I searched deeper within myself and found a well completely tapped of its willpower. Facing adversity, usually in the form of rain, each and every day left little room for appreciation of New England. That was a farewell I'd been ready to bid for some time.

Unable to completely leave my previous life behind, I refused to cancel my beachside plans: two weeks with friends on the New Jersey shore before tackling the southern half of the Appalachian Trail. I yearned for the soft sand between my toes and the soothing symphony of the crashing waves. A distinct counterpoint to *Main is Pain*.

7/5/17 – Campsite Behind The Little Red Hen, Andover, ME, 940 Miles Hiked - Day 83

The barista poured another cup of coffee with a smile as I returned one best I could. Since we'd conjured up yet another slackpacking scheme, I had plenty of time to enjoy a fresh brew. Yet an unclassified unease sat between my ribs. The best guess I could manage was being in the same place for too long, far away from the trail. Then a more obvious culprit came to mind: It was nearly a year to the day since Erica broke up with me.

My ex-girlfriend took up precious little mental real estate since our last exchange two months earlier. Erica made it clear that there wouldn't be any reconciling or closure.

I didn't get what I wanted but I got what I needed.

Answers and middle ground were unattainable. More importantly, I saw that the only person who could assure me that our love was real and our memories true is me. My contemplations went largely Erica-free for six whole states, and my brain had taken the final step towards healing itself. The freedom from contemplating my breakup made way for a happiness I'd long wondered were possible. Even through the pain, rain, and disdain of Appalachia.

But then the seal was ripped off by a longtime friend innocently asking me how Erica was doing. The spool was unraveled and I found myself reliving the days, weeks, and months following my unexpected breakup with Erica a year before.

At times in my bachelorhood I felt that I'd mastered a portfolio of skills that compel women to "try on" my lifestyle of honest and uninhibited sex at least a few times. 9 times out of 10 these women came to desire a continued platonic relationship with me. My longtime joke of "sex is how I make female friends" became startlingly accurate.

At the bar of the Little Red Hen, unable to respool the trepidations swirling my caffeinated mind, I found myself scrolling through text conversations to find that 13 of the top 20 females I was conversing with were former lovers.

Am I a bad person?

The age-old question was alive and well. What poor, innocent woman would I rope into a relationship next? How would I ensnare a good woman into my life to convince my own self of my goodness?

If someone that *good loves me, then surely, I'm good too.*

When Erica broke my heart she shattered that illusion.

"I literally *ache* for someone to call me a bad person," I'd confess to friends after Erica ended things.

I wanted someone to finally have the guts to tell me the painful truth. In desiring such a sabotaging label, I lashed out, attempting to make it easy for one to call me bad.

Days after the breakup I took a Georgetown grad student on a kayak trip in the Potomac, something I never got around to doing for Erica in nearly four years of dating despite her wishes to do so. I then fucked that girl in our shower and again on Erica's rug. At least at that point I was deliberately trying to avoid Erica's bed. Less than 24 hours after that I came upon the chest of a mutual lover of Erica and I.

I then successfully seduced two mutual friends of ours, secretly hoping Erica would find out. Little did I know I'd be the one to spill the tea directly. Once the resentment properly stewed, I took a girl home and had sex in Erica's bed before we cuddled throughout the night on the same pillow where my former roommate lay her head for a year and a half. I felt that I'd made a sound case for any jury to sentence me to bad-personhood.

I was like an arsonist proudly watching his work as sirens blared to the scene of the crime.

I knew I had to get away, to leave that apartment, to leave DC. Not that I had a choice about the apartment, which I adored. My inability to remain productive in other areas of my life while I cavorted about sticking my penis into any willing dance partner sickened me. It wasn't the promiscuity that cut me. It was my ineptitude at accomplishing any goal that wasn't a notch on my bedpost.

Moving back in with my parents in New York didn't slow me down as much as I'd expected, but it did the trick enough for me to resume a life of purpose and moderate income. Finally sex wasn't my primary objective, or my most frequented activity. I was down to a healthy frequency of 1-2 times per week, largely with the same woman.

Complete celibacy was finally thrust upon me when I set foot on the trail, marking the beginning of a two month hiatus from the deed. My body didn't take kindly at first to the sudden withdrawal. Within a week all my dreams were sex dreams and erections bordering on pain pressed against my sleeping pad every morning. But I did cool down, and soon masturbation was as far from my mind as I was from Mount Katahdin. Whether I liked it or not, this period was the medication I needed, bringing about the newfound discovery that I don't need sex physically and my esteem and mental well-being are also independent of my proclivity in bed. What started out as subconscious remodeling of my hierarchy of needs soon became a lucid rearrangement of my very soul. In this state of clearheadedness, I turned my thoughts inward at the Red Hen.

Do I miss sex? Yes.

Do I need sex? No.

Do I still distrust monogamy? Extremely.

Do I feel capable of initiating a healthy ethically non-monogamous relationship? Not yet. I'm still far too selfish and reveling in my independence.

My hand absentmindedly swirled the remaining coffee and felt a tinge of peace following my java-fueled reflections. The remainder of my self-work felt a bit more manageable.

I spotted Wonderboy and Scrappy through the window and tossed back the coffee. It was time to move on.

7/6/17 – Eddy Pond, ME, 951 Miles Hiked - Day 84

Fire crackled contentedly as the full moon presided over the lush valley of evergreens. A few feet beyond the chatty embers, boulders conceded to a glimmering pond reflecting the modest mountain beyond. Peepers and toads melodized once the thrushes retired to their nests. It was hard to imagine a more perfect camping spot for Maine to offer.

The scenery was even more impressive when held up against our extended stay in the one block town of Andover, ME. We again vowed to get back to the trail and sleep in the woods, away from the 24 hour church bells of the world.

"I could see how people get sucked into towns," reflected Scrappy in her tent.

"You mean like how we did in Delaware Water Gap? Or Rutland? Or Lincoln? Or Bethel?" I asked.

Yeah. We were living the phenomenon.

One wouldn't have to hike for very long before hearing a tale of thru-hikers going into town for pizza and ending up at a church hostel for weeks. I, myself, met several thru-hikers who stopped in a town for resupply only to hole up long term after yanking a HELP WANTED sign out of a window. We hadn't dropped off any resumes, but Wonderboy, Scrappy, and I all had trouble peeling our tramily away from hot daily breakfast in Andover. We all had an unspoken reluctance to go back to trekking with our packs like good little thru-hikers.

Once the fire by Eddy Pond needed no more tending, I scattered my belongings in its luminescence. I sewed, I glued, I condensed, I discarded. I cleaned everything. The newfound absence of dirt on my gear was extremely noticeable and spirit lifting.

I took my filthy rag to the pond and cleaned it as best as I could. Catching the moon bounce off the ripples, like melting neon lights, I tried to find a place to keep the sight in my mind.

Moments like this are the reward for carrying your pack. Stay close to the trail.

7/7/17 – Waterfall near Redington Lake, ME, 961 Miles Hiked - Day 85

I'd abandoned hope of catching Scrappy and Wonderboy once the sun turned all the conifers golden brown. A tale as old as time: they couldn't wake me up that morning. This was overwhelmingly the means by which we'd get separated throughout New England.

After bushwhacking through a hidden trail to get to a waterfall, I had no qualms about shedding all my clothing. The frigid torrents were exhilarating and I didn't even notice when my feet went numb. I pressed my head against a boulder and reveled in the sensation of water finding the easiest route around my shivering figure, knowing I had a fire waiting for me.

I pressed my butt against a smooth boulder and was thrilled to find that my idea for "nature's bidet" was in fact not ridiculous, but a stroke of genius.

Ramen worked in tandem with the fire to restore a comfortable core body temperature as I watched the falling water catch moonlight.

As I slurped a perfect portion of Ramen and felt its fiery broth drip down my torso, I had an odd feeling that I could see myself smiling. And it was a familiar smile.

In second grade, we took a field trip to a Buddhist monastery. I knew nothing of the theological philosophy, but I dug their style. The pagodas and pristinely manicured bushes enamored me and I felt a resounding peace walking the grounds. Coming up the rear of the class, I hung back to observe a man raking white sand in the garden. Beneath his bamboo hat, a unique smile could be seen as he worked. It was a smile unlike anything I'd ever seen. I didn't realize it at the time, but I was observing a moment of pure, unadulterated contentment. The man I watched happily labor away transcended happiness. Contentment was sowed into his very bones.

Maine had been wearing me down for hundreds of miles, but there was fight in me yet. It amazed me how much a little sun or a warm fire rejuvenated me whenever I needed it. I was still dreading the thousand miles that awaited me south of Harpers Ferry, but at least I was no longer questioning whether I was capable. I *knew* I was capable. I was content to let my journey unfold as it was meant to. To trust the universe.

The waterfall's white noise left my eyes heavy. I grinned in my sleeping bag at one last conscious thought: I wasn't just surviving in the wilderness, but *thriving* in it.

7/10/17 – Pierce Pond Lean-To, ME, 1,012 Miles Hiked - Day 88

The Appalachian Trail reached a point of ruggedness I'd not yet seen. I couldn't imagine it if I tried. Despite there being a well trodden path beneath my feet, everything was untamed and ferocious. Downed trees scraped my shins as I feebly climbed over them in the unforgiving heat. Horseflies screamed in my ears as I rose from the slick, jagged rocks that found a home on the footpath.

Quickly I was back to merely surviving.

The trail had again beaten me down, this time from starry eyed nudist waterfaller to a crestfallen, defeated, sack of skin. Each night I pitched my tent well aware that I wasn't working hard enough to catch my friends. I'd been eating their dust for four days. Every morning more and more belongings had succumbed to moisture. Luckily, the trail always provides.

I scraped out the last bits of a Trail Magic Mountain House meal watching a cluster of small mountains give way to hazy dusk. Silhouettes of hungry fish preceded ripples over the calm pond. As dazzling as the scene was, I had to observe it through a bug net. The mosquitoes and no-see-ums struggled to find chinks in my armor.

I couldn't maintain a pace to catch the day's last ferry ride to Caratunk, but luckily Harrison's Lodge was a stone's throw away. Fantasies of his legendary pancakes and coffee kept me going in the days prior, which featured a biblical thunderstorm and a face plant into a bog.

Once my tent was set up lakeside I dipped my foot into the temperate, clear water to check for leeches. I stripped off the unpleasant accouterments of my day's journey and plunged. The leech-free pond was my best bet for avoiding blood-suckers of the aerial variety.

The water initially felt crisp and then suddenly perfect, as if my body at once remembered all the steamy afternoons under the boiling sun. Floating beneath the dragonflies, I fantasized of all the delights waiting for me in the morning. Luxuries available at a lodge directly on the trail. No slackpacking required, nor risk of being sucked back into a town.

7/11/17 – Caratunk, ME, 1,017 Miles Hiked - Day 89

The dining room of Harrison's Lodge overlooked a pearly waterfall cascading into a stream. It bubbled beneath a ramshackle bridge composed of old dead branches, rope, and recycled railroad track nails.

Tim, who is an avid birder, pointed out that the waterfowl mother I saw during the previous day's sunset swim couldn't possibly be a loon with so many chicks. I couldn't even decipher "Merganser" through his thick Maine accent.

"Ayum-Yeee-Ahhhr-JEEE" he said through a smile, methodically flipping his fruit-filled flapjacks.

"Why was the lodge closed all those years?" I asked in response to Tim's mention of a recent grand re-opening.

"The waahf. She aahlways hated this place so she sahh tew it that I couldn't owuperate it agaaain until she was fully daahn and duhvorced. Keelled me to watch it gaathuhh so much dust fer nuuhthin'."

In my emotionally depleted state I felt my eyes well up. How could anyone divorce this kind, passionate human? Let alone drag it out over a dreadful five years, taking away his passion and livelihood all in one shot? I pictured a mean, awful wench of a woman before I remembered something: I didn't know her. I don't know Tim, either. This marvelous vivacious host could have been a terrible husband.

I don't truly know anyone. No one truly knows me.

That realization had been rattling around my head for some miles. I wasn't much closer to figuring out what to make of it as I watched Tim slide the flapjacks off his griddle.

A great judge of character was something I'd long prided myself on, but I came to see that this does not equal *knowing* someone. Character and essence are separate, and I believe essence can be masked and suited to various occasions. Just as I'd *known* hikers to be rude before they got comfortable and turned out to be as amiable as one can be. Just as the woman who professed to regard me as her favorite human for four years decided she wanted nothing to do with me for as long as we live. Was I *ever* Erica's favorite human? Top 10? I didn't truly know Erica and she didn't truly know me.

Tim didn't truly know his wife and she didn't truly know him.

The concept both delighted and terrified me, just like love itself. The last time I felt secure in love I wondered what stranger was sitting next to me.

"Love has a nasty habit of disappearing overnight." I muttered Paul McCartney's words through confused tears. Erica couldn't explain to me *why* we needed to break up.

"Love hasn't disappeared," she said with remarkably dry eyes. Erica was always a crier. "There *was* love, there will always *be* love. We're just not meant to keep sharing it with *each other*, not if we're going to be happy."

"I was happy. I think you're right when you say that someone out there can make me happier. But I don't want her. I want you." I wanted Erica's eyes to meet mine for the rest. She didn't want to invite a single moment of weakness. I continued, "I know I would have been happy with you. Maybe not my *happiest*. But genuinely happy. And that would have been good enough for me. More than good enough. I'm just sorry you didn't see that."

Butter oozed over the sides of my pancakes as I pondered a reality where I'll never truly know the person next to whom I lay my head. And I couldn't lay it there until I'd become ready to accept that intimidating fate.

A tapping lightly shook the window. I locked eyes with a

hummingbird, its majestic red breast plumed in and out.

I didn't want to hate Maine. Or the trail. Or anything.

I also didn't *know* Maine. We tend to forget, but it's supposed to be impossible to hate something you don't actually know. Acceptance, on the other hand? That requires very little knowing at all.

After breakfast, I returned to the trail. I walked among magnificently tall evergreens, the footpath playfully weaving in and out of them. To my right ran a crystal blue creek, destined to crash into the mighty Kennebec River at any moment. A river so mighty that thru-hikers had to be ferried to the other side by a man working what I considered to be a pretty sweet gig.

As I reached the shore, one of the hikers departing the ferry canoe took a wiffle ball bat out of his pack and held it as if to duel.

"Ooohh, hell yeah!" I said, pointing at it, instead of taking out my own wiffle ball bat and making light saber sounds which would have been the right thing to do. He then pulled out another and did some samurai moves. I laughed heartily and introduced myself.

"So Way," he said. When I looked puzzled he shook his head solemnly. "No way," he began. Then nodding and smiling he said, "Sooo Way."

This routine was very practiced. I nodded as if I comprehended it all.

"Why two bats?" I inquired.

"Chipmunk smashing, mainly. They're actually quite tasty."

Before I could even wonder whether he was kidding he revealed a tattoo on his calf of a chipmunk head with X's for eyes and yellow bats criss-crossing like a pirate flag.

"That's awesome," was all I could say. Though, the thought of smashing those little fur-balls seemed pretty un-awesome to me. At least he was eating them, though I would have preferred the butchering to be more humane and less America's Pastime.

"We're repeat offenders. Hiked '11, '13, and '15," So Way revealed, gesturing to his stunning and leggy female companion. I'd been trying to bag a tanned blonde my entire adult life and apparently I wasn't smashing enough rodents to get their attention.

"Wow! I can't imagine that. This trail makes me want to do so many other things!" I regretted saying that.

"I've done other trails and this is the best one."

The lady and So Way went on their own way, south towards Harrison's Lodge, and I was left with clean cut Greg, the good natured ferryman of the Kennebec River. He gave me brief instructions and we pushed the canoe out into the current. On the water, it felt like I left all the hate, frustration, and pain of the last few days on that rocky shore. I was reminded of how much I love water sports and instantly decided I wanted to aqua blaze in the south.

The term "aqua blazing" refers to choosing to travel by water in substitution of stomping past white blazes. In Shenandoah National Park the Appalachian Trail runs parallel to the Shenandoah River. The river is wide and gentle, all too inviting for a canoe or kayak. A small subset of hikers opt to take the much easier route through Shenandoah to give their feet a break. I already intended to join those ranks.

As I walked into the town (read: block) of Caratunk, it seemed for the first time in a while that things were gonna work out. I felt like a priest walking through the Red Light District, not letting my eyes stray too far, lest I be lured into another podunk town.

To my delight I saw the familiar bags of Wonderboy and Scrappy at my resupply destination.

Chapter Fifteen

1,050 Miles Hiked, 1,139 to Go
Days 93-115

7/15/17 - Shaw's Hiker Hostel, Monson, ME, 1,050 Miles Hiked - Day 93

"I've never seen this before in my life," remarked Poet, co-owner of Shaw's Hiker Hostel.

Shirtless in my pajamas, I felt an out of place pride welling up in me.

"Really?" I replied. "I find that so hard to believe! You meet just about every SOBO spotting your oasis at the end of the Hundred Mile Wilderness."

"Uh huh and I ain't never seen that," he said with a decisive point at a little invention of mine. "In the whole decade I've had a pulse on this trail."

Shaw's is a legendary place. Legendary places usually house legendary people. In 1977, Keith "Old Man" Shaw made a name for himself cooking massive breakfasts for the weary SOBO travelers who hadn't seen a brick building in 100 miles. And of course, all the NOBOs eager to get one last good meal in before the last test of will between them and Katahdin: The Hundred Mile Wilderness.

As its name might suggest, the Hundred Mile Wilderness is untamed land. At least along the trail between Monson and Katahdin, there are no traces of civilization. In that spirit, the trail maintenance is also noticeably less thorough.

Shaw passed away in 2004 and his son ran the hostel for a few years. It changed hands a couple more times before Poet and his wife Hippie Chick took the reins in 2014. They never strayed too far from the trail after their thru-hike in 2008.

Poet in particular earned notoriety in the same realm as Shaw, having even more flair with his pen than with his hands as he himself doles out heaps of breakfast in a packed dining area. He was most known for his gear-headed ways, and could nerd out with the best of 'em when it came to backpacking and survivalist equipment. Not only did he and Hippie Chick make a few shekels with a resupply shop, but a "Shakedown from Poet'" was something every SOBO had to endure. NOBOs often wanted to experience the ritual even though they were 95% of the way done and 95% settled into their ways and gear. Flip-floppers on the other hand had a lot to gain in my eyes, being roughly halfway done. A few key tips from Poet could be the deciding factor between a hiker making it or giving up.

"I mean it makes sense when you think about it," Poet began. "But even so, I've never seen it done. What made you do it?"

"I just wanted to get weight out of my pack," I shrugged.

"Right, the pack..." Poet trailed off. "Pack poles! You should call them Pack Poles! This could be huge!"

The objects of Poet's fascination were my trekking poles, which truly hadn't looked like any other poles I'd seen. I'd picked up a couple of pouches from resupply boxes, tied and glued them to my poles, and kept some things in there. After a while, water became so plentiful that I grew indignant about not carrying any. So one pouch housed my Smart Water bottle with a filter on the end of it. The other pouch housed some first aid supplies, snacks, candy, pot smoking paraphernalia; the handy essentials. To really complete the objective, I kept some gear in a large fanny pack as well which hung over my waist strap so I didn't feel its weight at all.

"Not a bad workout either, I see," pointed out Poet.

It's true, my upper arms were definitely less puny than the rest of my bony hiker frame. Carrying about a pound in each hand for a thousand miles did eventually add up to a modest gun show.

"Idaho, we could be rich!" Poet was pacing now. "I mean, I know some guys in the gear industry. We could send them this prototype and see what they come up with. Pack Poles! 'Get the weight off the pack, and into your poles!' I could really see it!"

"All right! Let's make some money!" I said with half hearted enthusiasm.

"Honey, I need you now! Whole group just arrived," beckoned Hippie Chick from across the lawn.

"We'll finish this later, don't forget, Mr. Pack Poles!"

I meandered the grounds a bit until I saw Wonderboy returning to the hostel.

"So a guy named Fancy Pants hands you a bag of mushrooms and your reaction is 'thanks, I have no further questions.'" My eyes darted from the colorful fungal assortment in Wonderboy's hands to his goofy auburn covered smile.

"Well, that's not his real name," Wonderboy reminded me.

"Oh, ok then," I said, reaching for my share of the goods.

We sat on the slope between the hostel and the owners' home across the way, waiting for the effects to kick in. Soon enough, the house was melting in and out of the ground against the dusky sky. The soft colors brought a sense of peace despite hikers wandering about us under the setting sun.

We left to explore the small yet charming town of Monson. We waded ever so slightly down a boat ramp into the murky depths of a small pond. The nearby street lamps cast a yellow glow over the black water and deep ribbits jounced the scene.

"What are those?" I asked.

"Bullfrogs, dude!" Wonderboy sounded shocked.

"I had no idea they could be this loud. I wanna see them!"

We traipsed up the ramp and headed for some cattails. Wonderboy successfully parted the tall grass to reveal a slimy monster sporting a neck as big as his body. With refined sight and my phone's illumination, I could see ripples cast out over the smooth water. Upon the subsequent protrusion I could see into his translucent body, the cold blood pulsating to endeavor an advantage over his competing gentleman callers.

In order to avoid frog-blocking, and to ensure adequate rest before the infamous Hundred Mile Wilderness, we returned to our tents and summoned sleep to eyelid bound kaleidoscopes.

7/16/17 - Little Wilson Falls, ME, 1,064 Miles Hiked - Day 94

It was hard to keep my hungover eyes open for my shuttle to the Hundred Mile Wilderness, but I did my best when a crisp rainbow presented itself over Maine's lush landscape. Feeling anxious and alone, I tried to take the sight as a sign of good things to come in this remote section of trail. Once my driver departed, the wilderness engulfed me fully, seeming to savor my solitude and trepidation.

Immediately the trail felt different. The path was quieter, like it held more secrets. The harmonization of mosquitoes and mutant-sized horse flies sounded like a chorus from hell. Beelzebub had no devil put aside for me. He'd be presiding over my pilgrimage himself.

7/17/17 - East Chairback Pond, ME, 1,084 Miles Hiked, Day 95

I went to sleep the night before wondering how much of the Wilderness I'd struggle through on my own. After a properly early start that morning, I nearly fell over when I heard a beast bounding towards me. Again I struggled to stay on my feet when Scooby landed her enormous paws on my chest. I brought a palm to my mouth.

"OOOOOH-WEE!"

After a few seconds I heard the same call echoing through the trees. Wonderboy was on the trail with arms stretched wide after his primal howl.

"'Bout damn time!" he said through his red beard, more scraggly

154

than ever.

"We were about to move on!" Scrappy said while cleaning up breakfast. "We took it really easy yesterday so you could catch us but started to think you never left Shaw's!"

After that, we traversed the Hundred Mile Wilderness together, Scooby scouting between us constantly, easily handling the extra miles those checkups required.

I sensed a reluctance from both my friends to keep up the usual pace. Scrappy was taking far more breaks than I was accustomed to seeing her take.

The trail went back and forth between dazzling us and beating us down. The untamed nature of it made for unique beauty, but also unchecked ferocity.

"I feel like I'm walking on a football field of wet bowling balls," I remarked to Wonderboy after a fresh spill into the mud.

A picturesque waterfall fell into a deep blue swimming hole and we couldn't resist its allure. We were tempted by many more breakpoints after that, but finally had to hold a safety meeting by a pristine lake with breathtaking views.

"Can't believe we're so close to Katahdin," I mused wistfully. "Been hearing about it for a thousand miles and we'll be standing atop it in just a few days."

My hiking companions began to squirm.

"I'm not ready," Scrappy confessed before a lengthy sigh. She threw a rock into the lake and continued, "I'm not ready for this to be over!"

Wonderboy was keeping his cards closer to his chest but I could see the same despondent look in his eyes, made even more blue by the vast lake.

Scooby couldn't share her emotions, but I knew she'd miss the trail most of all.

7/19/17 - Beach of Lower Jo-Mary Lake, ME, 1,120 Miles Hiked - Day 97

"Remember, we're going to the second beach." I looked back and forth between Wonderboy and Scrappy, preoccupied with packing up. "Second beach!"

"Ok, we heard you!" insisted Scrappy. "Second beach, the one--"

"With the mussels," I interrupted.

"That beach is also gonna have the most epic sunset of all our camping options," Wonderboy chimed in. "All the better for our shrooooomy adventure!"

I got the idea about mussels from the hiker companion app Guthook. Comments from other thru-hikers in Guthook indicated that fresh mussels could be harvested at the second of three beaches of Jo-Mary Lake.

I silenced the little voice in my head wondering whether introducing completely radical seafood into my diet was the best idea. Plucking those salty creatures fresh from the lake was too romantic a notion to pass up on.

Later that day, after my morning coffee finally hit my lower digestive system, I quickly paced under the canopy to catch up with my friends. Shortly after I spotted a large wild mushroom plucked from the ground and placed directly on the trail. Above it, "5:15" was spelled out with sticks.

My Fitbit shone 5:16 and I realized this message was for me. I extracted the magic mushrooms from my bag and popped them into my mouth. With even more purpose I hurried my feet along to catch up with the messengers.

Skepticism in full bloom, I stopped at the first beach to check for Wonderboy and Scrappy. Out on the peninsula overlooking the lake, I stared intently for 360 degrees with no sign of them anywhere. Yet I felt I could hear them. Last time I felt like I'd heard my friends I ended up being right, and I endangered myself for nothing after the fact.

"Probably just the drugs kicking in," I muttered aloud.

Onward I went, ever more determined to catch up. I was soon met with a large downed evergreen that had to be climbed over. Flies and mosquitoes descended on me and my heart sank from the top of the leveled trunk. Ahead I could see at least a dozen more fallen trees blocking my path. I took a moment to quickly throw on my bug net and pressed on, thoroughly annoyed that I had to view the world through standard definition while psilocybin coursed through my veins.

About six trees in, well into my mushroom trip, a branch snagged my bug suit, exposing my arm to the feasting hellions. Once on the ground, I removed my hood to inspect the tear. I saw in perfect clarity a horsefly land on my skin, chomp a noteworthy chunk of flesh, and fly away with traces of blood dripping behind it.

I raged on through the field of downed trees. After two miles, the trail opened back up and I reached the second beach. An empty shore awaited.

With flies dive bombing my neck, doing their best to press the mesh up against my sweaty skin to render it useless, I began to panic. I couldn't fixate on any one given thought or emotion with the constant ambushing. Then I found a horsefly trapped with me in the very mesh on my face that was meant to keep them out. I thrashed around until the bug was gone and tried to collect myself.

I threw my pack onto the sand. My headlamp served to keep the top of my net above my eyes then I had my buff from my nose to my neck. I left my eyes exposed because I was sick of looking at the world through mesh, which looked more like stained glass with my infinite perspiration. Long sleeve shirt under my bug net proved to be inadequate for the long mouthed mosquitoes in constant pursuit, so I had to layer up with my soon to be sweat soaked down jacket. Below the belt my zip offs were tucked into my Darn Tough socks, each finding a home in camo-printed Crocs.

My outfit eventually proved to be as effective as it was fashionable, save for the sushi bar mosquitoes made of my lower back when I knelt down to zip my pant legs to my shorts.

I manically gathered dry wood and set it ablaze. I cast damp driftwood onto it all, creating a thick cloud of smoke over the entire beach. The winged pests scattered and I disrobed down to my underwear. Lying next to the fire, I was able to recapture a sense of peace. This was especially important because clearly my friends didn't make it past the first beach, even after all my pestering that morning.

As the sun found refuge behind some clouds above the ridgeline, I turned my focus to the perfect explosion of pastels before me. Ashy mussel shells adorned the fire pit. It occurred to me that I should begin my harvest before darkness came.

I carefully surveyed the shore, not really knowing what to look for. Soon my fantasy seemed out of reach as I struggled to peer beyond the glare of my headlamp.

"Just one," I muttered aloud.

My grand feast was already up for bargain: I'd take a single catch. Just to say I did it.

I reached for what I expected to be another half-shell, but it was in fact a full mussel. I found some of his neighbors, more a few doors down, and before I knew it, I had a baker's dozen. I sloshed triumphantly towards my camp with the catch balled up in my shirt.

I placed three shells on a rock by the flames and prepared my pot to boil the rest. One of the meals I was carrying happened to be Spanish rice and I couldn't think of a better pairing. Water from a fireside shell sizzled and a great cloud of steam fell upon my face, whetting my already ravenous appetite. Beyond the hiss I could hear a rattle. Intertwined with the crackling fire, it made for an interesting song. "Hisssss POW!" It was haunting but immensely satisfying.

The boiled mussels proved to be the superior dish and complemented the rice even better than I'd anticipated.

Never before on the trail had I felt so independent, so equipped for survival, as that evening. I was able to repurpose the sadness I felt in being separated from my friends and remind myself of everything the Appalachian Trail still had left to offer me.

7/22/17 - Millinocket, ME, 1,168 Miles Hiked - Day 100

A shrill alarm woke me from the depths of my wet sleeping bag at 6 am sharp. I had a date with Mt. Katahdin, the great mountain. The heart of Baxter State Park in Maine.

Before I could lose the sliver of motivation, I unplugged the cap of my sleeping pad which rapidly became little more than a thin layer of latex between me and the coarse ground. The deflationary trick is one I learned from Wonderboy to get my ass moving in the morning.

As I gathered my damp belongings, the magnitude of the day began to set in. Katahdin is a mountain of incredible height, girth, and ancient mythology. The final terminus for NOBOs, the north-bound thru-hikers. A milestone of epic proportions for flip-floppers and south-bounders alike. For me, it meant no more Maine, and hopefully no more pain. Or I'd gladly settle for just *less* pain.

Since Wonderboy and Scrappy were NOBOs, Katahdin meant the end of their hike, and the end of our trail family. End of an era. My tramily was disbanding. The thought of returning to "lone wolf status" brought me great joy, but the thought of two friendships that will never again share proximity and routine was as painful as slipping my ravaged boots onto my mangled feet.

I felt the rose colored tint of immense affection for my hiking companions of 1,000 miles. Wonderboy's incessant lyrical rewriting, and Scrappy's simpering smile as she polished off a lion's share of snacks three days ahead of schedule. Scooby doing laps of sheer ecstasy around a tree, turning its bark into a scratching post when freed from the doggie pack she tried to avoid being strapped to every morning.

We hid our gear from the rain and trekked toward the home of Pamola, a revered deity of the Wabanaki Tribes. Katahdin did seem like a fitting home for the moose-eagle-man: head of a moose and the torso of a man, blessed with the wings and talons of an eagle. Four tribes native to New England believed that Pamola lived in a great wigwam within the mountain and was responsible for legendary nor-easters. Katahdin meant "Great Mountain" to the Penobscot tribe.

Pamola was believed to have taken prisoner or eaten any soul who attempted to climb Katahdin. The belief was so endemic that these tribes stopped trying to mount it altogether, with only two accounts of people surviving Pamola's wrath. A man and a woman both lived on after meeting the beast, only to die one year later when explicitly disobeying his orders. Then, as often happens in history, white people came and had to disprove a deeply held belief. So they climbed Katahdin and shocked the tribespeople upon their return.

It was easy to see why people would believe in Pamola for so long. The mountain impressively towers over all nearby peaks and can be seen from a great distance. The hot sun only provides momentary relief between icy gusts. Trees are warped and weathered, sticking out of jagged boulders and frozen gulches.

The harsh climate didn't dissuade my nostalgia for the northern half of the AT. I thought of all the hikers I met, for only a day or even a minute. The shared euphoria of seeing someone you never thought you'd lay eyes on again in your whole existence. It's a special feeling and it never failed to entrance me, even among those who were kind of annoying.

The trail is long, but it is narrow.

I thought of their new lives, how close they might be to their old lives, whether they're happy, whether they "got what they needed/healed/ate, prayed, loved." Whether they delight in the endless slew of questions from dead eyed suburbanites or loathe the conversations that could never begin to explain the tug of war in their heart when they laid their weathered hands on the sign at Katahdin's peak.

There was a thought brewing that kept coming back to me, finding more conviction as it traversed the corners of my mind.

"I've been here before," I said aloud as nostalgia turned to deja vu.

Of course I hadn't been there before. I hadn't even been to Maine prior to traversing the Mahoosucs in what felt like a three-day thunderstorm nearly a month prior. But the stillness and lush green of my surroundings gave me great clarity. I felt I'd been there before because the 5 mile jaunt was a perfectly analogous mini hike of my entire journey thus far. In many amazing ways, this footpath, from the campground in the shadow of Mt. Katahdin to its highest pinnacle, was a tiny perfectly chronological echo of my trek from West Virginia.

Its inception point, the campground of tourists and weekend warriors a footbridge away from the Ranger Station, was traced straight out of a mid-Atlantic staple of summer holiday: Harpers Ferry. The trail was smooth, easy on the body, and full of humans who don't have their trail legs. The stony path running parallel to the crystal clear stream was reminiscent of southern Rocksylvania. A return to smooth trail after the falls reflected the relief of entering the Garden State. Then the footpath gave way to manageable bouldering with no dirt to be found, much like the beautiful rocky bridge entering New York before Bear Mountain. A gentle earthy stretch was in essence the relief of Connecticut: the calm before the New England storm.

My soles began to throb on the foundation of conifers taking over the forest from their leafy cousins, bringing large sappy roots to the surface like the painful ground of *Massive-tree-roots*. All at once I found myself in a sea of utter green. A dozen shades of natural splendor. I was immediately taken back to the Green Mountains of Vermud. The Midsummer Night's Dream vibe was gone in a flash, just as tectonic shifted ranges of New Hampshire's White Mountains keep lush forestry to a bare minimum at its 4k+ peaks.

After three false summits, another calling card of New Hampshire's rapid elevation changes, I found myself walking among clouds. Cursing at 4,500 feet among the stratocumulus, only one state was on my mind: Maine. Perhaps it's because I could take in the entirety of it with only a slight turn of my head. The Mahoosucs, The Bigelows, The Whitecaps: every painful mile. Pamola forbade me to stand still and take in the ceaseless beauty of Maine's untouched wilderness. Without a doubt people hike back down Katahdin feeling that they felt the presence of god. To me, the presence of a Moose-Man-Eagle Deity of the native people was much more palpable in the biting winds above the treeline.

It was nearly time to bid farewell to rain, pain, and Maine's most highly evolved insects. The humid environment only tolerates the cream of the cream of the crop when it comes to human-feasting bugs. That's the joke of Maine: It may well be the most beautiful state on the whole trail, but you will have to offer up your blood, sweat, and tears to take it in.

Wonderboy and Scrappy made their way to Katahdin's sign only moments before I did, but I instinctively gave them a moment before my own approach. From a dozen yards away I could sense their sadness. Some part of them hadn't truly considered the sprawling emotions of leaving behind their new home. Nearing the end, they were more and more amenable to taking days off, and it felt as though they might just pack up and hike back to Georgia. Silence fell between the three of us when I laid my hands down next to theirs.

"Wow..." Wonderboy exhaled. "This is it."

"I wish we could *see* something." I lamented as the clouds grew denser in every direction.

"I can't believe it's over. I wish Scooby were here," Scrappy said.

"Sucks that she can't finish with you." I said, acknowledging the sad fact that dogs weren't allowed into Baxter State Park. "Feels like she deserves this moment more than I do, honestly."

Soon after we waited patiently for our Kodak moments and felt no guilt taking a little extra time. After all, we'd been walking a *lot* longer than these Marlas.

The hike down was quick and sadness turned to hunger. Scrappy's parents awaited us outside Baxter State Park with Scooby. They couldn't have been prouder of their daughter.

"How do you guys *feel?*" Inquired Scrappy's father while beaming.

"Tired." Wonderboy said with a smile.

"Hungry." I chimed in.

Scrappy's lovely parents dropped me off at the Appalachian Trail Cafe, where I'd soon be picked up for the first leg of my trip back to NY. We all chatted a bit longer but the moment couldn't be pushed off any more. Long drives were ahead.

I leaned down to wish Scooby farewell and had the distinct sense that she knew the journey was over for her. It was always clear to me how much that dog loved the AT. She truly had the presence of a pup made for the nomad life. It took Scooby a while to warm up to me on the trail but I could also gather that she knew we were saying goodbye and dreaded it. It's no secret that Wonderboy was her favorite, but she still appreciated my belly rubs. I proceeded to hug Scrappy, and then Wonderboy who was barely shy of unhuggable.

"Please. Please throw away these clothes." I pleaded.

"I'll think about it."

I waved through the kicked up dust and my heart felt heavy. Suddenly I was filled with regret about all the nights I purposefully created miles between me and my tramily just to get some alone time. I wished I cherished it all more.

Once seated inside, I ordered enough food for a small army. After taking my order, the server looked at me with a smirk.

"You finish your hike today?"

"Can't you smell it?" I retorted coolly.

She winked and handed me a Sharpie.

"There's still room on that ceiling tile over there."

I stepped on a chair and saw some familiar names scribbled into the industrial fiberglass slab. Deep sadness returned and I thought back to that karaoke bar in Rutland, VT. I could see all the smiling faces I thought I'd hike the next few hundred miles with. I hoped they all finished. I hoped they were all happy.

I inked my trademark signature and beamed at the handywork. It felt like I was signing a contract.

"I, Idaho Bones, pledge to finish this trail. No matter what."

Chapter Sixteen

1,178 Miles Hiked, 1,011 Miles to Go

Days 116-121

8/9/17 - Stealth Campsite near David Lesser Shelter, VA, 1,178 Miles Hiked - Day 116

Two weeks of hedonistic living later, I was back on the trail. The first day properly hiking again was rough. My feet were more accustomed to walking on sand than the forest floor. I could feel blood throbbing and pooling in my shoes. My heart, a thundering mess, wouldn't beat at a rate less than 130, even after taking a long break. My whole body was consumed by the intense radiating pain from the bottom up.

I tried to find some of that old magic in the trail. It wasn't anywhere. I couldn't stop thinking back to all the luxuries I'd had for two weeks and admonished myself for letting me get so soft. I expected to be in a place where I *craved* the trail, and all the life that comes with it. That I'd lie awake in my comfy bed, fully resentful of the gross and spoiled society I'd returned to. Chomping at the bit to return to my all too humble tent in my smelly and always slightly damp ~~sleeping~~ fart bag.

I did come to dislike the gross and spoiled society, but it didn't keep me up at night. I've always felt that way to an extent but that's never stopped me from storing food in a fridge or enjoying some conditioned air. No, my body didn't fight it. It gloried in the riches for two whole weeks. Just like how all food tastes so much better on the trail, all the creature comforts felt that much more decadent. The feeling of ice on my neck might as well have been the kiss of an angel. The jets of a jacuzzi shooting ripples of ecstasy across my skin. Every couch I sat on seemed to hug me as I shoveled snacks into my greedy mouth.

Everything. Was. Heavenly.

After mounting Katahdin, my mind gave no actual real estate to the notion of leaving the trail for good. My pride was tenaciously entangled around the completed trail. Even the threat of another 30 days of rain couldn't have trapped me in any of those hugging couches.

Surprisingly, I hadn't come to miss the trail after two weeks of comfort and sandy shores, but there wasn't a trace of shock to find myself back in Harpers Ferry poised to tackle another thousand miles.

I eased into the return, only barely crossing the threshold south into Virginia and seeking camp only eight miles in. The same distance I traveled out of Harpers Ferry four months prior, in the exact opposite direction.

Thanks to my two weeks of indulgence, it was almost as if I was starting the AT all over again. At least from a physical standpoint.

I followed a fading side trail at dusk and stumbled onto a lovely spot for my tent. Once I propped my feet up on my sleeping pad, I bit into the cold pizza I snagged before heading south out of Harpers Ferry. Letting it linger in my mouth, I closed my eyes and tried to remember just how perfect it was fresh out of the brick oven hours before.

8/13/17 - Tom Floyd Wayside Shelter, VA, 1,223 Miles Hiked - Day 120

Virginia's notorious *Roller Coaster*, over the course of 12.5 miles, serves up 3,500 feet of vertical high grade elevation change, largely over sharp rocks and ridges.

I couldn't make it more than a quarter mile at a time without stopping and gasping for air. The frequent stops gave me lots of time to think. I contemplated some self imposed anger.

Was it worth it?

In Maine, my body could've handled Virginia's Roller Coaster all in one shot. With every bout of dry heaving, I was wondering if I'd need two whole days. Was my premeditated two week halftime break worth losing my trail legs?

The largely beachside respite served as a mental life preserver for my time in the torrential New England downpours. The side trip was planned as far in advance as my thru-hike. So what purpose did it serve, then? Why did I build this into my journey?

The answer was as obvious as it was humiliating.

Fear of missing out.

To avoid FOMO, I sacrificed my trail legs in exchange for an ultimate frisbee tournament I deemed too fun to miss and a separate trip with old college buddies. Even Chris didn't have much in common with these friends anymore, let alone Idaho Bones. Yet they both chose to make a re-entry into thru-hiking all the harder. To make it all possible, I needed to reorient myself at my parents' house on Staten Island once I returned from Maine.

Being back on that angry little island served well to clean, fix, and replace gear. My time there tested my newly calmed temperament, and renewed concerns that I may revert back to my old self once I had to return and face civilization. With a roof over your head, daily dilemmas ironically are at least a few dozen more than *Walk. Or Don't.*

It was generally good to see my family, though that came with some challenges. My parents, mired in the strife of selling my grandmother's house and seeing to her well-being, didn't take much interest in my thru-hike. I empathized on an intellectual level, but I couldn't prevent some resentment from welling up inside.

In close quarters, I could plainly see all the damage my father suffered at the hands of his family. A man, not yet broken, but feeling the weight of a family that never stood a chance for united fronts or what could even pass as civility. A man lost in a web of manipulation and lies laced with short tempers. My dad has always been a little uptight, but overall he's a comedian, a kid at heart, a literal fucking puppeteer. Those masks gathered dust as the façade of a panicked grouch further set in during those first four months of my thru-hike.

After a few days on Staten Island, I was bound for Wildwood, NJ for the ultimate frisbee tournament. Wildwood was one big party, and thus served no ulterior motives. It was heartening to be back among friends and my old community, but in the end no higher purpose was served. Not that vacation needs to be fulfilling to be rejuvenating.

A bit south of the tournament, on Long Beach Island, NJ, things calmed down dramatically. I dug my toes into the shore every day with a gin and tonic in hand. I was often alone, which was both welcomed and lamented. I'd long been excited to lone wolf the southern hike, but this beach vacation was supposed to be a time of comradery. While I biked up and down the narrow island, my college buddies were in and out of weed naps, N64, and Elio's pizza back at the bayside beach house. I was disappointed to find a deficit of curiosity about my hike from my eternally stoned friends, and I found some resentment still bubbling from Staten Island.

Atop the final ascent of Virginia's Roller Coaster, I paused to glimpse dusk rolling in. I was still undecided on whether the extended holiday was worthwhile. Staring at the rapidly changing landscape, I remembered the danger of wishing any of my past to be altered. One alteration still seemed to suit me just fine: though the emotional ups and downs persisted, I was enjoying an SSRI-free mind. I even noticed more empathy since I stopped taking Lexapro. It was becoming easier to put myself in the shoes of others.

Unlike Wildwood, LBI did bring about a cerebral shift. Clean water at the turn of a wrist, electricity at the flick of a switch, warmth at the pull of a blanket. It was the first time I was alone with myself as Idaho Bones without fighting for survival.

Whenever I was separated from Wonderboy and Scrappy in New England, I was nursing wounds and gear was held together with tape. I was desperately avoiding raindrops. Oceanside, LBI was the first time Idaho Bones got to comfortably enjoy some time alone. It was quite agreeable. Ironically, every time I set my toes in the ocean, my mind kept coming back to an utterly landlocked place: Denver, Colorado. The city had been beckoning me for years and I was feeling more and more ready to take the call. A few weeks on the familiar East Coast did nothing to make Denver any less appealing.

As the days faded away on LBI, it was easier to accept my lone wolf vacation. The last day, just as I had every other evening, I did a tip toe past my friends playing video games. I rinsed off the beach and relocated my solitude to the bay in a kayak for the setting sun.

The usual ospreys and sandpipers awaited me on a remote little marshy island, as I tried to find waterways I hadn't navigated before. The water was peaceful as ever, and I positioned myself appropriately for the final sunset of my beach vacation.

As pink clouds surrounded the setting fireball I cracked my only pilsner and soaked in the scenery. Life had been distinctly easy for two whole weeks, when I felt my trail legs melt into the white pebbles by the ocean. Eventually I came to terms with the bittersweet anxiety of returning to the Appalachian Trail. I became soft as ever, unaware of how much time it would take to get back into shape.

The sky darkened as I drifted backwards in the bay, finishing the last sips of my beer, listening to the water splash the kayak's sides. Unhinged solitude had suited me rather well and part of me was surprised by that. For as long as I could remember I had a love interest, some casual sex to enjoy, a flirtation to explore. Having such crutches became deeply ingrained in my identity and sense of worth.

Virginia's rolling hills fell into shadow, just as the ospreys and sandpipers did in that bay. It was there in Appalachia that everything I learned in the northern half and on New Jersey's shores came full circle.

With no one to keep in mind, to answer to, to take care of, I had rekindled a love with myself.

8/14/17 - Thornton Gap, VA, 1,250 Miles Hiked - Day 121

I woke up thinking about the gripping audiobook that filled my ears the night before. I resisted the urge to pop my earbuds in to continue the tale. This morning, it was time to take in the AT with my undivided attention.

Most of us grow up to be expert consumerists. Even below the poverty line instant gratification can feel like a human right. The 20th Century taught us to want, need, and take in nearly every aspect of existence. I'd seen this disposition manifest itself in my hiking peers for over a thousand miles. Even unencumbered from the umbilical cord of mainstream society we feel entitled to information and snacks. Many a silence has fallen over shelters filled with munching trekkers who delight in the sliver of cell service.

Living with your constant thoughts can be overwhelming on a good day and debilitating on your worst. Solitude can't hold the door forever with anxiety and uncertainty banging on the other side. It's hard to judge anyone who feels the need to fill their days with music, podcasts, and audiobooks. After about a week I found the birds' chirpings and insect calls to lose their enamor significantly. After that I tore through 15 audiobooks and days' worth of podcasts.

Though I was filling my head with knowledge, back in Maine I resolved to mark sacred the first two hours of every day. During such times I would hike without stopping and would listen to nothing save for what the world had in mind. Whether that be a nest of blue jays overhead or 14 wheelers blaring beneath my feet. This was time to be present, completely in tune with the Appalachian Trail exactly as it were.

This subtle change had dramatic effects, and it was exactly what I needed for my return to thru-hiking. It brought on a renaissance of joy and wonder regarding my 2,200 mile home. I found myself gasping and breathing more fully. The whoosh of leaves blowing in the wind gave me goosebumps. I felt at one with the forest and grateful for her gifts.

Ears empty I proceeded south on a humid but temperate morning. All that could be heard were birds and my poles.

Suddenly my seclusion was compromised by a ruffling of leaves and I halted.

To my right, two stark black bear cubs clumsily hobbled up a hill. They stopped after a few yards and turned around inquisitively. One looked over her left shoulder. She appeared positively frightened and eager to create more distance between us. The female seemed to be waiting for her brother who had different plans. Looking over his right shoulder, I saw a snout covered in broken leaves. He cocked his head towards his sister, as curious as can be. But not afraid.

Half a second later heavy paws could be heard crushing earth to my left. 25 feet ahead, directly on the trail, a mother bear stared me down.

She grunted and a thick mist hung between us. A hardly noticeable nod from their mother was all the cubs needed to continue up the hill. The mama bear slowly followed the cubs without ever breaking eye contact. Her moves were deliberate and clear. Every bit of me understood that I was in her territory, and was to follow her lead.

She turned away halfway up the hill and with cubs out of my sight I was compelled to keep walking south.

On my third step the mother stood up briefly before pounding her front two paws into the dirt with a low, drawn out growl. Her eyes were intense as her head lowered. I instinctively dug my trekking poles into the ground between us, believing that any barrier was a good one for such a standoff.

It confused me that the mama bear would remain. Clearly I didn't know enough about the ursa genus but what I did know is that a mother would never willingly separate herself from her offspring. Ever. Something felt very wrong. My gut was telling me that she should have followed them, that a bear would never risk her cubs being attacked by some other danger just to do harm to me. Were my measly steps seen as that significant of a threat?

I went through an incredible gamut of thoughts in what must have only been three seconds: embarrassment in not knowing what to do, anger in lack of due diligence, confidence in my ability to maim the bear with my poles, and regret that I hadn't called my family in days.

My right hand reached up to free me from my pack for a 180 degree sprint but then there was another rustling of brush.

10 feet to my left a tiny bear bounded out from the ferns towards his mother. He halted briefly in front of her and she nudged his rear up towards the rest of his litter. She proceeded close behind him with eyes still fixed upon me and I resolved to not make the same mistake twice.

Mama bear finally out of sight over the hill, I turned to my left and clapped my poles together loudly. I waited with baited breath for another sound as my head darted nervously back and forth from the scene of my looming demise above and the green hill below.

I tip-toed along the trail with the same double take every few strides and when I felt the coast was truly clear I did indeed sprint.

I trekked to the next ranger station. At a safe distance, I could reminisce on how fucking adorable those tiny bears truly were.

Soon enough I found a friendly looking Ranger.

"Excuse me?" I inquired.

"Hi there! What can I do ya for?"

TOM was carved into the little gold plate over his left breast pocket and his broad, earnest smile was that of a man as simple as a three letter name. His deep wrinkles reflected a career of doing what he loved, so much that the application of sunscreen regularly escaped his mind as he whistled the days away.

"Well a few miles back, I came across a mama bear and her cubs." His eyes looked shocked but he was still smiling broadly. He rocked back a few inches but seemed to only do so because he thought the act would make me feel better. "I saw two cubs run up a nearby hill. The mother didn't follow. A bit later what I believe was a third cub popped out from a nearby bush." Now his eyebrows matched his eyes. I continued, "That's not possible, right? Did she adopt one or something?"

I knew what I saw but I still couldn't believe it. Some part of me thought that perhaps when locking eyes with mom, one of the cubs snuck around me to the other side. Or more terrifying, that there was in fact another mama in the vicinity and the families were traveling together. I'd seen a lot of nature documentaries and none of them featured a single mom working to put her *three* children through bear college.

"Oh, it's entirely possible! Downright common this year with all the rain and the mild winter. How many miles back?"

"Probably about 5 north of here."

"Ah, I bet you *did* see three. Sounds like you came across Madeline!" the Ranger said casually, as if bears with 50's housewife monikers were as common as rain.

"Wait, so bears can have three cubs??"

"They can have FOUR! Extremely uncommon, though. A standard winter and spring will yield two. But on a good year, the litter can double!"

My legs turned to jelly as I realized that I was in pretty much the only situation where black bears are extremely dangerous. They're adoringly called "giant chipmunks" by thru-hikers because they're so skittish and harmless. Days prior, I literally snapped at one to scare it away. I was snacking on a large boulder while he scavenged the ground beneath me, unaware of my presence. I popped a piece of beef into my mouth and snapped above my head. I then proceeded the universal "shoo" motion with practiced nonchalance. The bear looked up and then I saw the whites of his eyes in terror. His big dark butt raced down the hill. He evidently knew the most dangerous animal on Earth.

Facing the Ranger, I was embarrassed and furious with myself for not knowing the proper protocol. I couldn't bring myself to ask.

Reading the ghastly look on my face the Ranger continued:

"Anything else I can help you with?"

I shook my head as an unsteady smile formed on my chalk white face. I thanked him for the information and the next couple miles were a daze of self-directed profanities and head-swiveling. A reunion with Madeline and her three cubs was not on my agenda.

Chapter Seventeen

1,250 Miles Hiked, 939 to Go

Days 122-125

8/15/17 - Open Arms at the Edge of Town Hostel, Luray, VA, 1,250 Miles
Hiked - Day 122

Ever since I returned to the Appalachian Trail in Harpers Ferry, my
stomach seemed undecided on whether or not something was seriously
wrong. One day I'd be flirting with incontinence only to wake up the next
day with normal, solid excrement.

The night before, I arrived at Thornton Gap after pushing my
unwell body to the limit. I skipped right past what seemed to be a decent
campsite in favor of stealth camping near a bathroom with 21st century
plumbing. Four times I doubled back for encore deposits.

I awoke the next morning to the same light drizzle from days prior.
The rain was actually welcomed as a poor neighboring tree suffered the
wrath of my digestive system during the night. The constant spritzing made
cleaning up far easier than it might have been. To the best of my ability I
tried to cast the rancid waste into a cathole and abide by Leave No Trace.
Sharp pain in my stomach compelled me back to the familiar restroom of
yesterday.

"What the FUCK is wrong with me?" I asked myself after
thoroughly testing out the toilet's turbo flush feature for a hat trick.

Later that evening I'd meet Wonderboy at a hostel in Luray.
Fortunately for me, I didn't have to hike another step. My body had been
brought to the brink of collapse by the big miles the day before.

Wonderboy agreed to canoe with me for three days on the
Shenandoah River alongside the Appalachian Trail. Finally it was time for
my Aqua Blaze adventure. The snootiest of purists frown upon such a
substitute but my struggling belly and throbbing feet were in complete
agreement on the lower energy, lower altitude alternative.

As I waited for the hostel owner, Alison, to pick me up at Thornton
Gap as she promised me the day before, I debated running into the
bathroom one last time.

"Hi there, you Idaho?" she asked from her vehicle, catching me just steps from the restroom.

"Sure am!"

In the common room of the hostel, I plopped down on a recliner that I intended to remain in until Wonderboy's arrival.

Hours later I woke up to the sunset peeking through the blinds.

As I dangled string for the hostel's cat in the backyard, Wonderboy arrived. I found him descending his enormous Toyota Tacoma in a light blue button down shirt and light red chinos, both from the fashionable outdoor brand *Kuhl*. To my surprise, he still had his impressive ginger beard and long blonde (as he insists) locks to boot. I was expecting some sort of haircut and beard trim. Witnessing the typical array of hair wasn't quite as shocking as beholding the man in business casual attire. In Maine I bade him farewell in a shirt that had more in common with swiss cheese than textile.

Wonderboy was roughly a month out from his mournful completion of the AT at Mount Katahdin. Before he could even wash the stench off of a thru-hike, he had an interview scheduled with a crunchy granola school in his hometown of Atlanta. After his third round interview, he drove nearly 600 miles to Aqua Blaze with me. As gracious as I was, I suspected the yearning to taste the AT life again may have been more alluring than seeing his old buddy Mr. Bones.

"How'd the interview go?" I asked with arms stretched wide.

"Great, man! They want me to be a Spanish teacher, accountant, and carpenter. I think I'm gonna get it!" he said excitedly while immediately tossing a sleeping pad and bag into his truck bed. His canoe was taut over the cabin.

"What kind of school is this?" I asked. "Will you also be leading the weekly drum circle?"

"No, that's my buddy Dave's job."

"Hi, there!" Alison said under a bright porch light. "Will you be staying with us tonight?"

"Uummm...I was planning on sleeping in my truck." Wonderboy said through a grimace, pointing at the behemoth. Clearly the thru-hiker blood still ran deep within him weeks later.

"Oh...well we have plenty of room! I'd be happy to make you a bed." The hostel owner's tone was mostly confused, with hints of annoyance and desperation.

"Yeahhh I'd rather just sleep in my truck. How much would that cost me?"

"Cost you? To..." Clearly Alison was not expecting this inquiry. "Well I'm in the middle of cooking so let me get back to you!"

"Also let me know how much the firewood will cost us!" I blurted out with guilt. "Definitely gonna use lots of that!"

She forced a smile and bowed behind the screen door.

"Beer?" Wonderboy asked.

I caught a frosty Dale's tall boy and my excitement for the reunion boiled over. We made some hiker trash food and inhaled each carb-loaded bite. His presence was jovial and it was hard to pinpoint the added zest to it. The closest word that came to mind was hopefulness. A rush of it passed through me as well and washed away the anxiety I had about life after the trail.

"Dude. Are you fuckin' ready for the Smokies?" Wonderboy's vicarious tone ebbed over into his eyes. "I'm jealous, this is gonna be a sweet time to cross Clingman's Dome."

"Shouldn't be too bad in mid-October, right?"

"Hey, even if it is," Wonderboy began as he clapped me on the back in unexpected encouragement. "You'll finish, man."

He'd spent the grand majority of a thousand miles razzing me for being a "dirty flip-flopper."

"I mean, when I started in January, I was up to my knees in snow. I'm sure you flip-floppas can handle some flurries."

8/16/17 - Somewhere on the Shenandoah River, VA, 1,250 Miles Hiked - Day 123

We left the hostel to stock up on food and on the way to checkout filled our carts with a beer we'd never heard of before.

Hamm's.

America's Classic Beer. Born in the land of sky blue waters.

Why had I never even *heard* of America's Classic Beer? Especially at the low, low price of $11.99 per 24 pack?

We drove an hour south to Port Republic, our starting point on the Shenandoah River, and locked up the canoe with belongings hidden underneath.

"Take your oar, people are more likely to pick us up to hitch hike back to the canoe if we're holding paddles." Wonderboy said, getting back in the truck. When it was all said and done, this song and dance ensured that Wonderboy's truck would be waiting for us after our river excursion.

After raging back up Highway 340, Wonderboy threw the truck into park and we jogged back to the road. Three cars later, the oars proved to be useful as a river raft guide picked us up without hesitation. By noon we were finally on the river.

Immediately I was struck by the quietude. I'd become so accustomed to my poles scraping and squeaking, the groans of my overworked pack, the stomps and huffs and snot rockets. The tranquility of the Shenandoah Valley eluded me for many miles. Something about being on the water pulled me out of myself. The sound of the river gushing up against the smooth canoe sent me into a trance.

"Ok, after this, the only long-distance I ever wanna do is in a canoe. This is *amazing*."

"Heck yeah, man! This is my jam. Can't wait to get back out on the Chattahoochee this summer." Wonderboy said through a contagious auburn grin.

We let silence fall between us and quickly found a rhythm together. A pair of bald eagles passed overhead. I tossed Wonderboy a Hamm's and cracked my own.

"Holy shit," Wonderboy exclaimed after his first hefty gulp.

"What is happening right now?" I chugged another mouthful and looked wide-eyed at my friend.

"This is--"

"Actually fucking amazing!" I interrupted.

"What the--*why?*"

"I dunno, man. It could be the thru-hiker effect. You know, everything tasting better when you're on trail," I said while gulping down the rest of the can. "But I really don't think so!"

"This is so much better than I was expecting!" Wonderboy said with giddy laughter.

We let the gentle current carry us for a few miles as our exceptional metabolisms made quick work of the sweet nectar.

"Ok, we've gotta do *something* with the Hamm's." I said.

"What do you mean?" Wonderboy gestured to the built in cooler, still full of Hammy goodness. "I think we're on a good pace."

"No, I mean like...with a name like Hamm's? We've got weed, we've got wine. There's gotta be something there. We need to make Hamm's Sandwiches."

"Hamm's Sandwiches?" my friend inquired.

"Yeah, you know, like a strikeout. Do a hit from a bong, do a shot, chug a beer, blow out the smoke..." I trailed off. "I guess beer is the closest thing to bread that we have..." I knifed a hole into a can of Hamm's and angled it gently between my thighs.

"You're fucking insane, man." Wonderboy said while shaking his head, eyes resolutely on the obstacles ahead as he masterfully maneuvered them alone.

I lit a joint and dragged hard. I handed it to Wonderboy with a wink. I punctured the second Hamm's and downed it rapidly. Quickly, I sipped the wine and brought the second Hamm's to my mouth. It hadn't spilled a drop, a true testament to Wonderboy's river prowess. My lungs were begging for air but I was almost there and...

"GONE." I unleashed a smoky burp that actually hurt my esophagus as tears rolled down my cheeks. "That's how it's DONE!" I let out a few more unfortunate sounding burps and fell immediately backwards into the heart of the boat.

I woke to aggressive sunshine covered in sweat.

"Holy shit! How long have I been asleep?"

"I dunno, half hour?" Wonderboy said with a mocking smile as he navigated the current.

"Wow...ok. Maybe two beers is a little aggressive."

"You think?" The Shenandoah may as well have been filled with sarcasm.

"We just need a little tweaking! It's not ideal, but a sip of wine can be both slices of bread."

"Dude, I can't even do *that*." Wonderboy said with a head shake.

I took his oar and forced a beer into his hand. After much objection, Wonderboy spit up Hamm's only halfway into his sandwich's "meat."

"Well, maybe you're only meant to do Hamm's *sliders*."

I decided it was a good time to learn some tips from the river master. Mid lesson we crashed hard into a rock neither of us saw. Wonderboy offered some tips on spotting future hindrances and I noticed my feet were wet.

"What is happening?" I asked, holding out my cupped hand to show the problem.

"It would appear we've sprung a leak." Wonderboy said calmly.

"What the fuck? Isn't this thing like, *hard* plastic?"

"I don't know, Idaho! Just start looking for a good shore."

I was alarmed to find every port in sight to be a poor option. After about half a mile we found a viable shore that ended up being far more roots than initially met the eye.

"Well that escalated quickly." I huffed, hands on hips.

"Boat leaks aren't known for taking their sweet time," said Wonderboy, being much more useful and towing the canoe out of the current.

Wonderboy and I drained the vessel, flipped it, and put on headlamps to inspect. It turns out that the rear bench had a load-bearing piece that pressed down all weight into one spot. On the underside, whitened plastic around the hole made it clear that stress had been mounting for years. The compromised area couldn't withstand that last rock and we paid the price.

"We're gonna have to get pretty creative."

"Shit, my duct tape is taped onto my poles in your car," I said hopelessly.

"Y'know, Idaho...there are a lot of friends I would not want to get into this situation with. Most of 'em, actually...they'd panic. And be *fuckin'* useless. I'm glad you're the one with me."

As he laid out the limited belongings he had, looking for a solution, I tried not to let it show how touched I was.

"I actually had the same exact thought, man. I feel like we just intuitively knew we'd figure this out."

The truth was, I did always feel like an inferior thru-hiker to Scrappy and Wonderboy. They started earlier, rose earlier, and conquered a thousand more miles earlier. I couldn't blame them for the hazing, but I did yearn for those words of encouragement.

We stumbled onto our best solution rather quickly: my balled up underwear, tied up in several plastic bags from the grocery store, stuffed under the bench's crossbar. It was our hope that the tension caused by Wonderboy's weight would suffice to keep out *most* of the water.

Upon completion of our *Macgyver* solution, the dark crept in quickly. Continuing on for a better sleeping situation felt like a fool's errand. We both brought hammocks so conditions weren't bad enough to force us back out onto the water. Tragically there was no chance for a fire, so we enjoyed a Hamm's nightcap listening to the water flow between the tree roots.

8/17/17 - Somewhere *Else* on the Shenandoah River, VA, 1,250 Miles Hiked - Day 124

As if dozing off while suspended above moving water wasn't bizarre enough, I awoke to a mist so thick that I couldn't even see Wonderboy. The scene was mostly mesmerizing but also a little terrifying and I initially thought I was having a nightmare. I put on my slippery Crocs and carefully navigated the high ground to relieve myself.

While urinating I heard heavy rustling to my left. All I could see was an enormous brown blob through the cloudy mass between us. A moment away from clenching my kegels and running back to Wonderboy, antlers revealed that I was in the presence of a buck, not a bear. A breeze gently pushed transparent air into the clearing and I could see the male's finer details quite vividly. He had an impressive mane, and unlike just about every other deer I've ever seen, he didn't look like a complete idiot.

If there was any fear in him it couldn't be found in his dark eyes.

The humidity sent a chill down my spine and I audibly shivered. The buck decided to leave. I wasn't a threat, but he'd seen enough humans for one day. Who could blame him?

Wonderboy and I chowed down on our simple breakfasts and took the repaired canoe for a test drive.

"Seems to be holding up pretty well." Said Wonderboy, surveying the spot of the leak and finding it favorable.

We cut the tops off a couple beer cans to discard the inevitable water intake and by giving it attention every ten minutes or so, the issue was perfectly manageable. By and by we made it to the first portage.

We set down the canoe at our next docking point and walked to a diner a bit down the road. I ate a very mediocre burrito and we shuffled next door for a restock.

"More Hamm's!" I exclaimed, bringing the case to the register. Wonderboy shook his head in mild opposition to our added cargo.

Back on the water, we held up our cans to a couple fishermen who held up empty hands.

"Left the cooler in the car," one said with regret.

I reached into the cooler and threw two beers to our comrades.

"Haaaamm's a great day!"

They enthusiastically rescued the sudsy goodness with nets and cheersed.

At the next portage, we struggled to carry our vessel more than 30 yards at a time.

"Y'guys need a hand?"

A portly man with seemingly permanent sunburn leaned out of his truck.

"Oh, we're not with your river tour company, unfortunately," I said.

"I know that, does it look like I give a shit? You look miserable, get that thing on here."

We threw our belongings into the van and hoisted our craft onto the rack in tow. Wonderboy explained to the driver our predicament and his generosity continued as he offered to take Wonderboy into town for some T-Rex Tape. That left me to drink Hamm's in the riverside shade. I dozed off for a bit and awakened to find Wonderboy tearing off large pieces of impressive looking tape.

"Think that'll do it?" I asked, unhelpful as ever.

"I think it's the best chance we've got."

We layered the hole with 6 pieces of tape on each side and decided Plan A - Operation Undies should still be in effect to provide added tension. Remarkably, not a single drop leaked in and we were officially back on schedule.

The water grew clearer and fish jumping out of the water became downright commonplace. An Osprey swooped over the canoe and caught one in its talons.

"Yup. Canoe trips. That's what I want to do from now on."

I tried to check the weather in the late afternoon but my phone was unable to function in the scorching sun. I tucked the device under my thigh to cool. After another mile or so Wonderboy spotted a beautiful beach to stop at. I was eager to sleep on the soft sand rather than in my hammock. The excitement got the better of me as I jumped out of the canoe near shore and heard a heartbreaking *plop*.

My phone that already died whenever it caught a whiff of moisture fell into the murky shallows. I extracted the phone and instinctively shut it off before taking out the battery. In my heart I knew it was dead. Yet some thread of denial remained.

"The biggest bummer is that I've lost my camera," I said dejectedly beside the fire later that evening. "My old work phone is back in New York but it's several years older and the pictures fade in comparison."

"I'm sorry man, that blows," Wonderboy said between munches of his dinner.

"I guess the silver lining is, at times I've felt addicted to my phone out here. I expected I'd barely be on it. I suppose now I'll get the raw solitude I was hoping for."

As I closed my eyes that night, the vivid details of the buck from that morning came into focus. Something about the beast felt significant, but ambiguously so.

Suddenly an odd excitement came over me. I was about to be truly on my own. As a kid, nothing got my imagination humming louder than reading of Lewis and Clark's voyages. A pull to the Appalachian Trail was that it seemed like the closest thing to a proper adventure in the 21st Century. The Shenandoah fried my anchor to modern society.

I felt strangely free. Remembering Wonderboy's encouragement, I felt capable. Knowing the miles ahead of me, I felt like a timeless explorer.

8/18/17 - Blackrock Hut, VA, 1,305 Miles Hiked* - Day 125
*Yes, some of these miles were technically canoed, not hiked, but let's keep things simple.

I unzipped my tent after hearing several loud *MOOOOOs* and some splashing. My eyes fell onto exactly what it sounded like: a dozen or so cows taking a dip in the Shenandoah River.

I stood up for a better look. Every pair of bovine eyes fell onto me. They looked as surprised as I was, perhaps even with a hint of displeasure at my presence.

"What...on...*Earth?*" Wonderboy said, rousing from his hammock in the trees. "How many of them are there?"

We packed up camp as the cows weaved in and out of us, refusing to compromise their morning routine for a couple of idiots who could be eating them in the coming months. One was bold enough to try stealing a bit of food and it was hard to not feel some affection for the brazen steer.

Soon enough Wonderboy and I washed up on the shore where our river adventure began.

"I still can't get over you canoeing over 50 miles in the same attire from a life-changing interview."

"Hey now!" he snapped. "They haven't made the offer *yet.*"

"Oh, you're gonna get the job," I said confidently as Wonderboy pulled into the trailhead where we'd say our goodbyes.

"Dude, I can't thank you enough." I hugged the bearded man who made this all possible and was indeed impressed with the lack of body odor from his fancy, versatile outfit. "See you in Georgia?"

"See you in Georgia, dude. Byeeee."

Wonderboy lived 70 miles away from Springer Mountain, my final destination. That's where we'd meet again, merely 903 miles down the trail. No more rivers to bail out my soles.

And with that, I returned to lone wolf status. I climbed back up the ridge and found a westward facing lookout. The setting sun was still strong so I spread out all my belongings to dry and set up my hammock in the trees. I took out my phone to read, forgetting it was useless rubbish now.

A thrill was still within me, of seeing firsthand how I'd handle the life of a frontiersman. I had nothing more to guide me than the white blazes luring me southward. The ancient river's serenity and wisdom seemed to be within me now. I was tired, but the voyage also replenished me. Finally an absence left me *missing* the trail.

My eyes felt heavy as I watched the day fade away. Canoeing was harder than it looked.

Chapter Eighteen

1,325 Miles Hiked, 864 to Go

Days 126-140

8/19/17 - Charlottesville, VA, 1,325 Miles Hiked - Day 126

What was supposed to be a triumphant stopover in Charlottesville was a somber visit with a profound mourning in the air. Seven days earlier, a white supremacist drove through a crowd of civilians peacefully protesting in response to a "Unite the Right" rally. He injured 35 and killed a woman named Heather Heyer in what was ruled to be convicted first degree murder and an act of domestic terrorism.

A week after the city's tragedy, residents walked quietly through the pedestrian thoroughfare. Some stopped to pay their respects at a newly established vigil.

I was still without a working cell phone so much of what I heard that day I was hearing for the first time. 'Very fine people on both sides' were the words my president used to describe those heinous people the driver associated with.

My blood boiled and tears were at the ready. The fears of tyranny and hate were founded and real. How would our country survive three more years of this evil man?

Families and friends milled about, unable or unwilling to cancel their travel plans but unfit to conjure any of that carefree vacation spirit. Every laugh that filled the air seemed to swiftly find a muffling palm. Even children somehow knew to be on their best behavior.

I hated every single attendee of that Unite the Right Rally. My fists buzzed with rage staring into a photo of Heather Heyer. Anger turned to fear, which turned to hopelessness, which turned to anger. All churning within my tired veins.

The air felt heavier at the memorial site, but also supernaturally hollow. Like if I were to pluck a yellow maple leaf, arriving far earlier than what the season calls for, and drop it from my palm; if that leaf were to never quite finish its fall. Only barely past its time yet light on the breeze, never finding the rest it so badly desired.

A toad that cautiously approached the dying fire seemed to look me right in the eyes. At very least, he was aware of my presence and still decided to take two hops towards me. That was enough rapport for me.

In gazing at his bumpy skin, I found a scrap of gratitude for having no working phone. Throughout the day I'd noticed finer details of nature that seemed to elude me with such a distracting device. I pondered the unique situation of being totally unaware of anything happening to anyone not hiking the trail. Delightful, in some senses, terrifying in others.

I shuddered then, thinking back to a close call earlier in the day.

Cicada Killer wasps had become a daily occurrence since entering Virginia. Several times a day I would hear a loud and rapid succession of clicks and buzzes. Each time I'd follow that sound, I'd bear witness to a most brutal killing of a cicada. The efficient wasp would protrude its stinger, thrusting it up into the cicada's thorax, before endeavoring a butchering and feasting that at first made my stomach turn. After a few viewings, there was undeniably a satisfying savagery that I couldn't look away from.

A rattle in the late afternoon led me to believe I was in for another bout of blood lust. I leaned over into the tall weeds, expecting to see the same gruesome yet fascinating sight I'd become accustomed to, only to find an unfamiliar object shaking back and forth in a blur.

"Oh, fucking fuck, fuck me what the fuck??"

I jolted backwards, nearly falling off the trail. From a safe distance, I could see that the rattlesnake's head was less than a foot away from my gaping, stupid face a moment earlier.

The near death experience sent me into a tizzy of self-directed profanities and newfound focus.

"And what if something *did* happen?" I asked myself, unsure during my loudest tirade whether I was being rhetorical. "You don't even have a cell phone to call 911! Do you even know what to do in the event of a snake bite? You'd be dead right now!"

Then I saw a peculiar sight heading my way. Putting my rant on pause, I tried to decipher the oncomer through the corner of my eye. It looked like a man covered in face tattoos sucking a pacifier. Chains hung from a cut off denim vest, the clanking of which came to a halt when he sidestepped the trail with eyes fixed ahead.

"Thank you!" I said, only able to glance his way for a second as my feet decided to double time all on their own.

Everything my fleeting eyes saw earlier was true, with some added oddities. Following the rattlesnake near miss, adrenaline was calling the shots.

"Oh you ran into Man Baby?" a thru-hiker named Twisted asked at the following shelter. Twisted and I shared a good number of shelters by now, and him finding nothing strange about the situation didn't shock me. "Yeah, he likes this section of trail. I think he'll leave for the Smokies soon. Met him years ago, Beach Bum here just ran into him, too."

Needless to say, this brought no comfort to me.

"Someone got murdered here, almost three years ago to the day," shared Twisted, apparently fresh out of sweet nursery rhymes with which to serenade hikers. "Just came in and stabbed a thru-hiker, no motive whatsoever."

An ink-faced pacifier chain rocker seemed like a perfect candidate for an anniversary killing. There was only one way to get my mind off that possibility.

"Say, Twisted? What do you do if you're alone, a snake bites you, and you physically can't suck the venom out of your own wound?"

Finding no comfort in the ensuing shrug from Twisted, I went about my evening routines. Once the fire died, I watched thoughts run circles in my mind from the modest solace my sleeping bag provided.

Everything seemed connected. Charlottesville, the wasps, the snake, Man Baby. The stage of a random murder serving as my bed.

Fear. Uncertainty. Brutality.

It was hard to deny the raw chaos of life itself.

"Mom, we could die at any moment, anywhere, under any circumstances," I said in what my mother surely thought was a great comfort a year before my hike. "The odds of me dying in DC are roughly the same as me dying in the woods. Arguably higher, even! Considering the dive bars I frequent."

Those cicadas didn't expect to be skewered through the ass. The fear they must've felt as they dropped from the sky and fell to the ground... The wasps may well not even exist without a bump in the cicada population. The rattlesnake surely feared for its own life when a giant blob came into view. Somewhere along the way a giant baby decided he'd rather stand tall and dress how he felt than feign normalcy. And if he's anything like a real baby, he's scared of most things.

And surely Heather Heyer was scared before she was killed; she couldn't have possibly thought she was putting her own life on the line when she left that morning. Uncertain of exactly what was happening, watching her peers heartlessly mowed down mere moments before. The rally wouldn't even have happened without a bump in brazen, loud racism.

All of the protesters standing up for basic human rights, all being struck down by hate. The light fading from Heather's eyes, the fear she must've felt as she fell to the ground...

8/21/17 - Devil's Backbone Basecamp Brewpub, VA, 1,348 Miles Hiked - Day 128

I carefully read through my handwritten directions to the brewery, fearful that a mistake could leave me in the middle of nowhere.

No phone meant old school navigation, and it also meant no audible distractions from my darkest thoughts. In a few days I'd be ringing in the last year of my 20s alone. Not just without a girlfriend, but in all likelihood actually alone. No cake, no one to sing me happy birthday, no special cocktails, but alone walking through the woods.

I found that as appealing as finding some town and explaining to a bunch of strangers that it's my birthday.

The year prior I turned 28 with sincere excitement. I hosted a birthday BBQ in the courtyard of my luxury apartment complex, one last hurrah before I had to vacate as Erica had done. I was no longer rotting away in an office at the time, and I felt a great deal of optimism in heading back to New York to prepare for the Appalachian Trail. A happy and fulfilled life felt just around the corner for the first time in my adulthood.

This year, I was utterly indifferent about turning 29. The day was bound to pass, unnoticed by all but me, with a high chance of rain. For the first time since quitting it, I was pining for the positive effects of Lexapro.

Thumb out on Route 644, resigning myself to an uneventful 29th, I resolved to ring in 30 from a position of success and clarity. I wanted to be settled and fulfilled. Not the life I had before; I wanted a foundation laid on a steady bedrock of all the lessons I'd learned since quitting my job.

Before long I was jumping out of a flatbed outside of Devil's Backbone Basecamp Brewpub, one of the most highly anticipated stopovers for thru-hikers. I ordered a flight from the cute bartender, who slid a bonus taster of her favorite brew across the spectacular pine bar top. I took in the impressive taxidermy.

Two rams perched on boulders were to my left and a seven foot tall bear behind me facing the entrance. Turkeys, foxes, and bobcats were looking down on me. 19 Great American Beer Festival medals filled out the empty space. Beneath them was a chalkboard with the title "Farm to Food." Comprising the list were a dozen farms throughout Virginia that provide the raw ingredients for the food that Devil's Backbone is also well known for. I had no doubt that my notorious $5 hiker's breakfast the next morning would feature half the farms listed.

I took my remaining beers outside and plopped down on a picnic table alone to watch the sunset over the mountains from which I came. It was actually comforting then to be alone with the majestic view and know that it was mine alone. I reached for my phone to photograph the scene only to once again discover that I didn't have one.

8/22/17 - The Priest Shelter, VA, 1,362 Miles Hiked - Day 129

At the top of a massive climb in Virginia rests a marble notebook full of things you never wanted to know. Stories of people failing to wash their hands after not burying their shit. Tales of spurned employees of the service industry introducing you to their genitals in one way or another. Then a few squares mustering the courage to share that they "confess they're having a marvelous time, and hope you are too!"

Once you finally summit the 3,000 foot climb from either side of it, The Priest demands a confession from all who kneel.

I CONFESS that I'm having a lot less fun <u>on</u> the AT. I'm a dirty flip-flopper and made the mistake of taking two weeks off at the beach before my SOBO Flop. It made me soft and weak. I've done embarrassing miles since my aqua blaze of the Shenandoah River, a side effect of which is that I hate the act of HIKING even more. The highlights of my days are never during the <u>hike</u>. I've come to just see it as the grueling necessity for living this marvelous nomadic lifestyle.

It feels like the only way I can make it all the way to Georgia is to sacrifice the extra curricular activities that make this hike so special. If that's what it comes down to. I'm too proud to leave this trail unfinished.

One extra curricular activity eludes me. What a tragedy it is to walk this trail, in the best shape of my life, unable to find anyone who wants to zip together our sleeping bags. My trim physique and soon to be forgotten abs wasted on a life of celibacy. It's sad to think that the ladies of Appalachia seem determined to keep men out of their diet.

Well, I better get back to hiking. Thank you, Father. I'll get started on those Hail Marys straight away.

Blasphemously Yours,

8/25/17 - Beverly's House, Lexington, VA, 1,402 Miles Hiked - Day 132

Through a car's passenger side window, I spotted a house with an ill-fitting *US Post Office* sign hanging over the stubbornly residential front door. A Trail Angel generously offered to take me all the way there, which was fortunate because the establishment was open for a pathetic two hour window for the entire day. Inside waiting for me was my old work phone, shipped to this podunk town by my dear mother.

"It's actually pronounced 'Be-YOU-nuh Vista,'" the driver corrected me.

I laughed.

"No, I'm serious," she continued.

"But it's spelled 'Buena Vista.' I'm no Spanish expert but I know it's not pronounced like that."

"No, of course not. But back in the Civil War era, locals took to calling it that so as to spot slave sympathizers in town. If you pronounced it the *right* way..." She mimed a slicing at the neck to drive the point home.

I returned to the car after retrieving the package inside and shipping the damaged one home.

"I'm not leaving you in this sad excuse for a town. Let me at least take you to Lexington," she insisted.

"What's there?"

"Just about everything," my driver answered. "And at least there you're not *totally* outnumbered by racists."

I unloaded a refrain of gratitude and followed the sounds of live music down an alleyway. I navigated the crowded patio and plopped down my pack.

"Hey, look at that!" exclaimed a woman pointing to my Devil's Backbone hat, which matched her shirt. "Did you stay there?"

"Yup!" I said. "Camped there a few nights ago, met Brian and some others."

"Heck yeah! Well order anything you want and put it on *Devil's Backbone's* tab, ok? Gina, give this guy anything he wants."

"Wow it's almost like you knew it was my birthday!" I exclaimed.

"Today? Happy birthday!"

Several glasses were raised in my honor and I found myself with two beers, a bratwurst, and mac and cheese all under my nose. The band played anything close to Tom Petty for about an hour as I secured three more ales.

"How long you been out there?" a gentleman from a nearby table asked.

"Nearly five months now. I'm not moving too quickly," I answered.

"Last one done hiking wins! I'm Tracer. That was my trail name, anyway."

Tracer was a bartender from next door, and Lexington had an "all bartenders drink for free" policy. I had a pitcher all to myself while Tracer and his friends sang me happy birthday. Another bartender took us to his haunt, a fancy establishment where I felt thoroughly out of place in my dirty hiker attire.

"I hear it's your birthday."

I turned around to find a cute redhead with zealous eyes leaning against the bar.

"Shocked I made it," I said with a smile. "Bear nearly ate me a couple weeks back. You come here often?"

"Hardly ever," she said with a sigh. "Met my friends here, did the third wheel thing until they bailed. Figured sticking around for the rest of my drink was only slightly less sad than going home alone."

"Well people have been treating me pretty great all day, let me pay it forward. What're you drinking, --"

"Beverly."

"Beverly. I'm Idaho Bones."

I ordered a gin and tonic for the lady, who was still laughing at my unusual name. Ice could soon be heard ringing in both our empty glasses.

"I wouldn't recommend getting any closer, I'm in desperate need of a shower," I said before biting my lip.

"I could spare some soap and water."

Minutes later we were sucking face on her kitchen table. After a good wash and a sublime fuck, I dangled a cat toy while lying naked on her bed. Beverly snuggled up next to me after dimming her lights.

Free food and drinks, birthday sex, and a bosom to lay my head on? This whole *meandering into town with no plan* thing was looking pretty good. Perhaps I'd pretend my phone was broken just a bit longer and continue wandering blind into unfamiliar towns.

8/28/17 - Near Hanging Rock Hollow, VA, 1,443 Miles Hiked - Day 135

Two days prior, I rolled out of Beverly's bed ready to immerse myself in nature and put in proper miles. Day One was successful, but my digestive problems came back with a vengeance. I pressed on between unfortunate restroom breaks in the woods.

Finding some equilibrium the next day, I trekked with ferocity. I found myself walking along cliffs for several miles and felt compelled to take a break in the late afternoon with two men sitting by a fire.

"It's been a while since I've been in the mountains. I had a bad experience." My new friend Tom took a long pause. "Me and my buddy would go all the time, you know, and uh...one time he didn't make it back. We had a bad accident."

"Oh, my gosh. I'm so sorry." I couldn't find any other words.

"So they sent me to prison. He died and then I had to suffer all over again in prison. I just got out yesterday" Tom shared. "I've been up in the mountains ever since."

"Hey, good for you," I said, raising the beer he offered me earlier. "They call me Idaho Bones on the trail."

"Trevor, by the way," said his friend.

"They called me Owen in prison. Soon as I left, I wanted to be Tom again."

"You know, sometimes an identity is meant to be temporary," I said.

"So where you heading next?" Trevor inquired.

"South to Springer Mountain in Georgia, with more than a few stops along the way."

Tom paced around the fire.

"All our friends hated that I had to go away. Everybody that know us, they just fucking hate what happened. You know?"

I didn't know, and thankfully I remained silent.

"It was a double tragedy. I mean shit..." Tom began. "All the time we'd come out to these mountains, get high and shit. He didn't come home and I was holdin' the bag."

Tom went back and forth between rubbing his chin and his forehead.

"Kids around here must not know about this part of the forest. You don't see graffiti. And you know what? I really really hate that shit," shared Tom. "But the day I got out, at this place called Indian Rocks, Trevor here says 'Hey come around, you gotta see this.' And I walk around to the rock face and it says FREEDOM. Right into the mountain. And you know I say 'Man, I like *that*!' That's my buddy, the one that died, and I said '...He wrote that shit for me.'"

I didn't like the idea of someone spray painting anything, let alone the word "freedom," into a place called *Indian Rocks*. I elected to not spoil the moment.

"You think your kids will be out here some day?" I asked. "Getting into the same shenanigans as you guys?"

"I hope not," Tom said. "It's not the same no more. Somehow, cops are getting worse, racism's getting worse. I already worry about them. I had to sit my kids down, before I went to prison. Told 'em to do whatever a cop says, keep your mouth shut. We'll figure it out later but don't give them no reason to shoot."

My heart was breaking for so many good reasons. This man losing a friend, losing his freedom, worried about losing his kids to a broken society.

"You gonna try to get some more miles in?" Trevor asked me.

I didn't even realize I'd starting packing up to leave.

"Oh, yup. Just a few more miles. It was great meeting you both, thanks for the beer!"

They wished me luck and I began walking down the trail, still feeling heartbroken.

"Hey, Tom!" I shouted once I was turned around. "I'm sorry the world's done you wrong. I'm gonna do my little part to ensure your kids don't grow up in the same fucked up country."

As I pondered how to keep my promise to Tom, Heather Heyer came to mind again. Somehow, well into the 21st century, I was living in the country with allegedly the *most* freedom on the plant. Yet people of color couldn't march for their rights without being killed. And even their peers merely standing alongside them were whisked away to prison.

Something familiar happened then: Once I felt the pain of Heather and Tom, all my anger at the world and society hurricaned within me. My skin felt hot as if it had nowhere to go.

What do I do with this anger?

My body was turning on me...physically and emotionally.

9/2/17 - Stealth Campsite near Daleville, VA, 1,463 Miles Hiked - Day 140

After only six miles of that day's hike, I was sweating profusely onto the floor of a gas station bathroom. My pace became glacial in a heartbeat a few days prior.

The odor in the air was worse than putrid, and bad enough for me to consider finding a hospital. A sharp pain in my abdomen accompanied the gag-inducing smell and my heart raced with anxiety. I smiled nervously at the poor soul entering the restroom after me and picked up my pack.

Throughout this on again, off again ailment, I was still able to put in decent miles. As I walked under the shrill lights of the gas station, I knew that those days were over. Time to face facts. I couldn't make it to Georgia in this condition. And my health insurance was only good in New York.

I returned to the trail up the street and hiked a measly 50 yards just to get away from the road. Tears rolled down my cheeks as I accepted the only option that made any sense.

I needed to go home. Which felt more like leaving home. I was terribly afraid I'd never come back.

Chapter Nineteen

1,463 Miles Hiked, 726 to Go

Days 141-157

9/3/17 - Mom and Dad's House, Staten Island, NY, 1,463 Miles Hiked - Day 141

Under steady downpours, I opted for an Uber to pick up my rental car in Virginia.

Sheets of rain appropriately rumbled the Ford Escape as I undid every mile I'd hiked over the course of a month in just a few hours behind the wheel. It killed me to be passing the very same mountains I traversed on foot, heading north in a vessel burning a hole in my wallet. I spent much of my drive arranging doctor appointments and explaining my unfortunate situation to all who needed to know. Seven wet hours later I was handed a receipt for a balance $300 over my reservation quote.

"I'm terribly sorry about that, Mr. Veasey," said a representative as he furiously typed away on his desktop.

This did seem like the sort of thing that would happen to Mr. Veasey and not to Mr. Bones.

"Well whatever resolution you'll find, it won't be with me. You'll be hearing from someone by tomorrow at the latest. I've done everything I can and if you need anything moving forward, here's my card."

I threw the useless card, literally deemed useless by the man who handed it to me, into a trash can as I stomped to the car waiting for me outside Enterprise Rent-A-Car. My sopping pack slammed against the floor of the trunk before I slumped into the passenger seat.

"I don't like seeing you like this," Deanna said after picking up her big brother from Newark Airport. "I'm not used to it."

"Well I'm sorry you had to witness me discovering I'm a loser."

"See? That right there. Not helpful." She shook her head. "You sound like Dad."

I hated myself so much in that car. Once rock bottom was hit, I was forced to face acceptance deep within. There I found an unadulterated compassion for my father. I could see how hard it is to be optimistic or hold compassion for others when you're so deep and familiar with inward anger. Back home after Katahdin, I was able to clearly see the damage my dad suffered at the hands of his selfish family. Inflicting wounds on myself is what pushed me to finally understand it. How hard it must have been to ask about this liberating journey clearing my mind when *his* life continues to cloud more every day. How unthinkable to say he's proud when he's not proud of himself.

I walked in the door and watched the family dog Cinnamon deliriously sniff my smelly bag, unable to choose between one of her favorite humans and a bouquet of stenches. I showered, put on clean clothes, and wrote out a long promise to myself to show my parents nothing but gratitude and empathy during my unexpected time home.

9/4/17 – Mom and Dad's House, Staten Island, NY, 1,463 Miles Hiked - Day 142

After dropping off blood and stool samples with the doctor, I collapsed in my old twin bed to stare at the same cracked ceiling I'd been inspecting for the better part of the previous year. The purgatory between my old life in DC and the long awaited thru-hike departure was spent sleeping under half assed attempts at a spackling. Perhaps this time, I'd finally discover in its crevices the singular moment where things went wrong in my 20s. The hours ticked as my regrets tocked, beckoning the cuckoo to keep sleep at bay. In the blackness, I tried to conjure the specific green of the rich oak leaves I should have been waking up to the next morning. Then again, waking is for the dreaming. My eyes were restless.

I finally unfurled my sleeping bag across the carpet, filling every last inch of floor that remained in my modest domicile. My body found comfort in the familiar bag. A subtle but stubborn musk of the forest emanated from the nylon and I fell asleep.

9/10/17 - Doctor's Office, Staten Island, NY, 1,463 Miles Hiked - Day 148

After five days of prescribed rest, I returned to the doctor's office.

"Just like we thought, you have Giardia," he said with a nod. "So finish those medications and you'll be good to go."

"When can I go back to the trail?"

This was the important question. I largely expected the diagnosis he'd just given me. The biggest unknown was whether I'd be able to finish the AT.

"Whenever you're feeling up to it. My advice is take another few days to get your strength back. Your body will thank ya for it."

"I mean even while sick I was averaging ten miles a day," I said with a genuine laugh.

"I know, I'm looking forward to telling my doctor buddies about

191

that," the doctor said with wide eyes. "They'll never believe it, you're a freak of nature, I guess."

"Sure didn't feel like a freak of nature."

"Well..." the doctor trailed off. "I do have a theory about that. From the amount you told me you were drinkin', it's entirely possible that you were dehydrating your body enough with alcohol to avoid some side effects, like diarrhea."

"Really? I'd imagine that would've made everything worse," I said.

"Well it is just a theory, and it certainly wasn't *good* for you." He paused to write a prescription. "You've still got five days on the anti-parasitic and you already know you can't drink on that."

For a moment, I debated asking the doctor for a Lexapro prescription. However, once I was told I'd be returning to trail, I felt a tremendous weight lifted and perfectly capable of carrying on with my natural brain chemistry.

Relief and anticipation coursed through me. The Appalachian Trail wasn't going to be another unfinished project, after all.

Having just 21% of the miles remaining, I couldn't help thinking about life after the trail. That night I polished up my resume and made dinner for my family. I sent the new curriculum vitae off to some old bosses and colleagues, and would go on to apply for several jobs every day for the duration of my trip. Most of my applications were for Denver-based opportunities, but I couldn't help applying for DC-area positions as well.

Two years before my thru-hike, I stayed a few extra days after my Denver work trip. The city positively seduced me. It had a vibe like no other place I'd ever been. The whole population seemed to be buzzing with joie de vivre and gratitude for living there. The views, the beers, the marijuana: it all complemented the good spirits of the people. The more I hiked, the easier it was to picture my life in Colorado. Especially after traversing the entire east coast for five months. I was beginning to feel like I'd seen it all and that my time by the Atlantic should soon come to an end. A part of me felt like I'd be a happier, better person in the Rockies.

With my days on Staten Island numbered, now certain of my return to Appalachia, I had a distinct sense that everything was going to work out just fine.

9/17/17 - Staten Island DMV, NY, 1,463 Miles Hiked - Day 155

"Two days left on this rock," I whispered to myself in Staten Island's least sexy DMV as I anxiously awaited completion of my last chore before returning to Appalachia.

I hadn't seen the trail in two weeks and I missed it dearly. That longing I expected during the two week beach vacation boiled over a fire of restlessness now. I'd turned my recovery into something of a garnering of resources and mental space to enjoy the rest of my trek. I paid my car insurance through March, extended forbearance for my student loans until February, and set aside all funds necessary for upcoming expenses. After obtaining a new driver's license, little more than $600 remained in my bank account. My chest tightened to think of the two extra zeros I'd grown accustomed to seeing in there but at least I knew exactly what that money was for. It was to finish my hike, and nothing else.

It was scary to again be barreling towards penniless uncertainty. I had no choice but to warm up to the idea of trusting myself. I'd recovered from worse dips before in a rather quick turnaround. Time to test out all that newfound faith in the universe I supposedly cultivated on the trail.

As I'd done in the past after encountering life's biggest hurdles, I found resolve to dispel my self pity and return to the trail with the wind at my back. There's something powerful about feeling as though life has taken you to a dark place where you were never meant to be. You may have little to no recollection of how you got there, and you'll feel foolish the moment you discover that you don't have to stay. In fact, the exit is often clear as day, and your instincts stir to life to put the agony behind you.

I never thought I'd burn through my life's savings on this journey but completing it was priority #1. Once my final step was taken I could focus on eliminating student loan debt and securing land. It wouldn't be easy, but so long as I kept myself anchor free and disciplined, I could make headway on those endeavors in a few months.

Once home from the DMV, satisfied with my productivity, I fixed and cleaned my gear with great jubilation. The familiar societal distaste made the rose tinted return appear all the rosier.

Chapter Twenty

1,478 Miles Hiked, 711 to Go

Days 158-165

9/20/17 - John's Spring Shelter, VA, 1,478 Miles Hiked - Day 158

Storm clouds lingered from the torrential downpours of the prior day. They intimidated the countryside but spared the Blue Ridge Mountains any further precipitation. The sun pierced the impressive clouds, casting the range into a medley of blue and purple. It made an already enjoyable drive even better. I couldn't help staring at the majesty of the home I was returning to.

A few days after my last doctor visit, once the anti-parasitic medication was complete and I enjoyed my first solid bowel movement in several weeks, I booked a car rental to squire me back to the Appalachian Trail. I belted out song after song as I careened through Virginia, bringing all the zeal I was lacking after my midway beach vacation. The reunion was a nonstop fantasy. I wasn't going to let this last chance slip away. I was 726 miles away from finishing the most important undertaking in my life.

Feeling lucky, I loitered outside of Roanoke-Blacksburg Regional Airport after returning my trusty rental. There were two flights poised to land. I hoped that some starry eyed traveler, still drunk from vacation, would toss aside their better judgment and offer me a ride back from whence my stench came.

"You hiking the AT?" asked a gentleman fresh off the plane.

"I am!"

"Nice! I hiked SOBO back in 2010. After hiking through Roanoke I thought, 'Wow. This would be a cool place to live.' And now I live here!" he said with arms stretched out, reeking of that well traveled good mood I was counting on.

"Hell yeah, good for you! Any advice for getting back to the trail?" I inquired with my friendliest smile.

"Hmm...Uber's your best bet."

"Gotcha," I began, trying to hide my disappointment. "Figured as much but thought you might be privy to an inside scoop."

"Happy trails to you!"

"Damn," I whispered. "Thought I had him."

"Hey, you want a lift?" he bellowed.

"If you don't mind! Oh my god, that'd be amazing."

We pulled up near McAfee Knob Trailhead. He pulled out his wallet as I thanked him profusely. I couldn't take my eyes off a 20 he pulled out.

"Here, take some money," he offered with a smile.

"No, you've already done so, so much for me," I insisted, eyes still fixed on Mr. Jackson.

"Well, do you want it?"

"Of course I want it!" I paused. "I just feel bad taking it."

He thrust it into my hand.

"Take it, go to The Homeplace tomorrow for an all you can eat meal, on me."

I nodded.

"What's your trail name?"

"Geo," he said with a hat tip.

"Geo." I put my palms together and bowed. I prepared my sincerest voice. "I can't thank you enough."

I ambled to Johns Spring Shelter, not too far from where I was dropped off. Next to the trail journal hung a plaque. Displayed next to that was an article detailing the loving tribute a father paid to his son in the form of the shelter I was standing alone in. John Haranzo hiked the Appalachian Trail 11 years prior. Five years later, to the tragic surprise of a father he was very close to, John took his own life.

Frank couldn't come to terms with his son's suicide, but that didn't stop him from trying. He took to driving his son's old pickup, wearing his old hiking boots, walking the same steps John did those years ago. The loving father contacted the Roanoke Appalachian Trail Club in hopes of finding a way to memorialize his beloved son. For years the club wanted to replace the dilapidated Boy Scout Shelter near McAfee Knob. With a donation and the efforts of volunteers, Johns Spring Shelter was erected two years after Frank's loss.

Facing grief and pain head on, Frank made a habit of visiting the shelter every single week. He flips through the shelter's journal pages, reading the sweet words hikers etch into it in memory of his son. The article detailed his healing process:

"'We spent a lot of time together in the woods," he said, again fighting tears. "He was just a regular guy. He was my buddy and my friend.'"

John seemed like anything but a regular guy to me, to leave such a loving imprint on the father with three sons still walking the earth.

Unexpectedly I burst into tears. A deep sadness sprung forth from my chest of the world that seems content to take lives like John's. Like Heather Heyer's father, John's dad described him as a person who cared fiercely for others. John was a free spirit who only felt at peace in the woods. That part resonated clearly.

I'd crossed paths with a number individuals who committed suicide, even in high school. An "affliction" they all seemed to share was rejecting "the normal life." Whether it be 9-5s, college education, raising a nuclear family, something about the typical existence our society pushes on us was unlivable to them.

I didn't know John's struggles, not any better than I knew anyone else's experience who has struggled with suicide, but I did know in some large way he felt like a failure.

We owe it to ourselves to cultivate an existence that allows more definitions of success.

9/21/17 - Four Pines Hostel, VA, 1,488 Miles Hiked - Day 159

Nestled between two lush green mountain ranges, The Homeplace was as picturesque as it gets. White rocking chairs ran the perimeter of the L shaped deck. A suspended bench gently rocked in the breeze and two matching gazebos overlooked the meadows and countryside. A mish mash of livestock and agriculture filling in the valley may as well have been southern Italy.

I cautiously approached the door, feeling woefully out of place amidst tucked in checkered shirts and fancy hats. I could see myself getting married there much sooner than I could imagine picking ribs out of my teeth and scrubbing BBQ sauce out of my unruly beard.

Earlier in the day, some NOBO section hikers recounted their extravagant feast at The Homeplace the night before. It felt like a sign to use Geo's offering according to his wishes.

While waiting for an open seat in the dining room, I found myself solidifying plans for a Tinder date immediately after the meal. Once sufficiently stuffed, I met my date Lindsey in the parking lot and we explored the grounds.

"I love cows," Lindsey said while petting one. "I wish I didn't also love burgers."

I stole glances as we laughed and realized she was getting prettier by the second. She looked fantastically slim and sexy in her tight jeans.

"Love your sweater, by the way," I said, referring to the galaxy print hoodie being worn as a cardigan.

"Thanks, it's for kids! I got it at Target."

I felt like I was falling in love.

Lindsey drove us to a nearby trail she frequented and we smoked weed while discussing our past relationships. Conversation became easier and the stakes higher. Lindsey was just so refreshingly quirky and wonderful. I was smitten.

When she drove me to Four Pines Hostel my heart was positively racing. I couldn't remember the last time I was so nervous to kiss someone. She was practically glowing in the moonlight on the bench next to me.

"Look at those little wrists!" she said while grabbing my arm. "They're smaller than mine!"

"Boy, you really know how to romance a man," I retorted. "I bet you're a lot stronger than you look. Care to arm wrestle?"

Lindsey jumped beside a side table and propped up her dominant hand. I toyed with her a bit, letting her think she might take me down. She was indeed stronger than she looked. Once I finally pinned her down a moment of silence followed our shared laughter. I grabbed her by the neck and kissed her deeply. It was the best kiss I'd ever had, I couldn't believe the compatibility.

She dragged me to her car and eagerly jumped into the backseat of her Subaru. I was overwhelmed by the passion already between us as I convulsed into her neck, breathing in her opulent hair. I gently scratched her back as she continued to gyrate on my fading cock.

By some miracle we comfortably spooned in her back seat, conditioned air cooling our fiery skin. Begrudgingly we bade farewell and I went to sleep in the hostel wondering if in a most unusual circumstance I'd met my wife.

9/22/17 - Craig Creek, VA, 1,505 Miles Hiked - Day 160

I rose out of my Four Pines cot in a particularly good mood and threw my $10 donation into the empty coffee can. I made eggs and coffee to take in the lovely scenery outside the hostel. A chicken walked right up to me and I set down my toast to get a photo of the colorful fowl. With a little patience, I was able to snap some pretty portraits of my breakfast companion.

I returned to find none of the toast I'd left behind and significantly fewer eggs on my plate. The inspection was short lived: a rooster was gobbling down the rest of my bread. It seemed that he was also to blame for my egg shortage, which I found unpalatable but not enough to abandon my appetite altogether. I quickly whipped up a second breakfast and guarded it with my life.

The hike up to Dragon's Tooth was steep but perfectly reasonable, especially after a protein packed breakfast. I climbed to the very top of the rock formation and found a lizard running circles around me. He settled in at arm's length. My joint crackled and I blew smoke in the reptile's direction. He sat up, settled down, and I repeated the action. My new friend didn't seem bothered at all, and in my opinion, he was positively stoned.

From there I pushed on to a respectable 17 mile day. As I walked the challenging terrain, I felt relief that the capable, veteran hiker from the north was still in there. It was impossible to tell how long I was ill with Giardia, but it was long enough to cast serious doubt in my mind. Were the parasites to blame for my second half average of ~10 daily miles, or had I just grown wildly lazy? Were Wonderboy and Scrappy more responsible for my formidable northern half? Was I incapable of motivating myself?

My mind drifted over and over back to the shelter that served as a father's surviving memorial to his son. I thought of their closeness, and the pain in the man's heart to know his son was silently suffering. The article quoted the father as saying that his son would work menial jobs in between doing things he loved, such as the Appalachian Trail and attempting the Pacific's counterpart as well. It occurred to me that my life had parallels to the man who took his own life. After all, he appeared happy even to his own father, with whom he was close.

I wondered how to repair the relationship with my father. It's not that we weren't close, it's that our relationship's health seemed to completely depend on his own life satisfaction. Something seemed far out of reach when my dad was anchored by a dysfunctional family and an insufferable job. If there was a recent conflict involving his siblings and mother, and there usually was, it felt impossible to connect.

There was a resentment I'd been trying to shake off with every step but still carried it on my back. In those six months at home before leaving for the Appalachian Trail, I did everything I could imagine to make my parents' lives better and show them the magic of living in a clutter free, clean home. How coming home to disarray bounds the mind to reside in the same state.

The lack of cooperation drained me. Before long they were the people who came to mind when a book I was reading asked me to seek out "the energy vampires in my life."

I contemplated what Lindsey would think of a concept as absurd as Dracula sucking energy. Then I pondered how energizing my time with her was. Finally a path I'd been seeking for five months presented itself:

I was to blame for feeling an energy deficit while living with my parents. I came into their home and made changes in the name of efficiency, headspace, and Feng Shui. They didn't ask me to, they opened their home to their struggling son and found a moody, frustrated man-child who was seeking any means necessary to feel essential again.

It is unfair to offer unsolicited energy if one expects an equal or greater return.

A few miles later I found a splendidly flat spot. The red sun was already seeking rest and I gathered firewood. The moon peeked through the trees as the flames grew. I stared up at it and thought of every reason I was grateful for my parents.

9/23/17 - War Spur Shelter, VA, 1,522 Miles Hiked - Day 161

The Appalachian Trail had a lot more of two things than I anticipated: cell service and alcohol.

When my phone plunked into the Shenandoah River, I had a phone-free week thrust onto me. As a result, the trail felt more intimate to me and all the unique views and experiences along the way had no choice but to forgo being immortalized through my phone's lens. It was a daily lesson in mindfulness.

When the doctor warned me to avoid alcohol for the 10-day Giardia prescription period, I was feeling bold and decided to make it a clean 30 days. Alcohol was a staple of the northern half. It was hard to picture New England without whiskey. I nearly died pushing past Mahoosuc Notch for the hooch.

I was eager to see how the trail would feel without my other vice.

In the spirit of my month off from drinking and constant deliberation on sex addiction, I checked out an audiobook called *The Craving Mind* from the library. Author Judson Brewer, a former addict and renowned addiction specialist, describes cravings as waves. The way he lays out those episodes for addicts sounded familiar to my most severe moments of anxiety.

The craving comes. The person acknowledges, without judgment, notes, and calmly waits for "the wave" to pass, having "surfed" it.

Even in those darkest times, my crippling anxiety does inevitably pass. Every time.

With that in mind I tried to tackle the self critic that had come back into my head. He was stuck on lackluster miles, fast diminishing funds, and no plan for the future. I was lazy, anhedonic, and destined to fail in his words. It began to occur to me that this voice wasn't inescapable. The critic had gone away on his own many times, in fact. It seemed his departure was even hastier when counter efforts were nil.

Next time I'd detect the unwelcome presence, I'd think of my days of surfing Oahu's shores.

9/25/17 - Holy Family Catholic Church, Pearisburg, VA, 1,553 Miles Hiked - Day 163

As soon as I reached the dirt country road I knew I was gonna be in trouble. Four cars passed me over the course of an hour and none seemed remotely inclined to pick up a hitchhiker. Finally, a truck pulled up and asked me where I was going.

"Pearisburg."

"Well, we're visiting our friend down the road if you want a ride," shouted the driver, Brian, over his two passengers.

"Sure, I'll take anything in the right direction. Should I get in the back?"

"Yessir."

I jumped into the truck bed after my bag and trekking poles and slapped the side of the car. As the vehicle started moving, I realized I was sitting amongst a bed of circular saws and knives and various other sharp objects wondering what the fuck I'd gotten myself into. I tucked in behind my pack and desperately tried to remember which veins to protect most fiercely in the event of a sudden stop.

I made it to their destination epidermis intact. Their friend Whitey limped out of his trailer and as each of his guests did, offered me a beer.

"I'm on a medication where I can't drink," I lied, to keep things simple. My last dose was over a week prior but I was doing my best to hold strong for the full month sober. It wasn't easy, as apparently free offerings of alcohol grew in frequency as one got further south towards Springer Mountain.

These were real rednecks, real proud of it, with real thick accents. Soon enough all 30 "Outdoor Edition" camo Bush Lights to match their outfits were all accounted for and this spelled my departure.

Brian kept one hand around his beer and waved to every house and establishment we passed on our way into Pearisburg. He seemed to genuinely know everybody waving back at him from lots with TRUMP flags waving in the wind, and honked for most salutations. I was blown away witnessing a man practically begging for a DUI with a blaring horn. Even with the noticeable offenses, I felt like I got picked up by a pretty good group of guys.

Things had gotten a lot more murky in the realm of political ideology and my snap judgments of Trumpers. The majority of the trail magic I'd enjoyed was thanks to them.

By the time I was hopping into Brian's pickup, the trail had confirmed my fear that there is no reasoning with Trump's supporters. When I found myself locked in debate in New England, their eyes would gloss over when facts were presented and mental gymnastics dominated the mind to justify his actions. There was little to no room left for rational presentations or admissions of guilt.

After abandoning efforts to have productive discourse with my political counterparts, I tried to understand them. This mission proved to be as futile as the first. When asked how his presidency had benefited them directly, they immediately turned their attention to Obama's shortcomings. After listening patiently, I would bring up incidents of gross misconduct by the president and they all seemed to find that endearing, if not admirable. When asked if they'd feel comfortable with Trump spending time alone with their teenage daughters, there was always a moment of hesitation but in the end they decided they would indeed trust this poor excuse for a man.

"Maybe understanding isn't the way to coexist," I muttered to myself as Brian turned off the main road. "Maybe it's just acceptance. Seemingly unattainable, equally ineffable, unadulterated acceptance."

One of the books that rang in my ears under Appalachia's canopy was *Radical Acceptance*, by Tara Brach. It helped dumb down and bring home some of the Buddhist principles I honed in on while reading *The Craving Mind*. Though the notion would be tested repeatedly in the coming miles, Tara Brach's take on Buddhism preached one thing I immediately believed:

Acceptance is even more important than understanding in life.

The refrain set my logic-driven brain on fire. Learning and understanding were what my left brain lived for. Accepting without understanding did not yet compute.

Brian's truck creaked to a half and I was finally dropped off at Holy Family Catholic Church, a donation based hostel for thru-hikers. After getting my bed ready for the night, I walked over to Wal-Mart for the cheapest resupply I ever found. I crossed the parking lot and was taken aback by a voice in a nearby car.

"You want some angel dust?"

I glanced over at a burgundy Ford and something inside told me to squint and keep looking about. My feet involuntarily did a confused spin to exaggerate my attempts at spotting the voice. I shrugged and returned to the church with gusto.

"Well I will be hiking up to Angel's Rest Lookout shortly," I muttered nervously. "Maybe that was some sort of sign from god."

9/26/17 - Lindsey's Car, Angels Rest, VA, 1,565 Miles Hiked - Day 164

Hello!

I'm Mr. Kitty. I love people. I don't have a forever home, but I've been living here at the church hostel banking on the kindness of thru-hikers since May.

If you wouldn't mind looking out for me and emptying my litter box, it would be greatly appreciated.

The note gave all the context one needed to know upon seeing the black cat make itself at home at Holy Family Church Hostel.

"Ah, shoot," said Blaze, a thru-hiker I met back at Four Pines. "I forgot to get him food."

"I think there's some under the sink," I offered.

"Mr. Kitty ain't gonna eat that garbage. He deserves the good stuff."

Since his arrival, Blaze made it a personal mission to find a new home for the feline, who in my opinion was thriving at the hostel.

"I'd happily take him home but my wife won't have it," he said, shaking his head.

"You're married?" I asked, finding it hard to believe for numerous reasons.

"Technically," Blaze responded with a sigh. "She's a wild one. We decided to try a separation and she asked me what I'm gonna do. Told her I'm gonna go for a long fuckin' walk."

"There are worse places for that."

"This is the one my son would have wanted me to do," Blaze started. "I'm only still hiking because I can feel my son's spirit out here. And I know he doesn't want me to give up."

Sadness washed over me as Blaze's words reminded me of John's Spring Shelter, and of course my own regress in that department. His obsession with taking care of a perfectly capable cat also made more sense.

"I don't have many regrets but I wish I were a better father. That I had more time."

"Well it's not too late to be a better husband," I finally said. "Besides, I think Mr. Kitty has the lay of the land around here."

I stashed my pack at the Angel's Rest Trailhead and hitched south to double back without it. Lindsey met me later that evening and we parked her car at the Angel's Rest trailhead we'd hike up the following morning.

We sat on the hood of Lindsey's car. I lit a joint and handed it over. Lindsey dragged it with a coy smile and whipped her long blonde locks over her shoulder. Her eyes narrowed as she pulled me in to blow smoke into my expecting mouth. Her teeth trapped my lower lip before she gently sucked on it, pulling back slowly and barely opening her eyes.

The moon rose over the neighboring ridge, adding lustful color to her bare nipples.

"Um...the hood's still pretty hot," she said with a scrunched up nose.

I slid my right arm under her tiny frame, spun around clockwise, and pinned her up against the passenger side window, feet wrapped around my back. Immediately I felt cum drip off my balls already fit to burst as she dug nails in my side and teeth in my neck. Her intense gaze under the glaring moonbeams told me that she'd never done anything like this before, never taken someone inside of her out in the open for the world to see.

I returned Lindsey to the ground before bending her over the hood of the car we abandoned earlier. Kissing her was exquisitely easy for such a challenging position and my right hand found her clitoris. Several strained moans escaped as I pulled her hair hard and she soon convulsed in a delighted orgasm. My thrusts slowed along with her breaths. I sped up again as I neared the finish line and pulled out just in time for her to take me in her mouth.

She looked like a nocturnal angel while ensuring there was nothing left.

We sat on the roof of her car smoking the rest of the joint.

"Holy fuck was that hot. Would've been worth the indecent exposure charge," Lindsey said with lungs full.

A car passed and we giggled as the headlights illuminated the handprints on the hood of her car.

"You're only the fourth guy I've been with, you know," she said with a smile, already knowing the look that she'd find on my face. "I was with a guy who wasn't right for me for far too long. Finally called it quits for good a couple months back. I needed something like this. Crazy, passionate...just didn't know how to find it."

"There's an app for that," I quipped.

"Several, actually. Good thing I found you when I did. My step dad recently passed away. My mom lives in Costa Rica, I have to go help her soon."

"I'm really sorry to hear that. I hope your mom is ok."

"It's gonna be hard. But she will be," Lindsey said in practically a whisper. "She's a really strong woman."

In the lingering summer heat Lindsey suggested we lie naked in her trunk. She laid a mattress topper over the flattened out space which felt like a 5-star accommodation to me. We talked about life until she straddled me, pinning my hands overhead. Her brilliant waist-length curls effortlessly fell over her other shoulder with the whip of her head. She bit her lip and reached down to take me in seamlessly.

"You're wet again," I whispered.

"I was never dry."

9/27/17 - Lindsey's Car on CR 42, VA, 1,580 Miles Hiked - Day 165

A mixture of pleasure and pain greeted me with the morning sun as Lindsey's tongue was already at work on my exhausted cock. In the latest chapter of *The Legend of Lusty Lindsey*, she finely tuned her newfound skill of having multiple orgasms in the cowgirl position with the help of her pointer and middle fingers. By the third one it was basically a five minute quiver and I managed to synchronize my climax with hers. She pressed her clit down on my oozing shaft and grabbed me by the hair.

"I never knew sex could be this fucking *good*," she moaned before collapsing next to me.

We were able to keep our hands off each other long enough to hike up to Angel's Rest Lookout and smoke the devil's cabbage.

"It's moments like this that made me want to hike the Appalachian Trail," I confessed to her. "But they're too uncommon out here. Most people will go their whole hike without truly sitting still with a view like this. A quick break, sure. When I've sat at lookouts, I've seen hordes of thru-hikers come and go in minutes flat."

It was a crisp, blue day with just enough haze to electrify the honest hues of the surrounding Blue Ridge Mountains. A long rock beckoned us away from the trail like a plank hanging off a ship. At its tip, away from the brush, a river matched the sky. The New River, a young buck estimated to be anywhere from 10 to 360 million years old, is ironically considered to be the second oldest river in the whole world by geologists.

It's one of the few US rivers to flow northerly headwaters in North Carolina, coolly running its way into the Kenosha River in West Virginia.

The longer I stared, I could see the carved valley beyond the river's edge, giving way to the New River over millions of years. Lindsey stole my attention when she sat next to me with a beetle she'd been pursuing in the dirt for some time.

Not only did Lindsey fit so well against me, beetle crawling round and round her thumb, but I never hesitated to do things that most people would only do with someone they've been dating for a long time. I was constantly running whichever hand wasn't in hers through her hair. I never wanted her to be out of reach, and she rarely was. Never in my life was the beginning of something romantic so easy. It felt like we'd been together for as long as I could remember.

I thought of how Erica told me she hated holding hands early in our relationship. How it made her feel like a child being dragged to something awful. She eventually warmed up to the practice, but even then nothing was ever as easy as things were with Lindsey.

We left Angel's Rest to trod the next section pack free, and hitch-hiked to an all you can eat Chinese buffet. Then we dragged ourselves up Sugar Run Mountain to walk off the feast. I was thankful to have slackpacking back in my life as cheap calories churned in my belly. Lindsey stopped every few hundred feet to snack on a root, identify an obscure plant, or pick up a millipede. We finally made it to the cliffs for sunset. Against the pink sky she pointed out the key differences between ravens and crows, and explained why sharp shinned hawks were being chased by them.

"When I discovered ornithology, when I found out that this could be more than a hobby for me," she began. "That was the best day of my life."

We melted into each other as the sun did into the hills. Looking at the photos we'd taken together, Lindsey turned to me.

"It's so crazy that--" she began. "Never mind."

"Hey! You can't do that!" I protested.

"Well, it's just that..." She looked me in the eye and continued, "These pictures look like we've been together for years."

Chapter Twenty-One

1,597 Miles Hiked, 592 to Go

Days 166-167

9/28/17 - Helveys Mill Shelter, VA, 1,597 Miles Hiked - Day 166

Once Lindsey hit the road to return to Roanoke, as I stood in the gaseous wake of 36 hours of pure bliss, I took a deep breath and called my family.

"I still can't get Mark out of the fucking house," my father Mike bemoaned. "I don't know what to do."

My abandonment of the plan to flip my grandmother's house back in January lit a fire under the asses of my dad and his sister, Michelle. Arguably, the job befell to them anyway. When I initially unveiled my plan the year prior, my grandmother Mary Lou assured me she was on board.

"I don't need all this space, anyway," she had told me a year earlier, gesturing to the crumbling walls. Mary Lou hadn't fought me in my endeavor, but perhaps that's only because she didn't have to. Mark was literally beating her to the punch.

I adored my grandmother but I wasn't blind to her manipulative ways. I'd been caught in her web of lies, pinning family against one another while she masterfully played the victim. My dad was getting that version. His mother would insist to him and Michelle that she was ready to sell the house, that she wanted to sell as soon as possible. Then she'd cry to their brothers Mark and George that the house was being ripped away from her.

Her true feelings, whatever they were, were irrelevant. The reverse mortgage she signed up for meant nearly $1,000 was being flushed down the toilet every month. All the while, there was no plan to sustain care for Mary Lou, who couldn't care for herself anymore.

My dad had a full plate without including the eviction of Mark, who was now all alone in a very empty house. Mary Lou's bipolar, violent, alcoholic son held the steadfast conviction that he earned that house through years of what he deemed excellent caretaking. The rest of us considered his neglect for her dietary needs or safety the kind of squalor you'd see on a 60 Minutes segment.

In late summer, they had finally moved Mary Lou into my aunt Michelle's basement, a plan all outside parties vehemently objected to. As expected, all inside parties grew miserable and resentful. My grandma seemed to weaponize her incontinence when denied alcohol. Despite a

206

proven correlation between alcohol and gout, among other health issues, Mark never stopped pouring and Mary Lou never stopped raising the glass.

The whole operation was built to fail.

"I don't envy you," I said to my dad, feeling the good vibes of Lindsey's visit slipping away.

"We were gonna tell him, 'Mark, you can have $5,000 *right now* if you move out immediately.' We got an eviction notice as a backup," my father began. "Well he got it in the mail today. He actually just called, screaming, never calmed down. Said he's never leaving. So I never brought up the 5k."

For a year Mark had been insisting that moving out was as simple as packing a few bags. Predictably, every month he'd insist *this* was the month, no problem this time. My Dad knew better than to try renovating the house with Mark still under its roof. After all, Mike was the one who helped me patch holes in the wall hours before his brother made fresh ones.

"And George is about to be back on the streets again."

It was hard to hear the tremors in my father's voice. His other brother, George, was wrapping up his 13th stint in rehab before getting released into the world he's tried so hard to ruin for everyone he's related to.

"So facing down the barrel, I intend to take that $5,000 and put it towards a good eviction lawyer."

"A hitman might be more effective," I spat. He ignored my dark joke.

"Bus is here, I gotta go," he said.

"Love you, Dad," I said to no one.

I hiked and wondered what it must've been like for my father to hear his oldest child casually remark about the death of his brother. I hadn't hidden my anger towards Mark but there's a vast chasm between anger and indifference towards death. Did the comment even register in his crowded, troubled mind? It wasn't the first time I'd expressed apathy at the thought of Mark's demise.

My cousin Matt used to say the same about our Uncle George.

"Because as long as he's alive, he's a danger to all of us," Matt once said. "And the first to go will be my dad. Or grandma."

"Well you're right about the danger part." I stammered after an awkward silence. "But I simply can't wish the man *dead*. He's just so broken. I wish the man would disappear. Forever."

Apparently my line of thinking got through to Matt. Months later he was singing a different tune.

"I just wish George would get a job on some fucking boat. So far from here, far away from his triggers and alcohol," Matt remarked a year before my hike. "Start a whole new life for himself."

"So you don't want the bastard dead anymore?"

He shook his head.

"Well that does sound nice," I admitted. "Since that's not an option, I'd feel fine reading his obituary."

I sat in silence, feeling guilty that I came to feel the very same way about his father.

Matt made an impression on me the same moment I changed him. I came to find that death would be just to either and beneficial to most. They'd used up their fucking boats, their second chances.

Even on the trail I still couldn't work through it all. I dreamed often of either uncle, sometimes coming to blows, other times making amends, occasionally them pleading with me for forgiveness and me refusing to offer it.

Disowning Mark was never easy. It made my life easier, but at the cost of my soul. I remember finding a frisbee in my grandmother's car a few weeks after I broke his jaw at the trailer.

"Where did this come from?"

"Mark bought it," said my grandmother. "He said, 'Oh well if the boys will be up for a weekend, they'll need a frisbee.'"

I thought of Mark, who was living and working at the trailer before I punched his lights out. In a lot of ways the trailer was good for him, for a time at least. Then I came about and disrupted everything. I thought of him, probably struggling to get out those thoughtful words just recently having his jaw brace removed, watching his mother go away to a place that brought him some peace with the guy who ended that era. It was hard for me to imagine him somehow taking all that and selflessly buying me a gift.

I wondered whether he considered it any sort of peace offering, or instead the perceived easiest and cheapest way to get me to forget what he'd done. Even if that were the case, a frisbee would be a pretty shitty offering for half a lifetime of verbally abusing my friends and girlfriends. There was a lot more than a few tasteless utterances of the n-word behind that wallop of a punch.

When I stood over his lifeless body for those moments that felt like hours, I remembered the transgressions. I only hoped he'd open his eyes to spare my own soul the pain to come.

I blew a wispy blue plume into the early autumn air. The humidity preserved the suspended gray strands, still circling one another. The skunky aftertaste made me reach for a *Jolly Rancher.*

"No lollipoppy til the toppy." I muttered aloud, leaving the candy in my fanny pack.

I'd created a reward system where I'd pop a hard candy into my panting mouth once a hard climb was completed. After falling behind schedule due to Giardia the month prior, I employed an arsenal of tricks to battle my fickle discipline.

My sickness turned the change of season into a very real adversary and my bank account called for some rather dispiriting dietary restrictions. The vision of me taking my final steps at Springer Mountain, once crystal clear, was growing faint like the smoke before my eyes.

A few minutes into the ascension, my lungs were screaming as they couldn't find enough oxygen in my shallow breaths.

The climb wasn't easy, but it didn't justify this level of respiratory distress.

"No stoppy," I gasped. "Til the toppy."

I shook my head firmly as my entire body begged for another break. Beads of cold sweat fell off my chin. My extremities were pins and needles then something familiar happened.

Sounds in every direction seemed to be placed in a great many jars, one by one. From my mother I inherited the propensity to faint. This wasn't my first swooning rodeo. The hearing is always the first to go.

Blackness crept in from all peripheral corners and I knew time was running short. Blindness progressed and all I could hear was my pounding heart. I rounded a corner to discover a heroic boulder waiting for me. I sat down and found temporary relief. The straps around my torso dug into me like chains.

"I'm not taking my pack off!" I screamed, only hearing a whisper. "No stoppy til..."

Something was different from my standard fainting prelude. Typically the scene in front of me appeared normal until it vanished altogether in a fade to black. Never before had my color scheme as I know it been messed around with.

Gazing around, it looked as though someone turned the saturation knob all the way up in my eyeballs while turning down the resolution. Pixelated neon forestry resembled that of some 80s Nintendo role playing game and I appeared to be dangerously low on health points. Every green became a screaming yellow and brown was nowhere to be found. Dirt was cherry red and tree trunks an electric purple. There was no time to appreciate the psychedelic color tilt because some serious propaganda was at work in my mind.

If I close my eyes, my sight will never return to normal. I'll be living in the dungeon level of Mario Brothers if I don't go completely blind.

The second and obviously more frightening scenario had my full attention and I doubled down on my effort to avoid fainting altogether. The chronic knot in my shoulder tightened intensely but I was barely aware of it among the chaotic depletion of my other senses. I kept my eyes wide open as focus became increasingly blocky and colors resumed musical chairs. The last sound I heard was a *POP* in my brain and my distress surged.

"I can't take off my pack if I want to finish this fucking trail! I can't let this be another unfinished project," I strained aloud, hearing nothing.

One last attempt at a deep breath made me extra sleepy. My heavy eyes frantically scanned the bizarre, pixelated understory and tried to remember what it all looked like before. Nothingness continued its encroachment as the blacklight theme gave way.

"I can't bear..." I absentmindedly unclipped my pack. "...the thought of telling everyone..."

I took a deep, nurturing breath unencumbered by my straps.

"That this is just another failure..."

As air left my body in a smooth farewell my right elbow found the ground that was always waiting for me.

"I need to finish," I muttered weakly.

From my supine position I finally let go of the bright yellow tapestry and shut my eyes.

A leaf found rest atop my forehead. The gentle disruption roused me from a peaceful slumber.

"Where am I?" The familiar voice in my head demanded to know.

Sshhh.

"Where's my pack?"

It's right next to you. No need to worry.

"Am I hurt? Why am I lying *on* the trail?"

Everything will be fine if you just breathe.

"Phhhoooooo." I made my breath audible per the instructions of the many guided meditations I'd listened to. "Mmmmmmmhhhhhhhhoooooohhhhh."

I strained my diaphragm to the point of discomfort and employed every other muscle in my abdomen. Just like the leaf that woke me up, I found my own rest.

My eyes fixated on a single leaf in the forest above. A breeze relinquished it from its mother and I observed its every move. Seconds stretched on and on as I observed each pirouette and leap. There was a harmony with the other falling leaves. Independent yet united by tempo and fate. Gravity choreographed the dance and wind arranged the song.

I was completely present with the changing canopy.

Fused neurons of neuroses roared back to life.

"It took you *30 autumns* to do this. Every year the leaves dance for you and you've never been bothered enough to watch."

There's no need for that. Just. WALK.

My exhausted body kicked into autopilot and steps came one after the other for several miles. Ultimately my conscious mind needed answers.

A lookout is coming up soon. We can do some thinking there. Keep walking.

It felt paramount that I listen. My stride complied and I could glimpse a colorful valley beyond the thinning trees.

My mind was blank except for an observation that my steps were perfectly synced with my improved breathing. Before long I arrived at the lookout. That new voice in my head was gone but its guidance wasn't necessary. I knew this is where I was meant to stop. In a trance I placed my pack on the ground and sat cross-legged.

My eyes smoothly scanned the panorama of the colorful valley below. I was determined to really take in the scene. I knew that this view was exquisite but I faced the hard fact that I wasn't present with it. I wasn't really *seeing* anything. It bothered me that I felt so far away from the landscape. Yet I was determined to walk away with a mindful experience.

Eventually I found a hill down below. I could see it quite clearly and my eyes scanned over it dozens of times. It was the most wondrous piece of land I'd ever laid eyes on. I could vividly see the cultivation that took place to create such a dreamy bubble of earth. I caught the barest hint of a narrow trail that led into the thick wooded heart of it.

A vision came of a father telling his sons that it was fine for them to dirt bike. *On* the path.

"Staying on the path is what keeps this place beautiful." My imaginary patriarch advised.

Is that father me? I wondered

What if I went down there? What if I told the hill dwellers that I saw it from the knob and had to see if I could walk the grounds?

Perhaps my wife is there and that land becomes mine.

At that moment, I found my *breath.*

I'd been to my fair share of yoga classes. Over a two year period I meditated nearly every day. Those activities helped me find great calm but neither led to pure discovery of my *true* breath.

Countless instructors and meditative guides have whispered grand words and lovely koans into my ears which soothed my diaphragm and slowed my heart rate. Yet not a single one of those moments ever led to this. Had I ever really known what breath they were referring to, I would have gone mad trying to attain it. Ordinary mortals are always told we're breathing wrong. The greatness of *the* breath had never been accurately impressed upon me, but then again maybe that's the point. It cannot be summated. It cannot be understood. True breath must be felt.

I observed a perfect rhythm throughout my body and my breath was the bass drum of it. My forehead seemed to breathe on its own at the very spot a leaf fell upon earlier. It was timed perfectly with my lungs. The point on my forehead topped an axis. When tilted forward just so, it was in perfect alignment with my throat. I was surprised to find that my chin was also intersected by this constellation. Once I noticed that, I could sense another collinear point at the very center of my chest. Finally, the base of my nose joined in, joined by my diaphragm and trachea.

It felt like my soul put together a *Megazord*.

This has to be a chakra alignment, right? I wondered, embarrassed to discover that I really didn't know what a chakra *is*.

Briefly, my old habits took control. I rued all the moments I'd come close to this nirvanic feeling, missing it by a beat or passing moment of muscle tension. Thankfully the restraints of my past calmly bowed away, creating space for karmic realignment.

The sensations lasted for quite some time. I felt every beat of my heart and my breathing was perfect throughout. I seemed to be glowing. My mind's eye could see my tanned body radiating loving kindness into the valley. Suddenly I was able to feel colors.

I smiled toward the sun and I could *feel* red. This wasn't that moment we all experience every summer where our eyelids are insufficient from keeping out every UV ray, but it wasn't necessarily unlike it, either. It was as if every other frequency within my skin's spectrum made way for red to truly make itself known. When I turned towards the shadows I could *feel* blue. I knew nothing in that direction was actually blue yet the sensation was unequivocally blue. It was nothing short of incredible and I held that regard for several minutes.

After eventually swatting at black flies and yellow jackets, I could only regain a remnant of that impeccable breathing. I felt excited but cautious: *Yes, this is a big deal, but it's smart to not get carried away.*

Things had a perfect clarity that I had never known. I could love my parents for exactly who they are, without resentment. I envisioned my future in Denver, exploring brand new avenues of life and thriving. A glimpse of finishing the trail in triumphant and glorious fashion.

It was hard to believe that less than an hour prior I feared I was going blind. The trust I placed in my body and the universe led to a transcendent experience.

I was able to appreciate all the decisions I'd made to lead me to that moment on the cliff. I was able to see a prosperous future for myself. More importantly, I was finally able to see what a prosperous *past* I have.

Pride always stood in the way of reckoning with my past. Looking back had long filled me with shame and regret. It's not that I'd been unable to see the many great experiences I cultivated. The shadow cast by my remorse had always made it impossible to fully see the blessings of past selves shine bright. I always pictured my life as a scale. Soul-sucking jobs on the left and a fulfilling personal life on the other. As long as the scales tipped to the right, life was good.

That was a lie.

I noticed the cantankerous knot in my shoulder was gone.

A deep understanding of my body was reached on that cliff. A greater knowing of its wholeness and inter-connectivity. Once the spell was broken I effortlessly orchestrated cracks and pops in entirely new places. Joints and sore spots that would have previously been too timid and tense to allow manipulation before.

"This doesn't mean I suddenly have it all figured out," I reminded myself aloud. I am a student, just like every great Buddhist.

I left that cliff with less weight to bear. I'd spent so many years carrying internalized anger. Even on this hike I rarely looked back with pride on what I'd done to get myself there. It had become a habit to pick out flaws and put previous versions of myself through turmoil that I didn't deserve.

"Holy fucking shit, dude," were among the first enlightened words to come out of my mouth. "I've spent a year and a half just doing what I love every day. I was already living the life I wanted and I can finally look back and say 'thank you' to my previous selves. And mean it."

Not only was that anger futile; it was also making my once in a lifetime walk less joyful.

There's a well known Buddhist tale of two monks who come upon a river crossing to find a woman in distress. She is unable to cross the raging torrents on her own and asks for assistance. It is against the oath of a monk to ever touch a woman, which leads to a silent moment of uncertainty between the two men. The elder monk soon shrugs and takes the lady across on his shoulders.

The younger man remains silent in outrage for many, many miles. Unable to contain his incredulity any longer, he unleashes his tempered inquisition.

"How could you do that? How could you break your sacred vow? How will you ever reach Nirvana now?"

The wiser monk calmly responds, keeping his eyes on the path.

"I carried her across the river. I picked her up at one bank, and left her at the other. Why are you *still* carrying her?"

Chapter Twenty-Two

1,621 Miles Hiked, 568 to Go

Days 168-174

9/30/17 - Chestnut Knob Cabin, VA, 1,621 Miles Hiked - Day 168

After fainting on the trail, Fall's inauguration became infinitely more clear. Summer dawdled in the afternoon air but the scenery told a different story. A crunchy blanket of color turns the page.

A new level of silence enveloped me during the magical splashes of rust and red descending slowly unto the earth that birthed them. I walked among the confetti of earth tones and felt as though I myself were lighter.

The revelations of the previous day hung in my mind like the dying leaves in the crisp air. Often they'd be whisked away before settling into place. It felt like the root cause of my inward anger came from never actually looking back on what I'd done to get myself to the AT and being proud of it.

I began to see that I was already set up for success.

"Thank you," I said to my previous self, eyes tearing up. "I appreciate everything you've done to bring me to this moment in time."

After this moment of acceptance, the universe delivered. Something I did when I chose to take responsibility for my future paid off: my old boss replied with a job opportunity.

The favors I'd done for myself since quitting that awful job played out in front of my eyes. I saw clearly how I was actively reaping the rewards. And I loved myself for it. Finally.

The Craving Mind continued to pair well with *Radical Acceptance* by Tara Brach. That transformative experience, weaving together unconscious and conscious minds the day before, readied me to finally let Buddhism into my life.

I'd been drawn to Buddhism ever since childhood. Looking back, it vaguely felt like watching a crush from afar, never making a move because I deemed her too perfect, too idyllic, to be seduced by the likes of me.

I had made a point of staying away from religion in general. Buddhism is really the only doctrine that says, *Take this and run with it. Take this and live by your own moral code.* The selfless origin of that was such a draw for me. It's something that I found to be an ever absent component from religions that should be a tenant of them all. The idea that gospels and scripture are too delicate to be questioned by practitioners alarmed me. I've sat through hundreds of Catholic masses in my life and not once did I hear an ounce of doubt or objective analysis.

Perhaps there are more components of flexibility in major religions, but I hadn't seen or heard about them.

In high school history class, I came so close to making a move on Buddhism. I loved everything I was reading and hearing, and there was a cosmic pull I'd never felt before. Then something stopped me.

"The topic sentence of Buddhism," my history teacher capped off before moving onto the next religion in study. "Is that *Life is Suffering*."

Life is...suffering? Then why are Buddhists always so happy and calm?

Unfortunately for the Buddha's teachings, I was getting an incomplete picture. More unfortunate still, I had just gotten out of my emo phase and was at long last enjoying the attention of my female classmates after a late bout of puberty between my Junior and Senior years. I wasn't about to throw away good times with good looking women for more suffering.

The Craving Mind ended up being far, far more about Buddhism than I ever would have imagined. The audiobook, along with some ancillary research it inspired, taught me that the old *Life is Suffering* bumper sticker is a result of bad translation. A better word for dukkha, the Sanskrit word requiring a relabeling, is actually *unsatisfactoriness*. And Buddhism doesn't say that all life is unsatisfactory, not even close. It more accurately says that our *refusal* of unsatisfactoriness and constant desire to reduce our suffering and reject impermanence are what prevent us from becoming enlightened.

A-ha!

Reading and understanding that shifted something. Something that was much easier to shift when my chakras found their alignment all on their own. My gut, intuition, second sight, whatever it be called, felt profoundly in charge.

In the evening after my soul Megazord assembled, my heart raced upon seeing an email from my old boss, Brian. When I saw the word *Denver* in his email, I had goosebumps. I hadn't even revealed to Brian that I wished to move to Colorado, and this opportunity just so happened to be where my heart desired? The serendipitous nature of it made a return to DC quite hard to imagine.

Namaste...in Denver.

10/1/17 - Lick Branch Creek, VA, 1,636 Miles Hiked - Day 169

The near full moon left the mountaintop, the valley below, and the surrounding ranges all in an incandescent glow of gentle brilliance. I strolled the pasture with my hot tea in hand, easily taking in every feature of the plants and trees around me without the guiding light of my headlamp.

With the existential boiling point behind me, I contemplated how the previous few weeks served as an exercise to ritualistically strip myself down to reveal how simple and painless life can be. I was a couple days away from a month without masturbation or alcohol. I traded my heavier but more luxurious mattress for a much lighter one, ditched my comfy camping shoes, and left my hammock home during my Giardia recovery. I traded self-doubt and judgment for acceptance and pride. My bank statements revealed 10 days without a single transaction, holding firm at $600. With only $11 in my wallet, I fully expected to go another few days in that fashion.

I'd been answering so many questions I never even bothered to ask before. Can I live without sex? Is life still fun without alcohol? Can I view my own anger through the eyes of a Buddhist, with compassion and acceptance? Is mindfulness achievable if I don't know what life holds for me next?

10/2/17 - Relax Inn, Davis Valley, VA, 1,650 Miles Hiked - Day 170

Appropriately, I finished *The Craving Mind* right as I was walking up to a gas station to buy my first beer in a full month. I saw a hundred little reflections in the condensation on the Yuengling tall boy. Each version of myself staring back, digesting the work on addiction I'd just consumed. There were waves during my personal prohibition, as the book referenced, but they were few and far between. I wondered whether any of my alcoholic relatives ever went a whole month without imbibing as I'd done, whether they were capable and if so how they felt and acted.

There were stages in my life where I turned to alcohol for many things: social lubricant, anxiety antidote, and most frequently, nonsensical indicator for the extent to which I was living my life to the fullest. At the beginning of this trail, I was scared of what the hike might be like if I wasn't drinking with people. In my two-week midway break, scores of liquor coursed through my superhuman metabolism.

I ultimately felt that I'd been alcohol dependent at times, but never an alcoholic. For better or worse, the examples set for me projected that if a bottle of alcohol remains in your home untouched for any amount of time, then AA is not called for. There was a two year old bottle of rum waiting at home so I must be doing fine.

The Craving Mind turned my attention back to the ever elusive clarity on sex addiction. On trail, I completed a six week celibacy before crossing paths with Namita. Since my Giardia recovery began, I went four weeks without touching myself. It appeared that an addiction was not what I was facing.

The book turned out to be very different from what I was expecting. I was anticipating an intensely scientific read. Science was a pillar, but I was surprised to find a practical and approachable guide for bringing mindfulness into one's life. The author did a good job balancing science, research, and the statistics with the "do it yourself practices" of managing cravings and addictions and living a better life.

An empirical unwrapping that was brewing for a long time began with that fainting spell on the trail.

All these things I never considered living without, alcohol, sex, masturbation, porn, sexual attention, fell aside like dead skin.

It intrigued me that outside factors brought on my subtractions.

When I was sick from Giardia, sobriety was thrust upon me. I also wasn't much use as a lover and didn't feel like masturbating. So those potential addictions fell to the wayside. Social media became something to avoid, the terror of confessing to the world that I wouldn't be finishing my hike was paralyzing. Soon enough it all got easy.

The last nefarious layer was self judgment. The molting of which entailed a full bodily shutdown. Following that collapse, my internal dialogue was utterly transformed. It was the ultimate vindication to reach that point without Lexapro. I always knew I could reach a healthy mental state, where my inner critic wasn't calling the shots, and I did it without pharmaceutical help. Perhaps I wouldn't be able to remain there unassisted forever, but to even reach it for a few days was hugely validating.

As I reached for beer at the gas station's picnic table, one unstrippable thing lingered on. *Not so fast*, my mind stirred. There was an addiction lurking under all that decaying hide.

You're addicted to feeling desired.

A tightening in my chest told me it was true.

I realized I'd never in my life been truly alone. Even in elementary school I had "girlfriends." There was always someone to talk to, to flirt with, to bemoan the strife of young love, even if every word of it were through a screen and neither of us could muster the courage to hold hands. Once sex was brought into the equation, I never went two weeks without it before this hike and that's what made sex addiction emerge as the front-running candidate. That and an ominous but definitive endorsement from my ex-girlfriend. But that was never it. Sex meant worth, fun, value. Yet I could have forgone it if some doctor told me doing the deed would result in nausea and vomiting.

The allure of someone out there wanting me: *that's* what I could never stray too far from.

Long before *The Craving Mind* I knew my propensity to get caught up wrapping my ego and self worth into the interest realized from the opposite sex.

My low lows could often be attributed to not getting any attention from women or getting attention from the wrong women. I'd been single but never alone.

I didn't know what to do with that hard truth.

"Isn't everyone addicted to being desired?" I asked my fast warming beverage.

Everyone wants to feel wanted.

It takes up so much of everyone's time. I think most anyone not spending time accordingly is actually very sad and would like someone to desire them.

So what now? How much effort is it worth to put into fixing it?

My mind chased its own tail until my hand did something without my command.

Crack. Tssss.

It was a glorious malty beverage indeed.

10/3/17 - Partnership Shelter, VA, 1,657 Miles Hiked - Day 173

The Barn offered a "Hiker's Breakfast" to those passing through Rural Retreat, VA and I intended to take advantage of it. A headache and six remaining dollars were all I had to show for my break-fast from alcohol. And six bucks wasn't gonna cut it for a $5 breakfast.

"Time to finally whip out the debit card," I said to myself walking up to the front door.

A banging on the glass came from my right and I saw Twisted's wave through the glare.

"Never thought I'd see you again," I said as I approached his table.

"Idaho Fuckin' Bones, how's it hangin'?" he asked. I nearly reflexively waved the air in front of me because I was so used to happening upon Twisted with a cigarette between his pursed lips.

"You look great," I said. "You look...relieved."

"I am! Five thru-hikes in the books. Blasted through The Smokies," he said while picking up his coffee. "You shouldn't, though. They're beautiful right now, you're gonna love it."

"Hope the weather holds. I'm nervous it'll turn by then. I had to get off the trail. Fuckin' got Giardia."

"So that's what was wrong, huh? I remember you not feelin' so hot," he said between sips of coffee. He quickly stood up and slapped a ten on the table. "Gotta catch a bus! Breakfast on me. Lil' deposit into the Bank of Bones."

10/4/17 - Old Orchard Shelter, VA, 1,680 Miles Hiked - Day 172

I swirled a flask of scotch beneath my nose, the orange glow of the fire dancing amongst the sand blasted steel of the vessel.

"Wait as long as you can before you have kids," began my new friend, Dave. "They'll keep you young. I wish I figured that out before I got a family going."

Dave was generous with his scotch so long as he could bend your ear for a while.

"You know, I've never enjoyed scotch," I said before taking another swig. "But I think sitting close to a fire is making the difference. It's like my palate is ready for the smoke."

"Ready? You'll never be *ready*," Dave offered, still harping on the subject of offspring. "You see, the system's a trap. You want to retire? Well, once you get a woman pregnant, you'll sign a mortgage for a house to raise your family in. You sign that dotted line, you'll be working for 30 years. Guaranteed."

It was like Dave could read my thoughts. Every conspiracy theorized societal construct I'd bemoaned for a year and half were coming out of my companion with peaty undertones.

It was the first time liquor hit my lips in over a month and I imbibed slowly. Warm trickled down my core as I monitored my body. An ease welled up from my gut but no other tantamount breakthroughs presented themselves. Neither the inaugural beer nor Dave's fire water brought on any sort of euphoria. There was no grand relief to be off the wagon again.

In knowing that I didn't need alcohol, feeling no longing in its absence, and observing no pull to keep drinking, a general softness found its way in. I simply enjoyed the buzz, perhaps more keenly aware of how my organs received the gentle poison.

I handed Dave's joint back to him and left the floor open for more of his wisdom.

"I just hate who I've become. You take a job. You get promoted. You take another job. You find out one day down the line you've become someone you hate. Someone who can't appreciate the life you built."

Dave's words took me by surprise, and swiftly ended my meditative exercise. I was uncertain of what to make of the parallels between us.

"My wife asked me 'How far you hikin'? Yer not much cut out for it, ya know.' And I said 'As far as it takes to stop being an asshole.'"

"You miss your wife?" I asked.

"More than anything. And I miss my kids but I feel like I barely know 'em," he said, reaching for the scotch. "Wait as long as you can. They'll keep you young and you'll be so much smarter."

Sleep eluded me in the shelter. I thought about Dave's words, questioning their truth.

I'd always planned to start a family at 25. Life got in the way and with 30 being less than a year away, I wasn't even sure 35 would mark that parental inauguration. It freaked me out. It felt like yet another promise broken to myself.

Dave was the first person who made me feel like I was right on time. I'd been told to wait but never with such enthusiasm. My concerns of not being able to keep up with my children as they grew up lost some footing by that fire. It compounded the relief of the previous week's revelations.

Then I heard a gunshot.

I sat up, instantly in a sweat, reaching for my knife. I heard scratching behind me and whipped around. I extended the knife before turning on my headlamp. In the spotlight was a mouse picking up an acorn and scurrying up the stone wall. He parked his rodent butt in front of a small hole and plunged himself into it. The acorn stayed behind, leaving only the nut and four yellow teeth in view.

One final pull sent the acorn flying, back to the wooden planks from whence it came. The *crack* was extraordinarily loud, louder than the first, in fact. Which was...not a gunshot.

I watched the ritual again, in disbelief that such a minute activity could bring the calamity of a thunderstorm. With a great sigh I picked up my pack and walked out into the moonlight.

While setting up my tent, I heard several bouts of what sounded like a penny falling onto cardboard. Just a few thuds, nothing more.

For the second time in the night a change in perspective made all the difference.

10/5/17 - Thomas Knob Shelter, VA, 1,692 Miles Hiked - Day 173

Instinct kept my feet still.

My eyes told me there was nothing to fear but staring at those massive, lean muscles beneath an auburn mane left me paralyzed.

A snort and a kick preceded one wild pony's beeline towards me. She started licking my calf, tail waving enthusiastically. Suddenly the two others I was watching had a bit more interest. One found my other calf and I held out my hand for the other, fearing what he might engage if something wasn't presented.

For a good minute, I was a willing salt lick.

Once a certain level of rapport was reached I was petting all three on the noses and backing away slowly. I had 14 miles to go and from the look of things, distractions like this were at every turn.

Less than a mile later, a set of longhorns longer than me stood atop a disinterested, masticating bull with brilliant chestnut hair.

It was challenging to resist petting every wild pony in my path, but I was determined to get to the shelter before sunset. All along the way the panoramas beckoned the eyes. Grayson Highlands might've been the most beautiful section of trail I'd seen yet.

At 5,430 feet, the shelter came with a valley view that struck me in the moment as the most beautiful sight I'd ever seen. I breathed as slowly as I could, determined to take in every wrinkle and chute it had to offer. Once I'd finish scanning one direction, the reverse carried lustrous new colors that faded the old into oblivion.

It occurred to me at that moment that I was sitting at the same elevation as Denver, where I presumed spectacles like this were happened upon daily.

10/6/17 - Woodchuck Hostel, Damascus, VA, 1,715 Miles Hiked - Day 174

Under cover of darkness, I was sharing a joint with a strange fellow named Shaggy I'd crossed paths with before.

We sat atop a rock beside the Holston River, which runs right through Damascus.

"Wait a second," I began incredulously through coughs. "You were baptized by the 12 Tribes?"

Shaggy nodded solemnly.

"How did this happen? The guys from The Yellow Deli?" I pressed.

"Yep," Shaggy said, nodding. "I ran into this guy who was meeting up with Aysh."

"No way! I love Aysh!"

I couldn't wait to get an inside scoop on the Twelve Tribes of Israel from one who escaped the remote island they all seemed to be floating on. Plus I knew one of the key threads in this yarn personally. Aysh welcomed me in from torrential rain way back in Vermont, along with many other thru-hikers I'd met along my hike.

"Well Aysh didn't love me, at least not at first. Didn't wake up for my work for stay chores, so he played a trumpet in my face," began Shaggy. "I yelled, 'What the fuck? Why you bein' a fucking asshole right now?' He didn't like my words, pulled me aside before the gathering and said we couldn't proceed with it if we didn't find peace. I didn't want all that shit stoppin' cuzza me so I said we had peace. But afterwards we were cool. Asked me if I want to get baptized. So they baptize me, right? And I bounce, I start hikin' out. But then it gets cold so I go back. And they're like, kinda suspicious so I say to them, 'I wanna be a Holy Priest.'"

Shaggy took an exquisitely long rip.

"So a few months later, I'm ponytailed out and shit, and I'm like bein' fast tracked to Priest shit, you know? But then it got warm so I bounce."

"Again?" I asked.

"They didn't like that," Shaggy responded with a shaking head. "*This* year I go back, right? Aysh greets me, and I'm helping. I'm cool, they're cool. I'm still a born again believer, you know? That's why I got this tat before I even start hiking three years ago. It says '*Live to Die*' upside down."

He lowered his baggy shirt and we both knew something was wrong but neither immediately sure what. The chopper font beneath his ample chest hair had a different motto in mind.

"No, wait...It says *Die to Live*." He nodded. "The way most people see it, we just live and we die. But the way I view it, I needed to DIE...To live. I mean dying for my ego, dying from my selfishness, dying to the world. So they appreciated that. They were like, 'Wow, this is a real believer.'

"So Aysh and I, we were cool. The Elder came up, said he forgave me. So we cool. But this one Holy Priest, he comes to me, I think we're cool," Shaggy said. "Turns out, we're *not* cool! And I'm like, 'Bro, the ELDER forgave me, why can't you, bro?' Because that's what a true Priest does, they forgive."

My numbed lips held me back from pointing out that I was *talking* to a Priest unable to forgive. Knowing that if Shaggy hadn't learned by now the error in his own actions, my opinion wasn't about to shift his paradigms.

Besides, I'd heard glowing reviews about a brewery down the street.

I felt a twinge of guilt drinking again, but it also felt wrong to pass on a renowned peddler of the suds so close to the trail. Besides, overall I felt like I earned the right to drink in a carefree fashion for the rest of my miles. I proved myself and learned what I needed to.

I couldn't find a single wing-man/woman/Priest back at Woodchuck Hostel to accompany me to Damascus Brewery because everyone was too high to function.

Nearing the brewery's entrance solo, hearing an ear piercing rendition of *Sweet Child O Mine* made me want a beer immediately. I scanned the taps and found the undisputable choice: *Beaver Fever.* Any straggling bits of guilt about drinking again fell to the wayside upon seeing this serendipitous brew before me. Among the hillbillies of the south, the all too common affliction of Giardia is commonly referred to as...Beaver Fever.

The porter was gone with alarming swiftness halfway through the DJ singing Nickelback. The nodding heads and failed harmonies from the crowd left me wary of the bit of paper I deposited up front.

"Up next, we've got Idaho Pony singing Piano Man!"

The idea of the men with plaid cut offs, who could have easily held quorum, throwing their glasses at "the guy with the tiny horse last name" for singing anything but Country Roads, didn't exactly warm up my vocal chords.

Unexpectedly, I was met with unanimous applause and greeted at the bar by a largely toothless but jovial stringbean of a man after the performance.

"Can you sing more Billy Joel?" he inquired hopefully with profound twang.

"Not for free I can't," I clarified with light taps on my glass.

Two beers later, salsa music came on during the DJ's smoke break and the bartender was guiding me in her arms.

In my head, I was a Mariachi casanova. In reality, I couldn't be any more impressive than an elderly person managing to recall *The Electric Slide*.

Things were in and out after that unexpected waltz.

After my final number, *River of Dreams,* I was feeling inspired to pay another visit to the Holston River. Feeling lighter than I possibly ever had before I bounced among the rocks of the bank under the moonlight.

It was almost as if that falling leaf baptized me and I was born again to a new existence. It was clear on that bank that my remaining miles were full of trust in the universe.

The manifestations had unfolded throughout the day. Chris would have been too timid to ask for the story of Shaggy's disgraceful fall from priesthood. He was never brave enough to sing Billy Joel outside of a moving car. Chris would undoubtedly have made an excuse to avoid tripping over his two left feet in public when petitioned by a bartender.

Idaho Pony hadn't hesitated all day long.

"I'm not sure about a life after this,

God knows I've never been a spiritual man."

In the comfort of the torrents, I pulled out all the theatrics and gutsy key changes.

"Baptized by the fire,

I wade into the river,

That runs to the promised land..."

I drew out the final line while hopping safely along the dryer stones of the bank.

"In...the middle of the niiiiight."

I go walking in my sleep.

Chapter Twenty-Three

1,730 Miles Hiked, 459 to Go

Days 175-186

10/7/17 - Abingdon Gap Shelter, VA, 1,730 Miles Hiked - Day 175

Buddhism teaches that we are all asleep. The Buddha asks us to wake up from the slumber of ignorance and fully embrace the loving acceptance, the inherent Buddha-nature, that lies hidden in all of us. Monks believe and teach that there is nothing to attain for us. Not enlightenment, not loving kindness, not happiness. Rather, teachings such as The Four Noble Truths and the Eightfold Path are meant to help humans actualize the glories of The Buddha within themselves, discovering the nirvana we're all born with. The nirvana buried beneath the layers of our dukkha.

Our unsatisfactoriness.

It is not enough to open our eyes and behold dukkha. We must cultivate mindfulness and other simple yet challenging habits to truly feel loving kindness.

I climbed out of the valley nestling Damascus, up the mountains carved by the formidable Holston River's torrents. Looking back at it, I pondered the ways I'd been sleepwalking into rivers like the one Billy Joel sang about.

Radical Acceptance had already begun waking me up to a richer experience but having only recently started the audiobook, I was still clueless on my unique brand of tanha, or thirst.

At surface level, my thirst seemed to be that of a rock star's: sex and intoxicants. I scanned down my body for signs of truth but my radar was empty. I clocked myself on a variation: Feeling desired on one hand, looseness and escape on the other? The needle moved, but not resoundingly.

I sat with that unknowing for a while and scanned for guilt about my recent booze binges. I didn't find any and felt that my relationship with alcohol had shifted. At least for the moment.

I couldn't feel its pull but I had more questions.

Do you need it? No

Do you want it? Not right now, no.

Would you drink alcohol if it found its way to you? Probably a little. I was largely satisfied with the absence of craving.

Craving is another definition of dukkha, and the previous work on my reading list gave me plenty to contemplate on that subject. Yet I still couldn't complete the puzzle of it all and wondered whether I'd need a sangha, a community, to resume my introspective work.

The Appalachian Trail Community was a sangha of sorts, and it certainly brought critical perspective. My views on family, judiciary, and faith had all been challenged during my trek and I was better off for it.

Accountability.

That's what was missing. I was further away from figuring out how to create accountability on a solo hike than I was from understanding what I needed to be accountable *for*. Taking in the rich autumn colors that changed with every climb or descent, I concluded that I was bringing my trademark impatience to a process that takes Zen Masters a lifetime. Or several lifetimes if you believe in that sort of thing.

I set down my pad and sleeping bag and found a calm mind with the warmth they provided. Progress of any magnitude in understanding the mind deserved a peaceful slumber to follow.

The moon cast me in spotlight just before I could depart the waking world, leaving nowhere to hide for my anxious thoughts. Loving kindness was a repeated theme in the works I'd been taking in and the associated meditations always incited a tightness in my chest. I doubted I could ever forgive Mark or George, let alone bring their faces to mind as I summon the world to bring *them* reduced suffering.

The meditation calls for the cushion topper to bring feelings of inward compassion for one's self. Once achieved, the meditator should move on to a loved one to wish loving kindness upon. Easy enough. After that completion, the practitioner should bring a neutral face to mind, someone they neither hate nor love.

At some point, regardless of the variations of this meditation style that can be found, the objective is to ultimately bear those same loving and compassionate feelings for an enemy as were felt for self and the beloved.

Each time I'd taken this on, I procrastinated until it was time to bring an uncle into the picture. This time around, I dove right in. I pictured them joining my group of meditation subjects, suddenly carrying themselves with an unrecognizable grace. They had soft smiles on their faces and unbelievably, I didn't wish for them to leave. My mind settled in that place for a few minutes, observing my kin with a gentle curiosity. Then these words filled my head:

My uncles are asleep. Mark and George...are asleep. Erica is asleep.

Just like the teachings say, would you ever be mad at someone for simply sleeping?

I gasped. Luckily the heaving breath didn't take me out of the meditation. My parents came into the circle. Erica joined us. My other relatives met us there. Then rivals from college and high school, detested politicians, Philadelphia Eagles players: they all joined us.

I...I think I love them all? I can say with more certainty I want us all to suffer less.

Like a freight train, an image of Mark's lunacy before I broke his jaw careened into my consciousness, forcing my eyelids to snap open.

It was progress, but I still had resentment for both my uncles. At least I was beginning to see them through new eyes. My love for my parents seemed to level up in that bizarre meditative image. My eyes tenderly closed once more. I searched and I searched and I found no resentment for how they live or how they raised me. I accepted them exactly as they are. I was tempted to grab that feeling, but I was now wise enough to know that's a futile effort. The love and the acceptance slowly dissolved in between unconsciousness and the waking world. Gratitude for shaping me into Chris Veasey, and even Idaho Bones, was at its peak.

I held Erica in the same regard. Her suffering saddened me and I wanted it gone. No desire lingered to inflict pain, to get even. I wanted her to be happy and I accepted that for her that means cutting me out of her life. A force seemed to fly out of me into the night, to seek her out and bring her peace.

A satisfaction lingered on after the meditation, yet there was a nagging tug in my chest. After catching a glimpse of existence where I hate no one, I selfishly wanted that feeling back for good.

Previously, the disingenuous nature of the farce, of avoiding my uncles in my loving kindness meditations, always felt like a complete undoing of the good raked in the zen garden of my heart. I wished for a guide to show me the way, and to help me realize complete forgiveness.

10/10/17 - Lindsey's Car at Watauga Dam, TN, 1,758 Miles Hiked - Day 178

Lightning struck in all directions and I tucked into the shelter. I watched the surrounding squall drip down into the valley with no escape. There the gray clouds toggled to and fro like a gargantuan Newton's Cradle, washing every loose particle in its path into the dark depths of Watauga Lake.

In one final thunderous laugh, the monsoon dissipated, hiding the massive lake under a marble haze of clouds. They wisped in and out of the mountain cage as if to remind the sierras that mighty as they might be, nothing could truly contain an Atlantic storm.

Once it was clear that rain had no place in the evening's forecast, I hiked as fast as I could. Lindsey had gotten off work a few hours before and was speeding down 81 to my eager arms.

My mind hadn't fully sorted out what my ongoing trysts with Lindsey said in terms of my craving for sex and and being desired. Even if I deemed the relationship to be a setback, I doubt I would've had the resolve to end it. I was too smitten. Speaking of endings, the fling was certain to end soon and we both knew it.

Perhaps in a loophole, my brain found the impermanence of the romance to be deliciously Buddhist.

I'd been hiking through a tunnel of rhododendrons for some time and finally lost all vision. The whisking of wet droplets with other eerie sounds amalgamated voices in my ears. I extracted my headlamp but found the beam of light to only add to the fright, casting everything outside of its little circle into an even darker shade.

The thick, wet brush finally opened up to reveal Wilbur Dam Road and Lindsey's car parked there as she promised. I ran up to an empty car and my heart sank.

"Hoo! Hoo!"

I jumped back and raised my pole like a spear. Facing down the tip of it was a cackling blonde.

"What the hell are you doing?" I yelled as Lindsey split with laughter.

"I heard an owl so I followed its calls for a bit."

"Fuck, I hate night hiking," I squealed between huffs.

Lindsey pulled two icy Goses out of an adorable cooler. With three of her sandwiches in my belly, I pulled her in for a kiss to show my gratitude.

As usual, a night spent on and in her car was everything I wanted. I couldn't comprehend why this woman was willing to drive eight hours round trip to see me again but I couldn't be more thankful for it.

Since finding my true breath, the sex was predictably more exquisite. Our time together was even more electric as I was able to be utterly present with Lindsey, whereas before I still had distrust for the universe.

"Oh, that's a barred owl," said Lindsey.

"Can we go see it?" I asked. "I still haven't seen an owl in the wild, I'm dying to."

"They usually respond really well to calls, let me pull one up."

Soon we were blaring hoots John Cusack style. A few minutes, some rustlings, and a whooshing later, it felt like the bird was close enough to touch. Lindsey and I both shined our lights in the direction of what should have been unrequited love.

"He's looking for the real thing," Lindsey said. "He's smart enough to tell the difference."

10/11/17 - Lindsey's Car parked on 19E, TN, 1,773 Miles Hiked - Day 179

A faint rainbow came and went before me as water vapor soothed my crisped skin. I reached into the chilling depths of the currents before me and heard a voice.

"Why are you washing your clothes here?"

I turned around to find an adorable little girl playing with her *Frozen* dress. She had smiling eyes that looked lost beneath her stern, curious eyebrows. I wrung out my compression shorts and hung them next to the rest of my clothes on a line of paracord.

"Well to be honest, they're rather stinky," I said.

"Why don't you wash them at home?" she asked, cocking her head.

"Can I tell you a secret?" I asked quietly, leaning a bit closer. She halted her half waltz and leaned forward, bringing a hand up to her ear. "For now, this *is* my home."

"You live *here?* At the waterfall?" she exclaimed.

"You said you could keep a secret!" I admonished, hands on my hips, my own smile peeking around every corner of my disappointed mouth.

I saw a silent nod between the girl's mother and Lindsey. Undoubtedly a closer eye would have been kept on the girl if the half naked man hanging shoddy clothes at a major point of interest were here alone. But if his homely appearance was good enough for a girl like Lindsey, then surely he could share a few laughs with a Disney princess.

"You're gonna be a great dad," she said, earnestly inspecting an utterly ordinary leaf.

A short while later, what was a busy wading area was suddenly a misty ghost town. Lindsey's intoxicating presence swelled like the crashing torrents before us and her hands found me in kind. She took me into her mouth the way only a lover can. Her familiar gape having a place for every unique part of me, ushering me levels beyond what I thought before to be idyllic.

My eyes darted from the trail, to the waterfall, to the brightened rock face overlooking us, eventually finding her staring back up at me. It

230

felt like she wanted me to look at her in disbelief.

My knuckles whitened against the nylon and she never hesitated. The orgasm was outrageous, the whole thing incomprehensible to either of my flushed heads. It emphasized how truthful Lindsey was being in saying she could never get enough of me.

On the drive to pick up food later, I found myself bracing for impact. The dashboard was inches from my face once Lindsey's tires were done with their screeching halt.

Without a word, Lindsey beelined for a tree, leaving me and her abandoned car still on the road. When I realized she wasn't coming back anytime soon, I followed her.

"Oh fuck yeah!" she said, filling her arms with bright red mushrooms. "Grab some!"

"Nope, not gonna happen." I threw my hands up and started back for the car. "The goal of today was to smell *less* like fungus."

"These are called Beefsteak mushrooms. So tasty but I hardly ever see them around!"

Something overcame me as she bagged the Beefsteaks and threw them into the back of her car. I grabbed her narrow face, kissing her as deep as I possibly could. Whenever I thought we were done, our lips would call forward to one another, begging for it to last.

Without having to say it, I wanted Lindsey to know that I was falling for that part of her. I found the whimsical, curious nerd I was locking lips with to be perfect in all her bizarre quirks.

I never wanted her to hide the girl who brakes for rare mushrooms.

10/12/17 - Overmountain Shelter, TN, 1,805 Miles Hiked - Day 180

I awoke to a large leaf scraping its way down my face. I jolted forward to find there was no nylon barrier separating me from the wild woods of Tennessee. As the rapids of the nearby stream soothed me, I remembered and her face filled my mind. The sly smile of one of the most incredible women I have ever met.

Lindsey left me at 5:30 that morning. In a fatigued if not heartbroken trance, I found a magnificent campground adjacent to a brook. I decided my tent would be unnecessary for such a brief nap, and gave in to the constant white noise of the water and nearby traffic.

Four hours later I rose to my feet with a discomfort in the center of my waistline. I rubbed the tender area and remembered something.

"My clitoris doesn't have much sensation," Lindsey shared the night before in the sex filled air of her Subaru. "When I was younger, I used to hump everything. EVERYTHING."

"You know, that actually makes sense," I replied, stroking my beard. "When we have sex, you really grind your pelvic bone into me and I always wonder whether that hurts you. But you've just got a calloused clit so you can handle that kind of force."

"Can that be my superhero name? 'The Calloused Clit!'"

"You'll never find...The Calloused Clit! She's a ninja on a mission!" I'd continued.

Lindsey also told me the night before that she couldn't drive out to see me anymore. I already couldn't believe the time she was making for me so I put up no protest. Even though I didn't want to see my hooded vigilante disappear into the night.

I took in the magnificence of Roan Mountain all day long, setting left foot in North Carolina and right in Tennessee all the way. The day exhausted me but I lay awake in my sleeping bag that evening, wondering whether I'd ever see Lindsey again.

10/13/17 - Round Bald Mountain, TN, 1,810 Miles Hiked - Day 181

Before the magnificent peaks around Round Bald caught my attention, I scanned the parking area with creased brows. The lot was full. Even at 5 pm cars were circling before giving up and settling for a spot hundred yards down the road. Both shoulders of the road were packed on both sides. Slowly I resumed my stroll, trying to understand what all the fuss was about. A pack of teenage girls took turns snapping yoga poses before the dusky view. A man manned the sizzling grill while his friends played cornhole.

Soon enough I deduced that it was nothing more special than a balmy Friday night.

When I spotted the ghost of a footpath to a field of rhododendrons, my feet and trekking poles had minds of their own. I was on a tractor beam. The tightness in my chest twisted when I found bits of toilet paper hanging from branches. For a state that attracts Bonnaroo-like crowds on a run of the mill Friday night in mid-October, this whole "No privies" thing didn't seem to be working too well.

I walked through the maze until I found a firepit with two store bought logs sitting on top of ash. When I leaned down to inspect, I was immediately struck by pure silence; the rhododendrons were superb sound barriers. I couldn't remember the last time such peace found my ears. My knees burned in the uncomfortable position but I was determined to preserve that sense. They finally surrendered to the lush, welcoming moss below and again I was overtaken by nature's charms.

The trail provides.

An old stump was on the other side of the luxurious patch of nature's tempur pedic and I jumped aboard. Standing on my toes, I could take in Round Bald's meager colleagues below. A great white cloud sharpened the purpling pink contrast and began to drape over the ridgeline. It looked exactly like a slow motion waterfall. The mass swallowed every tree and rock in its path, leaving nothing more than a serene blanket to reflect the exploding sky.

I thought back to that hill where I found my breath and took in every feature of this natural wonder. Slowly my chakras fell into place as the cloud fell with grace. I couldn't align all seven, but to even come this far again gave me hope that soon complete chakric alignment could eventually be as second nature to me as gravity was for that cloud.

10/14/17 - Greasy Creek Friendly Hostel, NC, 1,821 Miles Hiked - Day 182

With a dead phone, I did my best to navigate my way to Greasy Creek Friendly Hostel from memory. Signs are banned in the National Forest. According to the information I had, the hostel owner set up subtle flags and spray painted rocks to guide hikers accordingly. At first I thought the situation was rather neat, as if I were navigating my way through a secret level in a video game or solving a mystery.

It didn't take long for those thoughts to turn to fear. Fear that I could be on the wrong trail. Then irrational fear took the wheel and I wondered whether I was walking into a trap set to lure hikers away for unthinkable sins.

Two pickups with the beds open parked like a V on both sides of the trail. I said hello in my friendliest tone. I could barely understand the gentleman standing against one truck. He was very cross-eyed and his nearby buddy was cross-eyed as well. There was a muffin-topped woman with an overall body type that could only be described as "cigarette ravaged" topped with stringy bleach blonde hair in a lazy pony tail.

"You hikin' the Appalachian Trail?" said a man in the other truck I hadn't really noticed before, and I nodded. "You comin' from Maine?"

"Actually I started in West Virginia--" my story was cut short upon noticing a shotgun in the man's hand.

I stumbled through explaining my flip-flop hike while catching sight of several more shotguns scattered around. None of the others had a hand on them, at least.

"I 'on't understand," the guy leaning on the truck confessed.

"It's complicated, I basically hiked from Maine," I said before a nervous laugh.

Ms. Muffin top eyed me up and down oddly and my feet began to shuffle.

"Y'know, I don' 'ear da best thangs bout that hostel, and I know iss real 'spensive..." The leaning man said. "If yer lookin fer nuttin' more'n a shower and a place ta stay, y'can do it at my place fer free."

"Thank you so much!" I said while still walking but turning to keep their gaze. "I'm supposed to meet some people at the hostel. If it sucks, I'll run it by them and come on back up here!"

"Thass fine, Imma come down there anyway, wanna ask bout that Chevy Blazer fer sale."

I waved to everyone and picked up the pace. Once I had my back turned I heard a very creepy voice.

"Beee caaaarefuuuul," Ms. Muffin offered in a bizarre tone.

In a less than stellar first impression, the hostel owner rattled off about 10 instructions for very specific places to leave very specific things before I could enter the premises. Once inside, commonsensical signs marked every instruction to bear in mind from "Don't pee in the shower" to "Only Ceecee can do the dishes."

"I don't work on the Sabbath," she began, as I immediately wondered what would happen in the sink following a Sunday morning breakfast. "I'd be happy to wash your clothes tonight if you like."

With some vinegar, a little Borax, and what would soon be ordained a Catholic miracle, Ceecee made my clothes smell like I'd been wearing them for 19 hours rather than 1900 miles.

10/17/17 - Little Laurel Shelter, NC, 1,896 Miles Hiked - Day 185

At 5 am, I was on the move. It was by far the earliest start time I'd achieved on the trail. I had a great motivator: today was my interview for the Denver job. My old boss, Brian, recommended me for the job and now it was time to convince the company's CEO that I was ready to reintegrate into society.

The quarter moon provided enough light to hike without my headlamp until the sun teased its way over the horizon. Frozen clumps of dirt shattered under my feet as I trudged over the 5,500 foot massif that was Big Bald Mountain. I noticed tiny, shiny mushrooms over the entire bald. Except they appeared to disappear once the morning glow was in all its glory.

I reached down to grab one but it melted in my hand. Thinking I must've peeled the ice clean off the little fungus, I reached for another unsuccessfully. Finally I got down on hands and knees to inspect the mysterious fungus only to find that there was no earthly spine at all. Ice appeared to grow out of the earth itself. Curly ribbons emanating through dirt.

I resumed a healthy clip to my pickup point and was taken to Nature's Inn by the owner. She agreed to take me to her lodging outfit for WiFi and drive me back to the trail afterwards, all for the low price of $15.

The interview went well as my bushy beard was a natural ice breaker.

"You're gonna shave that before you start, right?" Paige asked, giving me a clue that Brian's recommendation was highly valued.

Everything about the startup's CEO was drastic. She was intensely inquisitive, friendly, and ambitious. Paige said she'd be in touch soon and I was driven back to the trail.

By starting at an ungodly hour, I was able to easily tack on another 15 miles on the ridgeline, my mind racing with fantasies of a life in Denver. I imagined myself getting in on the ground floor of a rapidly growing company, working up to VP over the course of a few years. Such advancement would come only after staunchly establishing a work-life balance. I'd worked enough 80 hour weeks in my young life.

Something nagged at the back of my head and I pondered further still on the potential opportunity. I'd been writing over and over for nearly 2,000 miles: "No more desk jobs! They don't make you happy!"

"But it's not a desk job!" I told myself. "She's taking me on primarily for relationship building. Paige even said she didn't want to see me in the office. She wants me out schmoozing with clients!"

It felt right, but it didn't feel divine. Perhaps that was asking for too much but a priority of this hike was learning to trust my gut and the universe. To stop settling.

I extended my daydream a bit further, picturing myself buying land and cultivating it. Taking this job was the best way to achieve these goals quickly and advance my life.

"I'm meant to be in Colorado, I know it. If nothing else," I said with conviction while setting up my tent. "It's a free one way ticket to Denver."

10/18/17 - Hot Springs Campground, NC, 1,915 Miles Hiked - Day 186

NOBOs and SOBOs alike rave about Hot Springs, NC. There's delicious food, craft beer, and of course the town's namesake. Serving as the gate or the reward for The Smoky Mountains, it's a thru-hiker's oasis come true. The prospect of a couple days there was enough to wake me up early with a grin on my face.

Trail Domme, whom I hiked with in the north, was starting to doubt whether I'd ever catch up with her and her new southern-half tramily.

Right there in Hot Springs, we drank beers together under the moon reflecting on the French Broad.

"Took you long enough," she said. "You picked a good time to catch us."

"I'll say, that cabin is fancy," I agreed. "Good location, too. Right by the river."

Fox, Bubbles, and Spry had all flipped similar flops so we tried to determine whether this was our first time crossing paths. Bubbles and I clashed from the start. I tried not to take the friction personally. When your personality's as big as Idaho, people are bound to have bones to pick with you once in a while.

A dance party transpired in the cabin. I saw CEO Paige's number buzz in and I had to moonwalk out.

Paige apologized for calling so late and asked if I had a few minutes.

"I want to make you an offer, what do you think?"

"Wow! I wasn't expecting to hear from you so soon," I began.

That voice in my head rallying against another desk job made more and more sense throughout the day. I wanted to hear it out and chew on its talking points.

I searched my gut. I wanted to say yes to Paige. It wasn't as resounding as I'd hoped but it was clear enough. I wanted to be rid of the anxiety of the unknown. The prospect of enjoying every last step of my thru-hike with certainty of my livelihood was too alluring.

With a smile, I quietly re-entered the cabin. Fox brought the music to a dull roar.

"Hey Idaho, how did it go?" she asked expectantly.

"Guys," I began, hardly believing it all. "I'm moving to Denver."

Chapter Twenty-Four

1,915 Miles Hiked, 274 Miles to Go

Days 187-195

10/19/17 - Hot Springs Campground, 1,915 Miles Hiked - Day 187

Feeling a shade more ostentatious than I should, having a guaranteed paycheck in a month's time, I paraded about town walking on air, feeling the unthinkable weight of cash in my fanny pack. I got the extras at the springs. I bought a variety 12 pack of Colorado beer. At the counter a rooster approached me curiously.

"Name's Henry," gruffed the cashier.

"And how are you doing today, Henry?"

I picked up the bird and spun as if I were some smelly Disney princess.

"How lucky we are to be surrounded by asses sculpted by mountains," I remarked later that afternoon at the hot springs.

"Seriously, though! Appalachian Trail Diet doesn't disappoint," Trail Domme agreed.

Back at the cabin there was one posterior I couldn't seem to keep my eyes off of. They kept meeting hers in whatever spare time they had. Throughout the night I kept finding reasons to come to rest next to Fox. And she kept finding reasons to lean on me.

We were eventually left alone by the river to drunkenly grope each other under the careful but now very familiar watch of the moon.

10/20/17 - Max Patch, NC, 1,933 Miles Hiked - Day 189

My jaw spent the entire hike up Max Patch in the off position. It was the most arresting panoramic I'd ever taken in. Once atop, the hill seemed to be perfectly in the center of a crater of ranges with infinite earth tones. I parked my sleeping pad facing my favorite section and began to stretch and foam roll.

Some tall grass ahead flagstaffed the remnants of a purple spider web. Each strand extended in the gentle airstream, casting a music stanza in the breeze. In golden hour the strings were stark against the yellow sky. It occurred to me that catching sight of this silky display was every bit as beautiful as any mountain range in sight. But it was so ordinary! It could be found in any field any day. That's what made it even more beautiful.

A few hours later, shooting stars seemed to be dime a dozen as the sky was filled with them all night long. Fox and I lied on our backs watching the astral delight.

"It's so nice to share these moments with someone who gets it, you know?"

I reached my hand into hers across the grass.

"I do," she said. "I really do."

All those miles and nights alone on trail, without other thru-hiking companions, I was bound to wear out all my feelings of solitary joy. There's only so much prideful independence a man could chew on.

In a flurry of contemplations, I thought of all the little moments I'd only recently shared with Lindsey. A part of me felt that I was betraying Lindsey with Fox but that didn't actually feel like the truth. Whether I liked it or not, my romance with Lindsey had run its course. In that moment on Max Patch, my romance with Lindsey didn't feel any less genuine or meaningful.

Though Fox was a stranger, there was something in that moment together almost more intimate than the array of sunsets Lindsey and I took in together. I immediately recognized what made it so. Fox and I shared the same quest. Different, but very much the same.

After nearly 2,000 miles to ponder it, I decided that there was only one thing that could have made any waterfall, blushing moon, or sighing sunset better than it already was.

Someone seeing the exact sight you're looking at through weary eyes.

10/22/17 - Tri-corner Knob Shelter, NC, 1,967 Miles Hiked - Day 191

Fox hiked ahead while I procrastinated the 4,000 foot climb into The Great Smoky Mountains. I'd heard fond retellings of this infamous stretch of trail since my first day. It's not that I wasn't eager to take in their splendor. I was just feeling the pleasant aftereffects of Hot Springs and reluctant to take on the 18,000 feet of cumulative elevation gain in the Smokies.

Seven miles in at Mt. Cammerer, I couldn't resist a marvelously climbable rock with a clear view of the valley. Musty scents of tannins and flora filled the air as my retinas took in infinite shades and pastels. There was an ostensibly random tri-color of red, yellow, and green splashes. A closer inspection told a story of air streams and thermals among the maze

238

that is The Great Smoky Mountains. I'd only been above 5,000 feet a few times in my life and my ascent wasn't even close to over.

Lindsey remained on my mind. I knew she was pursuing other love interests with my encouragement but I wondered again if my tryst with Fox was a betrayal to either of them. I examined my feelings for Lindsey and it still felt like love, inexplicably. My affection for Fox was growing quickly and I wondered what to make of that. It seemed that for the second time in my life, I was finding love with two different lovers. That fact didn't scare me. What was alarming was how natural loving two people felt, and how *un*natural monogamy had seemed for a long time. I pondered love in the abstract. Something occurred to me.

Everyone comes to the AT to fall in love. Most thru-hikers fulfill that love, especially those who finish.

Purists fall in love with the trail.

I fell in love with adventure.

Some fall in love with another hiker.

Some fall in love with themselves, finding self-realization and acceptance.

I supposed some lucky soul walked these steps finding them all.

Love. No better word came to mind to describe the glue of the Appalachian Trail Community. It had been two and a half years since I resolved to thru-hike the AT right in the Conservancy in Harper's Ferry. In that moment, there was no doubt in my mind that the Conservancy employees loved the trail. John Haranzo loved the trail right up to taking his own life and his father's love became a monument right there on the footpath.

Unlike with Erica, this love I deliberated on atop that rock didn't feel like one that "has a nasty habit of disappearing overnight." Not quite unconditional, but not one easily dissolved, either.

A frigid gust took me out of my romantic meditation and it felt like autumn finally arrived in that instant. Dark clouds cast the foliage into gray and I scrambled for the shelter, still 10 miles away.

10/23/17 - Tri-corner Knob Shelter, NC, 1,967 Miles Hiked - Day 192

During my initial ascent into the Smokies, a tank top was all I needed. My attire remained unchanged until my bird's eye view over the valley. I arrived at Tri-corner Shelter at 6 pm with every layer I had protecting my tan arms, still warm from the sunburn at Max Patch. It began to pour shortly thereafter. Fox nabbed us a spot by the already roaring fire as both levels of the double decker shelter were packed like sardine cans.

"How cold is it right now?" I asked Fox.

She held up her Garmin device , showing 28° on its LED screen. In eight hours the mercury dropped by 40.

Fox and I slept well enough, the embers lingering till morning, giving us some reprieve from the overnight low.

"Supposed to rain all day, high of 35," she said, handing me a mocha.

"No," I said. "I don't care if it puts me behind schedule. Just no."

Spry's leg was dizzyingly restless, his eyes fixed on the sheets spilling off the roof. He had a friend meeting him in Gatlinburg. With no cell service to adjust his plans, he didn't seem to have a choice but to hike the 15 miles in weather fit for Noah's Ark.

"Yeah, I don't think it's worth it," Fox said with a sigh.

"Fuck it. It's only 15 miles," Spry sighed.

"And a warm bed tonight!" I encouraged.

He layered up with nylon and grit. Spry left the four of us in a wake of guilt as we shared the narrow dry space with other cowards for the day. The only comfort was that it did indeed pour down on the shelter all day long.

Despite the extended fire, the air felt icier than freezing with near-full humidity.

Once a hint of darkness crept in, Fox and I popped in our earplugs and enjoyed our double sleeping bag system a good two hours earlier than usual.

10/24/17 - Mt Collins Shelter, NC, 1,986 Miles Hiked - Day 193

I woke up to darkness but my buzzing Fitbit cast my breath in a bluish white. My eyes fixed on the interior of my sleeping bag, drawn shut, haunted by the ghosts of my slumber. I wiggled my toes, confirming their numbness. A rapid knocking felt out of place until I realized my shoulder blades were shuddering against the frozen wood. Between then and Fox's alarm, I was somewhere between dreadful frost crestfallen wakefulness and confused bitter sleep.

Without delay I heard her little teeth rattle as she trembled in my arms.

I grabbed Fox's Garmin which must've been broken because it said 12°.

"This is crazy, right?" I asked Fox who was nodding. "Are we going to be okay? Should we bail at Newfound Gap?"

Recollections of other thru-hikers suffering frostbite haunted me as

I slipped my frigid socks onto my shaking hands.

The crunch of the frozen ground echoed among the icicles of the imposing branches.

10/25/17 - Silers Bald Shelter, NC, 1,994 Miles Hiked - Day 194

Newfound Gap wasn't what I'd call balmy, but at 5,000 feet it was survivable.

"The shelter's a little less than a thousand feet up," I said to Fox. "I can't see it being as bad as last night."

Bubbles and Trail Domme had just hitched out to meet Spry and we were contemplating our fates.

"It says it's supposed to get down to 10 here, though," Fox said with concern.

"Fuck."

That was really cold. 20 lower than what my cheap sleeping bag was even rated for. "I'll get off if you want, I just want to get The Smokies over with at this point. I don't wanna get sucked into another town, it may *never* warm back up."

We snacked and called for a safety meeting.

"Worst case scenario, you know I can get a fire going."

There was little joy in the four miles after the gap. Clouds came and went, sending a newfound chill with each pass. The clouds thickened as we descended over the half mile side trail to Mt. Collins Shelter. Never before on the trail had I felt so haunted. The cold, silent air seemed capable of hiding anything from me.

"You guys should set up your tent in the shelter if it's free standing," a fellow long-distance hiker offered. "You get a few extra degrees."

With little else to do we huddled in our tent. It somehow felt so much colder than the night before.

"Negative one."

I could practically see the horrific words spelled in Fox's breath. They evaporated into a sadistic smile and brought nothing good with it.

Freeing my head the next morning, a drop of water fell onto my forehead. Dazed, I ran my fingers over icy droplets of condensation, waiting to plunge down from the roof of Fox's tent. I found my sleeping bag drenched.

The human brain can be a marvelous thing. It detached me from dragging frozen socks over my red, desperate feet. I even took in a sight or two leading up to the Appalachian Trail's highest point in Clingman's

Dome, up at 6,800 feet. Had I not cut Fox off that morning, she would have told me that it was still below zero, and would remain there for the rest of the day.

I had to keep proving to myself that I wasn't experiencing a hypothermia-induced dream, never in my life did something feel so unreal. At well over a thousand feet above mile-high, there wasn't a sight to behold, not a farsighted one, anyway. A white nimbus pillow encapsulated the entire peak and snow gently fell. It was perfectly peaceful.

"You're gonna be so mad," Fox said, showing me her phone.

"What am I looking at?"

Before I finished my question, an owl fell from a snowy branch and spread its hypnotic wings over the width of her screen.

"This can't be real," I muttered.

"No, seriously. I just took it! You missed it by a few minutes."

Walking Clingman's descent, it suddenly felt like I hopped off the end of a staircase into Spring. It couldn't be autumn, because in autumn you're warm then cold. No, this had to be the work of the Mayqueen.

A great pile of snow fell in front of me, yanking me out of my trance.

I looked up at the green behemoth, its branches yearning to shake off the unseasonable squall as efficiently as possible. After all, the tree was looking onto a valley whose leaves still blew in the wind. They were hardly recognizable now, but they were clinging on for dear life and putting on a technicolor show.

Gazing through snow covered branches at those rich autumn colors, I regained all of my senses.

"No one gets to see this sight," I said with a quiver. "No one gets this."

Once the sun had its fill for the day, the biting evening winds stole their opportunity. We seemed to be on the right side of Clingman's now, but that didn't mean comfort necessarily. A mere five miles later we were lured to Silers Bald shelter.

We found an old yet sturdy man fanning flames in the firepit. His daughter handled the introductions and told us it was his 64th birthday. Pride of such a gallant birthday and a beautiful daughter glowed like the inferno he brought to life. Fox and I intended to hike another six miles to the next shelter but the fire's pull was too strong. Countless Marlas packed in, shivering.

Before the sun had given up entirely, the temperature was climbing back up to single digits.

10/26/17 - Birch Spring Campsite, NC, 2,018 Miles Hiked - Day 195

I'd had it with shelters and Marlas and I simply wanted some semblance of the trail I was admiring a week before. Camping typically wasn't allowed in The Smokies but apparently no one got around to building a lean-to between Mollier's and Fontana Dam. There was a campsite five miles beyond. At 3,800 feet, the site was 3,000 lower than Clingman's, 1,400 below the previous night's shelter, and 600 beneath where I was standing. Then there was the added benefit of being five miles closer to town the next morning.

I arrived at Birch Spring to find the only two campsites with a fire ring occupied. I followed a long forgotten trail to what looked like a fort, realizing that it made a perfect visual block to build my own fire pit, since technically flames were only allowed in the designated fire rings.

The act of building a pit brought me great joy. It was thrilling to think of all the hikers in its future. I'd built maybe a dozen fire pits on the Appalachian Trail and such a legacy warmed my heart. It also felt like a small but barely appropriate 'fuck you' to the overly micro-managing park service who had been forcing us to sardine up with tourists all week long.

Fox arrived shortly thereafter. The 17 mile slog was longer than the previous two days combined and we felt it. Fox fell asleep in my arms as I stared into the first of what I hoped would be many campfires for my little creation.

Chapter Twenty-Five

2,031 Miles Hiked, 158 Miles to Go

Days 196-201

10/27/17 - Appalachian Inn, Robbinsville, NC, 2,031 Miles Hiked - Day 196

The hike down from The Great Smoky Mountains restored the spirit. It got a degree warmer every few minutes which felt like Athena was breathing life into us. It had gotten down to 2° overnight. An hour after leaving camp I was down to one long sleeve shirt and nothing more.

By the time I arrived at Fontana Dam, a measly 1,800 feet high, I couldn't get clothes off fast enough.

"71 degrees," Fox shared, coming to expect my hourly temperature inquisitions.

"69 degree swing," I said smiling, catching her eyes roll before I could even finish. "Nice."

In actuality it was a surreal experience, feeling that mercurial shift in a matter of hours. I removed my last shirt to lie on the dam's wall, taking every last bit of Vitamin D I could manage before hunger set in.

Fontana Village was a proper ghost town, every soul vacated for the off season save for one convenience store and the post office.

After hiking a few miles out of town, we were fortunate to get picked up by a privately contracted mailman, an occupation I'd just learned existed.

"Sah yew tew a few taahms on muh route, figyured yew woon't find no ride fer hwile," he grunted, moving mail to make room for his passengers. "Juss gotta finish mah sheeuhft, then I'll take *yew*, anywhere yew liike."

He winked at Fox in the rear view mirror and she reflexively kissed my cheek.

"Seen't a lotta buhrs?" the driver asked, filling the awkward silence.

"Yup, saw a bear a couple days ago," I answered. "Seen a lot more than I thought I would on this hike."

"Oh yeah, they're errywhurr. Ruhl easy to get a buhr huntin' purrmit this yeeuhr."

He drove recklessly through the neighborhoods, his butt more on the passenger seat than on the driver's, as the mailboxes were on that side of the rickety vehicle. When he had to get out at one box, I counted three different types of camouflage from head to toe.

I carried the conversation, repeatedly whispering what he was saying to Fox who couldn't understand the man. At a certain point, I would've been smart to stop playing translator.

"Y'gots tew soak tha buhr meats in buuuttermilk o'ernight. Dat takes tha gamey taste raht owut."

"You said you have a dog?" Fox said, desperate to steer the conversation away from dead bears.

"S'right, three of 'em," he responded. "Might be two by the weekend, m'oldest one ain't doin' so hot."

"Oh no!" she said. "What's wrong with him?"

"Lost a chunk of his leyug, otha day," he said. "Got snatched up bah the buhr I'm soakin' in buttermilk tonight."

His laugh was haunting and Fox was resolutely silent for the rest of the ride. It's not that I approved of bear hunting, or needless dog euthanasia. I just didn't want to be dropped off in the middle of buhr huntin' country.

We walked up the steps of the Appalachian Inn and instinctively went through the motions of such a fancy establishment, kicking off our boots and leaving everything on the steps. Fox's dad insisted she stay at a bed and breakfast after narrowly avoiding frostbite.

Traumatic memories from The Smokies played slowly in my mind as I breathed in the eucalyptus from the clawfoot tub. It was suddenly impossible to believe that my body suffered through an entire day below zero at all in my life, let alone three days before. I sat up and pulled the plug, watching the gray brine melt away into the pipes. I relinquished the tub to Fox.

I strolled the room gloriously naked, taking in unbelievable foliage in the mountains through our window.

I sprawled out over the Victorian bed and passed into something of a slumber. Fox woke me up with a firm grasp on my penis who was way ahead of the game, and gentle, fragrant kisses on my neck.

"Holy fuck," I gasped minutes later. "That was a lot of firsts for us."

"What do you mean?" She laughed and plopped her adorable chin on my chest. Her damp, brilliant red locks rolled opulently over my softened skin.

"Well that was the first time we were properly clean for the deed, first off," I said, pausing to let her laughs fill the room. "I don't think you've ever been able to ride me with so much freedom and vertical space before. And most importantly: we've never been able to lie naked comfortably afterwards. Our standard postscript is to scramble back into our dusty sleeping bags!"

"Wow, you're right," Fox said, taking it all in. She ran her newly groomed nails down from my lips and whispered, "All the more reason to do it again."

10/28/17 - Nantahala Outdoor Center, NC,

Fox and I proceeded to get softer and softer. We dined on an egg frittata bake filled with fresh vegetables. Bracketing the picturesque feature were homemade applesauce and freshly baked banana nut muffins. As the rain pounded the roof with baked sugar hanging in the air, it was hard to imagine leaving the quaint haven.

"Supposed to be like this all day," Fox sighed.

I grabbed the remaining muffins and braced myself for the elements. There were no views to behold, no moments to relish, in the ten cold miles to Nantahala Outdoor Center.

Fox and I had free rein over all the non-perishables left at the NOC by an entire season of thru-hikers. We mixed and matched and filled up as our clothes dried. Once fed, we splashed over to the River's End Restaurant for some beers.

The real estate of our table overlooking the Nantahala River was made even more prime by The Great Pumpkin Pursuit. Daylong rain and near freezing temperatures didn't deter the hundred participants of one of the NOC's proudest traditions. We watched from the safety of our warm riverside table as kayakers edged one another out for gourds floating beside them.

Entrants would retrieve a pumpkin from the icy depths and trade it in for a plethora of prizes. I was told those ranged from a toothbrush to an all inclusive river raft guide for four.

Once their pumpkin was traded in, the kayakers would find volunteers nearby with fleece blankets. I sipped my porter, wondering how mad someone would have to be for something like that. Then I remembered my Appalachian trek was far madder.

10/29/17 - Wesser Bald Shelter, NC, 2,061 Miles Hiked - Day 198

The climb out of the NOC was steep, but doable. The calorie spend was actually appreciated, warming the body with each step. Then, much like that first day in The Smokies, the weather turned quickly.

Sharp, icy snow battered my cheeks and saw to it that my

numb-yet-glove-laden hands wouldn't get their sensation back anytime soon. My toes and fingers were threatening frostbite right up to the shelter, where I found Will and Austin whom we met at the NOC. They offered to move their tents to sandwich Fox and I, right there in the shelter, hopefully proving to be mutually beneficial. An hour into my hibernation, the toe warmers purchased at the NOC were about as warm as a nun.

10/30/17 - Gooder Grove Hostel, Franklin, NC, 2,077 Miles Hiked

The gesture from Will and Austin was as appreciated as it was fruitless. The four of us found very little sleep. We all woke up with wet sleeping bags and dampened spirits.

I inspected the damage before reaching for my two liter Sawyer bag which spent the night next to me in our tent. It was a block of ice.

Having gone full Marla already, Fox and I decided to dive right back into the comforts of civilization. Gooder Grove Hostel in Franklin, NC was our destination and the 16 miles to get there were a frigid blur.

As we got our bodies back to a reasonable temperature, our phones buzzed with a text from Trail Domme:

Yooooo we're getting to Franklin tomorrow just in time for Halloween. Ya'll ready to raaaaage?

10/31/17 - Haven's Budget Inn, Franklin, NC, 2,077 Miles Hiked - Day 200

We began Halloween night at a hiker-friendly bar called Mixers. We were donning masks that Fox's mom sent us for Halloween. The five of us played bar games as Fox quickly got to a level of intoxication I'd never seen before. It was highly amusing, with the added benefit of her being more outgoing and sassy. It turned me on.

We all proceeded to McDonald's to find that only the drive-thru was open. We tried to walk-thru but found no success, and were equally failures at trying to hitch through it. We settled for a gas station where I reluctantly purchased a microwave cheesesteak.

I face planted on the bed at Haven's Budget Inn to find some concerning features of the comforter spread.

"Have any of you made ramen since we got here?" I asked, lifting a fistful of crunched up Maruchen into the air and letting the crumbs fall back onto the cheap fabric. Everyone shook their drunken heads. "Cool, instead of complimentary mints, we get noodle bits."

It honestly wasn't too surprising. The motel was your textbook horror movie intro with dead flies hanging from every ceiling corner. The concierge surely had a fear of dentists and showed no remorse for charging us more than the rate given over the phone. A Coke machine with a font not seen in the last two decades must have been some sort of drop off point because people kept coming and going with happy looks on their faces. I happened to know on good authority that the machine was broken and 75 cents richer after my arrival.

We all drunkenly finished our junk food and got ready for bed. Fox and I retreated into the adjacent mini suite AKA adjoining closet and crawled into the squeaky bed. Instantly I passed out.

"Idaho, I'm about to fuck your girl. You should probably wake up."

The voice sounded far away but the words were clear. The message less so.

A few glances back and forth across the mysterious ceiling put a few more pieces together. A girl giggling. Then a different girl giggling.

That right there...that's the unmistakable sound of two women navigating each other's bodies.

I rolled over and Trail Domme grabbed me by the chin for a deep kiss. Fox kissed my neck and my hands met Trail Domme's to disrobe Fox.

The three of us seamlessly weaved in and out of one another, kissing and sucking while clothes found the floor. The two women groped at each other intensely and found their respective ways down to the clitoral realm. Things picked up quickly and soon they were knuckle deep in one another trying desperately to keep quiet.

Fox reached back for my head to make sure I didn't feel forgotten and shoved her tongue deep into my mouth. Her hand moved adoringly down my side before she grabbed my throbbing cock and thrust it into her incredibly lubricated pussy. Trail Domme continued to rub Fox's clit as I penetrated deep and pulled her hair. I came hard and somehow managed to let out nothing more than a gasp. Trail Domme eagerly went between Fox's legs to taste what had transpired while we kissed affectionately.

"Fox, come lick this cum off with me."

Trail Domme licked up and down my wavering shaft which was soon back at attention.

Trail Domme came up to kiss Fox. Hard as ever, I slid back inside Fox solely for the purpose of bringing her to orgasm. I figured after getting her off, we could focus on the hero, Trail Domme. She'd been imploring us to simultaneously lick her and it would've been rude not to.

It turns out that I had vastly underestimated how arousing this all was because rather soon into my motions I ejaculated for a second time. It was a complete surprise, especially considering just how intoxicated I'd gotten. Accepting my fate, I penetrated Fox with my two best fingers and felt the massive accumulation of two extremely excited loads of cum between my cooperating fingers. Though she'd gotten close several times, I was finally able to push Fox over the edge while Trail Domme grabbed her by the throat.

"Lick my fucking clit already," Trail Domme said, truly living up to her name.

Fox and I made our way down to the foot of the bed and got to work. We both fingered Trail Domme simultaneously as I pinched her nipple with my other hand. Fox utilized another finger and that seemed to be the secret sauce. Both hands over her mouth, air escaped Trail Domme in heaping quantities, indicating one helluva orgasm. I recognized the breathing pattern from that church backyard back in Maine.

"Fuuuuuck," Trail Domme said with a heaving sigh. "I fuckin' *needed* that."

Within minutes of each other, Trail Domme and Fox both slumbered, each with a hand on my chest. My body was worn but my mind raced on what to make of the events that had transpired since Lindsey enthusiastically bound into my life. My desire for non-monogamy was a liability that did damage of still unknown proportions in my relationship with Erica. It seemed to play a role in our sudden and mysterious demise. Soon before the split I discovered that my resistance to monogamy made Erica feel inadequate. She feared I'd *never* be satisfied, and it consequently made me feel like I had to hide if not eliminate my desire for a non-monogamous lifestyle.

I'd been fearing that disclosure of my non-monogamous inclinations would make dating very challenging and could cost me a soulmate in the process. Lying between two women who didn't see my unorthodox nature as a problem, heart still full from a third in Lindsey, I finally saw that trusting my truth and being open and honest moving forward only enhanced my odds for a happy wife and a happy life.

11/1/17 - Fairfield Ridge, NC, 2,103 Miles Hiked - Day 201

Fox and I woke up feeling especially frisky after our wild night. Shortly after our friends left the shared motel room for an ambitiously early start, we were rinsing off sex under the hot shower.

A few miles in we stopped for a safety meeting by a waterfall. Something about the way Fox blew out smoke and whipped her fiery hair back riled me up. I pinned her up against a boulder for another round and we both joyfully screamed into the wet abyss knowing that no one could hear our orgasmic exclamations. Putting some solid distance behind us, Fox and I took in the best view of the day in the early afternoon. Inspiration found us again as she sucked my sore but eager cock. I couldn't believe I was getting such astounding lip service within view of cascading mountains. Right as she was about to win Round 5 in 24 hours I stopped her.

"I don't think I should be the only one that gets to take in this view." I bent her over another rock and pulled her hair to bring her neck within biting reach.

"It's like we're having another threesome with this view," she gasped with a fistful of my hair and I filled her up again.

To this day I feel ashamed and incredibly naive to think it acceptable to fill a woman living in the woods with four loads of cum. She never asked me to pull out but the fact that it didn't occur to me as a courtesy still makes me cringe. I can only imagine what the physics of all that play out to be. At the ripe old age of 29 it was as if I thought some magic uterine fairy came to collect deposits of semen for change under your pillow.

If Fox did have an issue, it wasn't dire enough to keep her from going for another.

The entire day piled onto a mountain of evidence that group play was actually like tonic for my one on one sex with a primary partner. After every threesome, Erica and I would enjoy three times as much sex as usual in the following weeks. I'd jokingly called group sex a Lazarus Pit, a mythical fountain of youth and revitalization, for my sex drive.

I felt with conviction that if I could find a woman on board with semi-regular group play, that a genuinely happy relationship could thrive.

Fox and I were enjoying an incredible bond, and the fruits of a shiny and new physical relationship. However, our post trail fates were destined to transpire a thousand miles away from each other. It was unspoken, but we both knew that our romance would end at Springer Mountain with our final steps.

As the sun began to set we found a flat spot at the top of a climb with a breathtaking view. Fox set up the tent while I gathered stones and wood for a fire. We finished dinner just before the sun settled on the horizon and we applauded ourselves for a day well spent. A slow kiss brought my battered penis back to life.

On the sleeping pad next to the fire, Fox took the sixth of Idaho's bones under the dusk sky. Thankfully this time, it finally occurred to him to pull out. It also crossed his mind that it's going to be a challenge to go back to fucking in a boring old bed.

Chapter Twenty-Six

11/2/17 - The Helendorf Inn, Helen, GA, 2,126 Miles Hiked - Day 202

Right on time, the rose tinted glasses found their shiniest hue. A return to appropriate temperatures fostered warmth inside and out. A sunrise from Kelly Knob was the true catalyst. A star of pure red rising on the horizon line with just enough clouds to stare at it head on. The nearby clouds caught all sorts of wavelengths of color to create something straight out of Edvard Munch.

I walked beneath the rusty canopy feeling unbelievably whole. My mind harkened back to my first week. With ease I could notice every little thing about the forest and see nothing as ordinary. Finding a miracle in every leaf, splendor in the bubbling stream, I basked in it all.

I wondered whether I'd ever fully recapture that initial honeymoon phase of being completely smitten with nature. The mountain laurel above my head, with their *come hither* branches, begged me to remain. They spun an inviting tunnel of curved and intertwining striped bark with hardly any understory beneath. Strolling through literally felt like walking into another world.

This section of trail is deplorably referred to as *The Green Tunnel*. While I understood the frustration in seldom catching a worthy view, I also found the laurels overhead to be enchanting, even protecting.

The day's climbs brought fulfillment. I relished in truly feeling the climb, welcoming the challenge of gaining elevation. I made a game of focusing on one part of the body at a time as I worked toward the sky.

Undoubtedly the prolific sexcapades of the previous 48 hours had something to do with my sunny disposition.

I debated just how realistic it would be to end up with a woman who also appreciated the rejuvenating effects of group sex. There had to be some bisexual woman out there for me with the mindset of, *Wait, I get to enjoy both genders at the same time, and the added bonus of that is that I get fucked six times in 24 hours? And I cum every time? Yeah, I'm in.*

I posed the hypothetical to Fox in the most ethereal sense I could muster.

"I could see that being fun long term," she said. She remained silent for a while, seeming to further chew on it and said, "Yeah, wow. That sounds ideal, actually."

Her nonchalant agreement to a dynamic I still worried was one in a million filled me with hope. It also brought gratitude for bringing such a marvelous woman into my life. The trail is long but it is narrow.

Little by little my post trail life was coming into focus. I was finally getting off the East Coast, moving to a state that had been beckoning me for over four years. I vowed to maintain a strict work-life balance in a job that afforded me the freedom to travel back to New York frequently. I intended to take advantage of that perk often to see my family. I couldn't wait to reestablish those relationships, to take accountability for my part in my family trauma. I would cultivate loving kindness for them all and accept them as they are.

The last piece was trickier. What was necessary to find romantic fulfillment?

A few months into my relationship with Erica, I divulged that I wasn't cut out for monogamy. Every woman I slept with since our breakup knew that fact well. All I knew was what *wasn't* going to make me happy. What about what *was* going to make me happy long term?

I liked the idea of non-monogamy romantically but it also scared me. What if I scared off the woman I'm meant to be with with such an unorthodox prerequisite? What if they find someone better while exercising their right to see other partners? What if seeking my own partners outside the relationship consumes my life and ruins our relationship?

Fox's enthusiasm for non-monogamy was a far more significant catalyst for me than I realized at the time. It reminded me that there were others out there "not cut out for monogamy." Even Lindsey expressed doubts about being with one person forever and confessed how badly she wanted other lovers during her four year relationship. Then of course there was Trail Domme, who seemed primed to push the boundaries of non-monogamy much further than I'd ever imagined.

More clearly than ever, I could see that sex wasn't an addiction for me. It was an unexplained, unorthodox mystery that I hadn't yet solved.

I wasn't alone, and I intended to explore that world even further.

Contemplating that exploration made the miles zip by. Fox and I walked into Helen, GA, which greatly exceeded our expectations. We'd heard the quaint town was modeled after a Bavarian village, but we didn't expect to find ourselves amidst a plaza that seemed to teleport us to Germany. What should have been campy and tacky was charming and debonair.

"Too bad you guys didn't hike a little faster," the bartender said, filling two liter steins with beer. "Helen has the longest Oktoberfest in the world. And you missed it by one day."

"No fucking way," I bemoaned. "Oktoberfest has been on my bucket list since high school. And this place is pretty damn close!"

"You two hiking the Appalachian Trail?" asked a tired looking but handsome fellow from a few seats down. We nodded and he turned to the bartender and said, "Put all their drinks on me, the rest of the night. You got any hats left, Victor?"

Victor searched the bar and pulled out a wool Bavarian hat.

"Here." Our generous friend poked a pin into the hat and handed it over. "When you do make it to Oktoberfest in Germany, make sure this pin is visible. It'll get you free Paulaner just about anywhere you can find bratwurst."

11/3/17 - Jacks Knob, GA, 2,140 Miles Hiked - Day 203

I came across a very old man section hiking and was instantly struck by something that was hard to put my finger on. After only a few exchanges I realized why he seemed so familiar: this is ME.

It felt distinctly like I was crossing paths with a future version of myself.

This gentleman certainly oozed with that enviable energy we all find in the occasional octogenarian who seems to never sleep. His joie de vivre was the aura of the man I'd been yearning to become.

The encounter brought on reflection about my future.

I still very much felt like my LIFE was on my back. I simply carried it from place to place.

I searched within and found myself to be the happiest I'd ever been. Better yet, this life seemed so much easier, even with the numb toes and lack of level surfaces.

Could I bring that simplicity with me to Denver?

Even between jobs, I could rent out my apartment and wander from place to place. Right? For a few hundred bucks I can ramble for weeks, or even months.

It was crazy to know that the option was there.

The whole of my scalp was tingling as I played out hypotheticals in my mind. The sensation felt warm and satisfied. All day my eyes were on the verge of tears being so completely filled with gratitude and wonder.

Around a turn I left the guarding laurels and stared at the endless haze of Georgia's mountains.

In that moment, I wished as hard as I could for everyone to go out and do this.

Whatever the equivalent of this is for you, I want you to have it. I want you to see that it's not as impossible as it seems. I appreciate that we can't all do what I've done but find a way to do something for yourself that awakens the soul. You're not stuck. None of us are truly stuck.

"Is that loving kindness?" I asked no one.

I walked on, thinking how everyone could afford a reminder that life goes on without us. It is humbling as it is painful to realize that life resumes unabated in our absence.

Everything goes on without us.

Coming out to the Appalachian Trail made me see in real time what life would be like if I were dead.

How would all my friends be doing if I just...disappeared?

JUST FINE.

They weren't even thinking of me often, I was sure of it. It was a hard truth to accept but it also brought humility and freedom.

For someone as neurotic and anxiety prone as I was, it was sensational to take a bit of the pressure off.

Whatever we choose to do with our time, whether it be long term or short term, things will carry on. We may as well enjoy whatever it is that we're doing. We may as well have a good time because life is too short to suffer through it and life will go on.

11/4/17 - Blood Mountain, GA, 2,158 Miles Hiked - Day 204

Rain dripped from the lowest pair of boots in sight. There were at least 120 pairs of them hanging from the trees.

Neels Gap is notorious for the theatrics of thru-hikers tossing their no longer necessary footwear into the trees, casting with them their hopes and dreams of mounting Katahdin. Overwhelmingly, those boots belonged to NOBOs, who make up the vast majority of AT thru-hikers. The whole of them was a monument to people who whipped out the credit card and embarked on a fantastic and wet adventure they were ill-equipped for. I guess there's something to be said for these boot tossers. At least they figured out mere days in, fresh out from Springer Mountain, that they made a mistake and had a flair for the dramatic. After climbing Blood Mountain from the other direction, it wasn't hard to imagine tackling the imposing giant from the south, without trail legs, and being tempted to cast my boots into the sky.

As I waited for Fox, a distant thought began to tug at me. Why would anyone throw brand new boots into the trees? Even if the Appalachian Trail was more than you could chew, it's not like you'd suddenly hate any form of hiking! Keep your boots, go home, find a more palatable means of bonding with nature.

What made far more sense to me was the thought of SOBOs getting a new pair of boots shipped to them, or tossing up their old ruddy shoes for a new pair at the outfitter beneath the trees.

As a romantic, I loved the sight and the sentiment. As a pragmatist, I couldn't buy it.

11/5/17 - Gooch Gap, GA, 2,173 Miles Hiked - Day 205

"Not all your ideas are meant for you."

A highly respected life coach and close friend said that to me a year before. She tried explaining to me that I'd accrued a resume of unfinished projects because I'm not meant to execute my ideas myself.

The concept seemed reasonable, but also frustratingly perplexing. Who's going to take my ideas? Who will see them through?

Then again, I wasn't seeing them through. A piece of me died with each initiative gone by the wayside.

The Appalachian Trail did little to slow the idea machine. My phone's circuits were filled with hours of elevator pitches on everything from a musical choreographed on rolling chairs to an alarm clock that plays porn first thing in the morning. You know, for America's most sophisticated bachelor residing in mother's basement.

The gears began to turn on how this concept could work for me (the entrusting of ideas, not PornAlarm.com). With this job in Denver, I could be seen as something of a consultant in a couple years' time. With a shiny eggshell business card sporting the big c-word, I could hand it out ad nauseam until something sticks.

The dread of finishing the trail had grown steadily since The Smokies.

I daydreamed about my future apartment a great deal, mind you. It was hard to imagine taking on a random roommate after vagabonding for a year and half. A fireplace was a must have, and a balcony of course. Idaho Bones can't be expected to remain inside all day, let alone go without the comforting cracks and pops of a fire. He needs a smooth transition, a detoxing period. Well actually, more of a re-toxing period.

The apartment felt deserved. A haven in which to cultivate a new life for myself was deserved. The job, however, was a murkier matter.

Am I betraying myself? How many times have I written in black ink on this hike that I can never return to a desk job? I swore off sales, and now I'm going back? Sure my future boss said it's different, but they've all said that.

The jovial bounce in my step couldn't sustain the sudden heaviness in my chest. A job like this, that's an anchor. A 12 month lease, that's a pretty heavy anchor. I can't drive clients in my beat up '03 Camry, a new car will be a five year anchor, if not more.

I was supposed to be embracing a new way of life, never settling for anything again. I certainly wasn't going to negotiate with monogamy, no sir.

Denver felt right.

The job offer? That seemed like a sinister way to plant my wandering feet into quicksand.

I'd been stuck for so long. How could I ensure I never get stuck again?

11/6/17 - Springer Mountain, GA, Southern Terminus - AT, 2,189 Miles Hiked - Day 206

After a subtle but tender kiss from Fox, we slowly ambled to my soaked tent. We shifted uneasily between holding hands and putting arms around each other, feeling eyes upon us.

"We should do an ass out hug," I offered comedically, wishing I'd taken the time to be sentimental at Springer Mountain's plaque when we were alone.

"I can only handle so many awkward situations," she protested with the giggle I'd come to adore while I patted her between shoulder blades.

"Well this is me," I gestured to the sad, sopping structure. "I'd invite you upstairs for coffee but I know you're allergic to cats."

She laughed and pulled me in for one last kiss with the back of her head firmly fixed upon her mother and aunt.

"I'm really gonna miss you," I said for probably the dozenth time since morning.

She gave me a smile that made me weak in the knees and started back for the car. I plopped down in my tent and felt an ambiguous but certain sadness creep into my mind. The rain appropriately picked up. I absentmindedly unlaced my right shoe and watched the car back out of its spot.

"Oh shit. WAIT!" I bellowed as I fumbled for my fanny pack. It was stuck, of course. I finally freed it from my pack as the car turned slowly out of the lot.

"WAAAAIT!" I mimicked my words with my long flailing arms as I was relieved to see the brake lights come on. Fox quickly vacated the car. As heavy precipitation drenched her fiery locks I sensed she was expecting a mammoth of a Hollywood smooch to follow the pursuant dramatae. Instead I kissed her sweetly on the cheek between rushed breaths.

"Here!" I handed her a piece of paper with *Fox* written on it.

"Oh," she said with a perplexed look. "Thanks."

"No problem, safe driving!"

A large part of me did want to land that pucker but I felt that I'd embarrassed myself already.

"I knew I was going to forget to give her that," I muttered to no one, annoyed that I'd passed on a handful of perfectly good moments early in the day.

Upon returning to my tent the sadness was more pronounced. The newfound yearning for Fox's continued presence stirred with a sudden yet sharp sense that my purpose had been lost. As I prepared to plop down into a tent devoid of meaning or direction or right to be there...I felt cold tears trickle on the edges of my eyes. The dark corners of my mind conjured up all the ways I'd been a fool.

How dare I welcome so agreeably the conclusion of the greatest adventure of my entire life? What is so fundamentally wrong with me that I can't fully experience such a rich and spiritual life any longer? How could I be so imprudent to wish away every wet, uphill mile on the last day of a life I'd been planning for years and years?

Like Pavlov's Dogs hearing the bells of their next meal I felt shame before I properly even had the chance to lay into myself.

Then I heard one of the only noises that could snap me out of such a cantankerous mood: the soothing and oddly proximate hooting of a Barred Owl.

Brown droplets scattered as I yanked tight my untied laces. Humidity and haste snagged the sleeves of my raincoat as I quietly treaded the brush towards the source of the call. I kept my eyes firmly fixed on what my mind perceived to be its perch. I walked carefully and skillfully so as to not disturb the creature. Since this hike's maiden steps, nearly seven months ago, I had been wishing wholeheartedly to see an owl in the wild. Many nights have featured their echoing calls. A number of those evenings included an earnest effort to find the source in pitch black darkness. All I had to show for it were near misses. No encounters.

As I neared ever quieter the hoots ceased. For three sequences a far off owl's calls went unanswered. From previous hunts, that's how I knew I was rather close. I resolved to not look down so help me --

Enormous wings fell down from the tree I zeroed in on. They quickly ascended back into the high branches of a tree roughly 50 feet ahead of me. I kept my gaze glued to the tree it disappeared into and then it happened. The owl looked me right in the eye.

Its pupils were a color I'd either seen a million times or never once before. A vibrant blend of gray, brown, and white, forming an ancient amalgam of wisdom and evolution. The stare was only for an instant but a lifetime passed in its wake.

The great raptor turned its head and fell gracefully to the earth. In a flash its wings were spread wide, revealing stark black feathery tips across its majestic span. There was a peculiar hypnotism in watching such a sublime bird of prey soar with lofty elegance beneath the canopy. The owl I'd been waiting for flew out of sight and everything changed.

This fellowship with wilderness...my natural adventure, a rugged tryst. Finishing the Appalachian Trail isn't the end. It is only the beginning.

The Appalachian Trail forgets no one. Days will come when remembering brings pain. Yet a sore sole knows not the agony of a sore soul.

About the Author

Chris Veasey is an adventurer, non-traditionalist, and a lifelong storyteller. His uncompromising New York core can be found beneath layers of mountain-calmed temperament and reverence for the English language. Always taught to be practical, he gave up trying to make a profession of entertainment soon after college and opted for safe desk jobs and relationships in our nation's capital. Catching a foul whiff of 30 years old, Mr. Veasey packed his bags and walked away from it all for an entirely impractical hobo epoch.

After a lifetime of normalcy, the liberation taught him that living an unorthodox life is nothing to be ashamed of. In fact, this is where his newfound happiness stemmed from. Discovering that there is no direct correlation between playing it safe and contentment is what compelled Chris to write the very book you've come across.

The story he tells is one of nonconformity and trust in the universe, written as a hope that you too will be able to find your own "unstuck" self.

Future Works

If all goes according to plan, Uncivilized will be the first book in a trilogy. Keep an eye out for these follow-up titles:

UNATTACHED

An Evolution Into Polyamory After Challenging Societal Constructs

RECIVILIZED

Reacclimating to Society After Finding Oneself in the Wilderness

Milton Keynes UK
Ingram Content Group UK Ltd.
UKHW010655261023
431376UK00004B/279